One woman juror broke down in tears and wept openly as the verdict was delivered. The decision had not been an easy one for the jury. One of them had been discharged from service, after becoming ill during the trial. It had taken the eleven that remained nearly twelve hours' deliberation and an overnight stay in a hotel to decide that the small brown-haired woman in the dock was guilty of murder.

There is only one sentence for murder. Sara Thornton was led from the court to begin her life term.

While the family of the man she had killed smiled with relief and congratulated each other, Sara's sister left the court to tell Sara's ten-year-old daughter that her mother would not be coming home.

In prison Sara refused to accept her guilt and slowly and surely she convinced others of the injustice of her case. Now thousands of people across the country have signed petitions and attended demonstrations to show their support for her fight. From inside jail she continues that fight for recognition, understanding and justice.

Jennifer Nadel is a qualified barrister and a journalist. She has reported on legal, political and social issues for the BBC and Channel Four News, and has followed Sara Thornton's case closely since Sara's first appeal. She now works as ITN's Home Affairs Correspondent.

SARA THORNTON

The Story of a Woman Who Killed

Jennifer Nadel

VICTOR GOLLANCZ

LONDON

First published in Great Britain 1993
by Victor Gollancz
an imprint of Cassell
Villiers House, 41/47 Strand, London WC2N 5JE

A Gollancz Paperback Original

A catalogue record for this book is available from
the British Library

ISBN 0 575 05581 2

Photoset in Great Britain by
Rowland Phototypesetting Ltd, Bury St Edmunds, Suffolk
Printed by Guernsey Press Co. Ltd,
Guernsey, Channel Isles

Contents

For all those who have had to fight or
who are now fighting for justice.

Acknowledgements

Few who have known Sara Thornton have remained unaffected by her. In writing this book I have interviewed as many people who knew her or her husband, Malcolm, as possible. Many of them were initially reluctant to talk about her and her case and I am grateful to those who did. It would take too much space to name them all, but I would like to thank them for their help. In particular I'd like to thank Malcolm Thornton's sisters, sons and former wives for their assistance and trust, which I know were not easy to give.

I'm also very grateful to Ed Fitzgerald, Rohit Sanghvi and Gareth Pierce for their patience and help with the legal aspects of Sara's case; to Dr Max Glatt, Dr Gill Mezey and Dr Henrietta Bullard for their advice on the psychiatric dimensions of the story and to Julie Bindel of Justice for Women for her patience and assistance. I would also like to thank Sara's sister, Billi, who shared many painful memories and endured what must have seemed like an endless stream of intrusive questions in order to make this book as accurate as possible.

Thanks also to my employers at ITN for their encouragement and enthusiasm despite the project involving my absence from work, and to my colleagues in the Home Affairs Bureau, especially Malcolm Munro and Harry Smith, who covered for me during my absences and made it possible for me to complete the book. I am also grateful to my former producer, Trish Powell, for her support, encouragement and inspiration and to ITN's news information department for their help with research; also to the computer team for their much-needed technical assistance.

A very special debt of gratitude is owed to Emma Hewitt, who researched and helped to write this book. She provided wisdom, insight, skill and immeasurable doses of patience. Without her help the book would never have been written and I am very grateful to her, as I am to my mother, sisters and Lewis Gordon for their advice and support. Thanks also to the many others who helped us, among them: Jason Isaacs, Ben Emmerson, Ann Shamash, Sue Bindali, Jeremy Horder, Chris Tchaikovsky of Women in Prison, Harriet Wistrich, Southall Black Sisters, Colin Port of Warwickshire Police; Ken Matthews and John Cole from TNT and Kiranjit Ahluwalia.

Finally, and most importantly, I need to thank Sara Thornton herself for having the courage to let me write this book. It was written on the strict understanding that she would give me full access to every aspect of her case and retain no control whatsoever over what I wrote. That she felt able to give me such a free hand reflects not only her courage but also the faith she has in the strength of her own case.

JN

Foreword

by Helena Kennedy, QC

Truth can often be a casualty in the conduct of criminal trials. The characters involved in the cases and ensuing headlines are polarized into heroes and villains, good guys and bad guys, innocent victims and monstrous sadists. The imperfect, infinitely variable human beings who appear in the courtroom rarely warrant such simple characterization but complexity only muddies the waters of denunciation. It is so much easier if the dramatis personae of the proceedings are clearly identifiable – evokers of sympathetic sighs or deserving of the hiss and boo.

Sara Thornton has suffered the consequences of being both demonized and idealized, as indeed has Malcolm Thornton, the husband she killed.

Many people were angry at her conviction for murder and consequent life sentence, because she herself had been the victim of serious abuse at the hands of her alcoholic spouse. At the time there was a growing sense that the law was failing to take account of the reality of women's lives: the handling of rape cases and domestic violence seemed to epitomize the shortcomings of the legal system, and feminist lawyers and criminologists were showing increasing concern about how our jurisprudence presents a particular perspective that excludes that of women. Legal definitions of self-defence and provocation and tests such as that of the 'reasonable man' seemed to have been created without the woman on the Clapham omnibus in mind. So it came about that Sara Thornton's appeal became the focus of arguments that were already entering the mainstream of legal debate.

Campaigners use a shorthand in which there is no space for the postscript or coda. In the publicity surrounding Sara Thornton's case a great deal of attention understandably focused on the violent behaviour of the man she killed. Malcolm Thornton became the vessel into which was poured all the outrage about violence against women. He was depicted as a vicious brute with no redeeming features. However, Malcolm's family publicly refuted his portrait as the real offender and proclaimed him a decent man with something of a drink problem who was only capable of violence when pushed to the limits. This, then, was a case that clearly revealed the problems inherent in applying male-created law to women's experiences without contextualizing the events in light of the history of a particular relationship. It also exposed the vital need for a genuine understanding of domestic violence in our courts.

When Sara Thornton herself began to articulate the ways in which the system failed and infantilized her, she became a striking emblem of the need for reform. She was Rapunzel, imprisoned in the law's dark tower, but her release would be secured not by a noble prince or Law Lord but by the power of women's anger and the support of enlightened men. Her separation from her child heightened the wretchedness of her situation. She came to symbolize the multiple ways in which womanhood is wronged by the judicial system: lawyers, judges, legal principles and all.

After initially promoting her as a deserving victim, sections of the press began to turn, reiterating the arguments produced at her trial, when she was accused of being feckless, wanton, narcissistic, volatile and unstable (but not unstable enough to diminish her responsibility for a calculated crime). There were also suggestions of poor mothering, drug-taking, abortions and flirtatious behaviour.

Anyone who enters the public arena (and is lionized) can face a reversal in their fortunes but women have a special burden to bear. Female victims are expected to fulfil specific expectations, and the more that was known about Sara Thornton the more she defied the popular profile of the 'victim'. This was no cowed, passive individual but a spirited, independent woman. Most curious of all was the fact that she stayed with the man who was abusing her. Even those who should understand the complex dynamic that develops in a violent relationship found it difficult to comprehend that she of all women did not leave. Her own capacity for survival became a testament to her guilt.

She too found it hard at first to explain why she remained in the relationship. The fact is that many abused women minimize the horror of what is happening to them as a stratagem for their own emotional survival. Coupled with misplaced self-blaming, a profound sense of failure, and a genuine concern for the partner who is the abuser, battered women often surrender their autonomy and become incapable of taking the enormous step of leaving home. The issue for many is one of financial resources, but emotional paralysis can be an even more powerful inhibitor.

In twenty years of working within the criminal justice system I have come to believe that domestic abuse, both physical and sexual, is one of the most far-reaching problems in our society. An enormous proportion of women within our prisons have been abused, and significant numbers of women within mental health institutions have had similar experiences. Quite as significant is the extent to which male offenders, particularly violent ones, were subjected to abuse as children or were brought up within violent homes. There is no doubt in my mind that domestic violence should be the most pressing concern of the police, the courts and policy-makers, but until some horrendous tragedy occurs it is still relegated to the low end of the criminal scale. The idea that there are acceptable levels of violence within the home poisons the response of the law enforcers.

Jennifer Nadel has searched painstakingly for truth in her account of Sara Thornton's life and trial. She has made the imperfections of the legal system plain to see, yet unfortunately there are no simple remedies. No lawyer ever guarantees that different choices would necessarily have produced different results. The real problem lies in the attitudes that endorse the failure of the law.

Sara Thornton's case has been a watershed that has set the stage for subsequent successful cases. Now at least there is a growing awareness of the need to contextualize domestic killings where there is a history of violence, and the courts have finally begun to sanction the calling of expert testimony in appropriate cases to explain the impact of sustained abuse. Furthermore, debate is at last taking place about whether there should be a change in the definition of provocation so that 'sudden and temporary loss of self control' does not exclude the seemingly deliberate actions of a battered woman who may have lost control long before. My own feeling is that instead of expanding the definition we should perhaps be thinking of reappraising the whole defence. It seems extraordinary to me that the law is more prepared to accept a degree of exculpation when a killing is carried out in anger rather than in despair.

The Thornton case has also added fuel to the call for the removal of the mandatory life sentence that follows a conviction for murder. This change would at least provide a safety net in the event of a battered woman being found guilty, allowing a judge the discretion to pass a greatly reduced sentence because of mitigating circumstances.

'It's a fascinating case. I just wish the facts were better.' This is one of those wry legal asides which is unfunny to the outside world but which articulates one of the fundamental problems of test cases. Few trials simply and perfectly present an issue for resolution by the courts: layers of real life get in the way. All the complexities of the human condition, the imperfections of real men and women, confront the legal niceties. But a legal system is worth nothing if it cannot absorb diversity and embrace difference. It is in such tensions that justice is forged and that is the challenge we must meet if confidence in the system is ever to be restored.

1 · Deceptive Beginnings

At night the corridors echo with the sobs of women, women who know that it will be many years before they can again share the solitude of the night with those they love. Sometimes sleep is impossible, at other times it comes in fitful spurts, and occasionally as a deep and welcome escape from the brutality of prison. For Sara, the nights are a time to think and a time to try to come to terms with how it was that she ended another's life. Haunted by dreams of the man she loved and killed, she picks through the embers of her life, trying to find if not an explanation, then at least an understanding. With that process has come a growing sense of internal freedom, a sense that her struggle for understanding and justice began long before her trial and that in fact it is something she has been searching for for much of her life.

Little in Sara's early life could have prepared her for what she was to face as an adult. She had few of the normal mundane experiences which equip children for the decisions they will have to make in later life. Her childhood was exceptional and unusual, marked by upheavals, emotional intensity and the lack of any real opportunity to put down roots.

No childhood is ever perfect, of course. Outwardly, though, Sara's had a fairy-tale beginning of material privilege and apparent plenty that could not have been further removed from the concrete confinement she was later to find herself in. Born in Nuneaton on 12 January 1955, she was whisked off by her parents, when she was just six months old, to one of the most beautiful parts of the world.

Sara's parents lived and worked in the South Pacific – her father, Richard Cooper, was an administrator for the British Government, and her mother, Jane, was a marine biologist. The home to which they took their baby daughter was on the island of Tarawa, one of the more than forty tiny outcrops of land near where the equator meets the international dateline, which make up the Gilbert and Ellice Islands. Tarawa was only 2½ miles long and half a mile wide. The nearest major city was 2500 miles away in Australia. The islands had been annexed by the British a century before and, as Tarawa's magistrate and virtually only white resident, Richard was viewed as something of a dignitary. Even so, the family's home was basic: bare walls and a thatched roof with no internal ceiling. Kerosene lamps provided light; windows were simply square holes cut out of the concrete walls. The long white beach, dotted with coconut palms, was just a stone's-throw from the house.

Unlike many of the surrounding islands, Tarawa did have a wireless receiver. Richard had been on an official tour of some of the more remote islands when Sara was born, and did not discover he had become a father until he returned to Tarawa and received a radio message telling him Jane had given birth. Sara's arrival into the world had been less than smooth. Jane's pregnancy had been a difficult one, and as there was no hospital on Tarawa she decided to return to England. That proved to be no simple undertaking: indeed, Sara's family were to tease her afterwards that even before birth she had caused complications. Just getting to Australia involved taking a series of colonial ships. Once in Melbourne, Jane was able to catch a plane, but air travel was still relatively unsophisticated. The weather was bad and the crew, feeling it was too risky to have a pregnant woman on board, decided to drop Jane off in Bangkok. This she refused, however, insisting with characteristic forthrightness that if she was going to be jettisoned it would be somewhere where British currency was accepted. When Jane's father, Gerald Austin, arrived at Heathrow to collect her, he was told she had been dropped off in Calcutta and taken to a clinic where she was instructed that it would be unsafe for her to travel any further unaccompanied. Gerald Austin was as devoted to his daughter as he was later to prove to be to his grand-daughter, Sara. He dropped everything and flew out to Calcutta to collect Jane, whose advanced state of pregnancy made the journey home very difficult. As she was unable to fly because of the pregnancy they were forced to take a train across India, a ship up the Suez Canal, a train across Europe, a ship to Dover and another train to Victoria where they were met by Jane's mother, Luisa. A week later Sara Elizabeth Cooper was born, healthy and seemingly unperturbed by the epic journey her mother had just completed.

Taking a more direct and orthodox route, Richard flew back to England to be with his wife and daughter. After six months they decided that Sara was strong enough to make the journey back to the South Pacific. Nuneaton's local newspapers all carried stories of the brave young couple who were taking their baby daughter to live in the equatorial wilds. The family of three boarded a P & O ship bound for Australia.

Sara's parents were in many ways the archetypal 1950s' colonial couple. Both were well educated and well bred. Jane was born in the Midlands of a wealthy family of hat-makers – the details of her early life and marriage to Richard were recorded by her father in a personal diary he wrote after he retired. The family factory in the Leicestershire town of Atherstone was a major employer and so Jane had grown up with a sense of privilege and status. She had been a sickly child, however, plagued by asthma and a severe allergy to milk. Possibly because of her ill-health she had become pampered, with a strong streak of stubbornness that Sara too was to inherit. Determined not to let her physical vulnerability hold her back, Jane became an accomplished horsewoman and skier, and despite repeated interruptions to her education caused by the war and her ill-health, she excelled academically. She was moved from school to school, in part because of the danger of bombing and in part because she was very fussy about her surroundings. She was accepted at the fashionable girls' public school, Roedean, but insisted on leaving after only five minutes, horrified at the thought of sharing a bathroom with other girls. Eventually, after her allergies became unmanageable, she ended up in Switzerland, from where she went to university, first in Paris and then in Dublin. By then she had blossomed into a bright and fiercely independent woman

– petite and attractive, her most dominant characteristic was her intellect. It was while she was in Dublin that she met Sara's father, Richard; at the same time she came down with polio.

In his diary Sara's grandfather records how Richard fell madly in love with Jane but could not persuade her to marry him. Both Richard's parents had lived in India, where he spent the first five years of his life before being sent to live with his grandmother in Cumberland, moving to Guernsey with his parents when they eventually returned from India. Richard trained as an economist and decided he wanted to work abroad in the developing world. He was offered a job in the civil service and posted to the Pacific. It was only weeks before his departure that Jane relented and agreed to marry him.

Their first home was on Christmas Island, which between 1957 and 1958 was to become the testing-ground for Britain's early nuclear weapons. Four hydrogen bombs and two atomic bombs were exploded there, turning the once idyllic atoll into a deadly nuclear waste-ground. Four years before the first bomb was exploded there Jane became pregnant and the couple decided to move to Tarawa.

Tarawa was a tropical paradise for children. Remote and safe, it provided a world of physical freedom which children brought up in England can only dream about. With the sea just seconds from the house, Sara was able to swim before she could walk, and she learned to speak the islanders' native Gilbertese before she learned English. There were none of the traditional luxuries that she would have enjoyed had she been brought up in England. 'We had no toys as such. There was a local store, which was nothing more than a large shack made of shiny corrugated iron. The sun glistened on it, it stood alone, a magical, glistening, special place, full of luxuries such as scent and nail-varnish. My doll was a bottle. A square bottle of clear glass with a long neck. To dress her I made frocks out of a strip of cloth, with a hole cut in the middle. The hole fitted around the neck and my doll was dressed.'

All the family lacked was another child. Jane became pregnant, but after she miscarried quite late in the pregnancy, she was advised that she would not be able to have another child. So, when Sara was three, the family returned to England to adopt a second child. They were in touch with a couple who were expecting a baby that they had already agreed to put up for adoption. On 17 May 1958 Barbara Ann was born. Sara is on record as saying, 'Take her back to the shops and get me a boy.' But Billi (as Barbara was later to be nicknamed) was to become Sara's closest companion and her staunchest ally in the years ahead.

The family of four returned to Tarawa. Their home was run by two local men, Arenga and Ranimooui, who cooked and did odd jobs. Sara and Billi were looked after by a young Gilbertese woman, Nee Morcora. Richard's work as an administrator kept him very busy, and he spent a considerable amount of time travelling from island to island. Jane had started to work as a marine biologist for the Hawaii Marine Laboratories. The Americans had also decided that the remoteness of the islands made them a perfect nuclear testing-ground and they exploded a number of atomic bombs above Johnston Island, the latest in 1958. Jane and Richard had both witnessed that explosion, even though they were hundreds of miles from the Island where it took place. Sara remembers her mother saying it was one of the most frightening things she had ever seen. For the islanders, though, it was even worse; not only would they later have to cope with the environmental devastation wrought by the explosion, but at the time no one thought to explain to them what was happening. When the explosion simply took place with no warning, some of the Gilbertese committed suicide and others went to the beach to meet their maker, believing that the end of the world had come.

Jane's work involved identifying the toxins caused by the resulting fall-out in the fish and other marine life. She loved her work and Sara remembers how her mother would spend most of the day out on the rocks collecting specimens, dressed in old trousers held up by one of Richard's ties and a large conical fisherman's hat made out of pandanus leaves. Her children spent their time playing outside under the safe and watchful eye of Nee Morcora.

However, for Sara and Billi, this tropical family idyll was not all it seemed. While from their parents' point of view both children were given a loving and supportive home, both Sara and Billi's perceptions of their childhood, as is often the case, were very different. Beneath the surface they felt there were tensions which would ultimately estrange both daughters from their father and damage Sara emotionally, setting her on a desperate quest to win the parental love and respect she felt she lacked. Neither daughter ever felt able to secure the affection or the approval of their father. It was something that always seemed to be held tantalizingly out of their grasp, leaving them with deep-seated feelings of inadequacy. His children remember him as the archetypal Englishman, mild-mannered and correct, sometimes detached and often seemingly aloof. They always felt that they disappointed him and somehow failed to live up to his expectations.

Their mother, on the other hand, was a forceful, intelligent and very independent woman. She was also very strict. To her children it seemed that the strictness often bordered on the sadistic. It is unclear what difficulties she was experiencing in her life, but whatever they were, she seems to have taken many of them out on her children. Her rules were rigid and not to be broken. Her discipline was supplemented by a readiness to use physical force. Both children lived in fear of her wrath, which gave their lives a sense of constant peril and arbitrariness. It seemed to them that they could never do anything right. They remember being slapped daily while their father was at work. Billi would turn her head whenever her mother went to slap her, which saved her from the stinging pain of being hit across the face, but the perpetual blows to the side of her head eventually damaged her ear-drum. Sara remembers making a swing with Billi out of a nylon washing-line, on the branch of a flame tree. Their mother came out of the house and angrily told them to take it down. Sara tried to do so, but the girls' weight had made the slip-knots very tight and she couldn't untie them. When Jane came out to make sure the children had done what she'd asked, she was furious. They tried to explain but she wouldn't listen, she took the cord down herself and whipped Sara with it. It seemed to both children that no matter how hard they both tried to conform to their mother's rules, they were unable to please her, and that led to their developing a constant feeling of failure.

Sara and Billi say that their father denies his wife's actions, but it seems likely that what they remember as cruelty would have appeared to any adult observer as nothing other than normal disciplinary behaviour. Although both sisters' memories are strongest about their mother, for Sara it was certainly her relationship with her father that was to prove most influential. Family photographs show father and daughter standing side by side in a manner which belies none of the emotional turmoil which Sara now associates with that period. While Richard Cooper believes that the childhood he provided Sara with was normal and loving, she remembers it as a period when she hankered for closeness and expressions of emotion that she feels she was denied, an experience she was later to describe as having scarred her with a permanent sense of never quite being lovable. Billi too cannot remember many moments of affection, but both sisters do remember rows – rows between their parents, rows which seemed to them to punctuate almost every day. Raised voices and anger were something both children came to expect and to dread. They turned to each other for comfort and developed an alliance against the adult world. As with most children, they both hated their parents' arguments, doubtless interpreting them as far more serious than they actually were, and would cower from them in a neighbouring room. But as with all children the familiar becomes comforting; they would actually grow uneasy if a few days went by without rows. They remember it as a frightening and disturbing environment, but it was the only world they knew.

As is often the case, both children developed ways of coping with that adult world which were quite different. While Billi withdrew and detached herself, becoming something of a stoic, Sara enmeshed herself in her parents' emotional cycle, mirroring and rivalling her mother in her volatility and becoming rebellious and provocative. Both children would constantly attempt to create a diversion to try to stop their parents arguing. It would usually be Sara who would make a noise or hide to try to distract them. Sometimes she would jump out of the window and run to the beach. Then it would be up to Billi to break up her parents' argument by telling them that Sara had run away. Sara quickly learned that to get attention she often needed to resort to extrovert and outlandish behaviour. But although she got her parents' attention she felt they didn't give her what she and Billi both desperately wanted – expressions of love and approval. That was something they felt both parents always withheld, which made them want it all the more.

To some degree Sara was able to get the love and attention she felt her parents didn't give her from the staff they employed. Nee Morcora was the person she looked to for affection and support. 'I don't remember any love, affection or kindness from either of my parents. Cuddles came from Nee Morcora. . . . I loved her very much. . . . It is her love I remember, her dark warm skin holding me, her hair which I buried my face in.' But Nee Morcora moved to another island when Sara was six, leaving her and Billi feeling that they had no one to turn to, although Sara did also develop a close relationship with the cook Arenga's family. His daughter became her best friend and she spent a lot of time with the family, speaking Gilbertese while she was with them.

Initially Sara's education consisted of her father teaching her to read, giving her what she recalls as a rare moment of closeness with him, but eventually she was sent to a local Gilbertese school. Classes were carried out with the children sitting cross-legged on the floor, writing on a slate. At playtime they would crowd around a well and wait for the water to be pulled up and mixed with the local 'Sunshine' powdered milk. Later she was sent to another school on a nearby island where there were other European children, but she didn't fit in, recalling that 'They were more English whereas I felt more native.' Every day Jane would be waiting with her bicycle to collect Sara from the launch that brought her to and from school. Sara would sit on a special seat in the back holding on to the sides as she was not allowed to hold on to her mother.

Sara's happiest moments were when she was out of the house. It was then that she enjoyed a real sense of freedom. Although her memories of her early childhood are patchy, she remembers one day quite clearly, a day that at the time seemed no more significant than any other. The sun was typically blisteringly hot and the sea a piercing tropical blue. Sara was standing on the small island jetty while down below her, bobbing on top of the waves, defiantly out of her grasp, floated her underwear. She knew her mother would not be pleased. The loss had occurred in the middle of a tricky manoeuvre. The jetty doubled as the public loo. Sara had watched with fascination as normally sedate adult women suspended themselves over the edge to relieve themselves into the waters below. It seemed simple enough, and although Sara had been warned against trying it, she squatted down over the edge, having first carefully removed her under-wear. All had gone according to plan, and if it hadn't been for the rogue gust of wind that blew her knickers into the sea, Sara's premature excursion into adulthood would have been flawless. She spent the day without her knickers, terrified that her mother would discover she had disobeyed her. But at the same time Sara also felt proud of the assertion of independence that their absence represented. From that day on she would often go with-out knickers, she says, as a gesture of defiance and liberation. Thirty years later, on trial for the murder of her husband, in the sombre and oppressive surroundings of a British Crown Court, her habit of going without underwear was to baffle and offend those in authority. She was asked by the lawyer prosecuting her, 'You don't always wear underwear, do you, Mrs Thornton?' to which she merely replied, 'No, I don't.'

As well as feeling disapproval from her mother, Sara was haunted by feelings of inadequacy in relation to her father. As children often do, she interpreted his aloofness as a rejection of her, and the insecurity that resulted from this often left her feel-ing 'second-best'. As she was later to recall, everyday childhood experiences took on a deeper significance (not shared by adult observers) as a result of their emotional context. 'I remember quite clearly an early example of this feeling of being second-best, not quite up to standards, which became a part of my life. I must have been five or six years old. The four of us, my father, my mother, my sister Billi and I, were playing hide-and-seek. My mother hid, behind the hen house I think, and my sister found her. "Aren't you clever?" they said to her. "What wonderful eyesight." "She's the clever one" and "This is the one we'll have to watch" were the remarks that followed. It wasn't the fact that I had not found my mother first that hurt me, it was the manner in which my parents discussed Billi and ignored me, as if we were laboratory animals, totally devoid of feelings. I felt a failure and swallowed the feeling of guilt and shame that their behaviour aroused in me. It was a pattern that was to be repeated for the rest of my life.'

When Sara was six the family made another visit to England. At that time the civil service insisted that their employees take six months' leave every three years: this was the Coopers' second leave, the first having been when they went to adopt Billi. Jane decided that she would cruise home via Australia with the girls; Richard would stay on in Tarawa until the last minute and then fly back to join them. Sara remembers the cruise as quite a happy experience, mainly, she says, because they were rarely alone with their mother who was nicer to them in the company of other people. 'I noticed at an early age that she behaved in a different way in public than she did in private. It didn't take long for me and Billi to imitate her, so to the outside world we had a caring relationship with our mother, but the reality was very different.' The journey was full of organized games, barbecues, magic and fancy-dress shows. For the first time Sara and Billi found themselves in a completely European environment, which was a new and difficult adjustment. Sara remembers feeling like an outsider. They entered a fancy-dress competition and Jane worked very hard to create national Gilbertese outfits for them, with grass skirts and coral necklaces. She painted their nails bright red and Sara remembers feeling like a queen. They won the competition.

At the end of the night Sara wept when her mother took off her nail polish and remembers her saying, 'Only sluts wear red nail varnish.' This confused her and made her feel dirty for having worn it, and her moment of triumph became tarnished with guilt.

As the ship neared the dateline, the crew prepared for the ceremony of Neptune. People who had not crossed the dateline before were draped in sausages, Sara remembers, and man-handled into the swimming-pool, to the delight of all the children on board. As the weather became colder and they neared England, the crew changed their tropical white uniforms for a more sombre black, and Sara and Billi's excitement grew. The thing they were most looking forward to was being with their maternal grandparents.

Having proved to be Sara's guardian angels before her birth, Gerald and Louisa Austin were to continue to watch over both Sara and Billi and to try to shield them from their mother's harshness throughout their childhood. Sara adored her grand-mother and was captivated by her individualism and eccentricity, characteristics which she herself was later to develop. It was her grandmother, always immaculately dressed, who was later to teach her about cosmetics, hair-styling and fashion. Luisa Austin was by all accounts an unconventional woman who began eating yogurt and practising yoga long before either became fashion-able, and she stuck with these habits well into her seventies.

Sara has vivid memories of the joy and excitement of driving in her grandfather's car from Southampton to her grandparents' home in Atherstone. 'As we drove into the driveway of Arden House I would be on the edge of my seat, ready to be first out of the car. . . . Arden House was a special house. Gran always kept apples under the stairs wrapped in tissue paper. The smell of her make-up, the scent of the floor polish . . . all these smells meant security, love and kindness which came in the shape of Gran and sometimes Grandpa. She loved me, praised me, appreciated me, in the way I felt children should be appreciated. I never felt frightened of Gran.'

After spending time with the Austins, the family went on

to Guernsey, where Richard's parents lived. It was there that another of those small childhood incidents took place that still bewilders Sara to this day. Her mother continued to suffer from asthma and took pains to avoid cow's milk in any form. One day, when Sara and Billi were helping their grandmother prepare the family's tea, they noticed that she had spread butter on the scones she was going to serve to their mother; this, they knew, could spark off her allergy. At the ages of four and six, they had already developed such strong feelings against their mother that they agreed in whispers not to say anything, and if they were lucky she might die. They watched their grandmother carry in the scones and they watched their mother eat them. When Jane failed to succumb to butter-poisoning and nothing happened they couldn't believe it, and the incident reinforced their belief that their mother was an all-powerful, invincible force. Years later, when Sara had a child of her own, she related her memory of the incident to her father. 'He dismissed it completely, saying she was pumped full of steroids at that time and so could have eaten pounds of butter without it affecting her.' For Sara, though, the incident shows that 'Somehow, by the age of six years, I had come to actively dislike my mother to such a degree that I would not have minded if she died.'

After making the rounds to see more relatives and friends the leave eventually came to an end and the family travelled back to the Gilberts. Two years later, when Sara was eight and Billi five, Richard was offered a job in Fiji. It was a step up from his job in Tarawa as Fiji was a bigger and more economically sophisticated island. The move was to be the beginning of a series of difficult and painful departures in Sara and Billi's lives. Tarawa was the only home they had ever known and saying goodbye was hard for them. Jane decided to make the journey to Fiji a working trip. So she and her daughters took a series of boats, stopping off at all the smaller islands along the way, where Jane collected specimens. All Sara remembers of this journey is being briefly reunited with Nee Morcora who lived on one of the islands they'd stopped off at.

On their arrival in Fiji's capital, Suva, all the girls wanted was an ice-cream. 'I was eight years old and I was wise enough to know that Fiji offered delights unknown in the Gilberts.' They arrived ahead of Richard and stayed in an exclusive area reserved for Government employees. Sara remembers the white bungalows and long expanses of grass possessing a deep quiet and an aura of respectability. But the peace of the Government compound was quickly exchanged, after Richard's arrival, for a less attractive and somewhat cramped permanent apartment.

That Christmas Sara's grandparents, Gerald and Louisa, came from England to visit. Gerald was upset to find the family living in such cramped conditions. He felt Fiji's Governor had 'failed to do his duty by Dick' and at the first available opportunity he decided to try to make amends for Richard's employer's oversight. Gerald was a proud and dedicated Freemason. He soon discovered that even thousands of miles into the South Pacific the Brotherhood was active, and he was invited to attend a meeting of the local Masonic Lodge where he met a man whose wife had a house to sell. Luckily for the Coopers it was perfect. With Gerald's help they arranged an overdraft at the bank and moved in. As Sara recalls, 'Twenty-eight Statham Street was a single-storey structure standing on stilts, and about a mile from the sea. There were houses closer to the sea, but my parents didn't want one for fear of tidal waves. The house was set in its own grounds, with coconut trees along one side, and a hedge separating it from the neighbours. It stood on stilts at the front, because the ground from the sea sloped up at such an alarming rate. Underneath the house lived fleas and crabs, but this didn't stop my sister and I playing under it for hours. The ground had dried to a fine silky dust, which was perfect for making mud pies, for sifting through a sieve for hours on end with no particular idea in mind.'

It was after they had settled into their new home that their life in Fiji began in earnest. Just as there were Masons on Fiji, there was another familiarly English institution – a pony club. Jane, who was passionate about horses, announced that Sara was going to learn to ride and bought her a pony called Toffee Apple. Sara was small for her age, agile and seemingly fearless.

She learned to ride quickly. Toffee Apple was kept with an Indian family called the Singhs who lived just up the road. They had a large plot of land which they rented out, and it was Dhurup, the eldest of their four boys, who did most to teach Sara to ride. The Singhs treated her as one of the family and she spent endless hours roaming the fields and scrub around their house on the end of Dhurup's leading reins.

Sara went to the local school where for the first time she started to make friends with European children. At the beginning she was asked to stay the night and spend time in other children's homes, but as time went by these invitations dwindled because Sara could rarely reciprocate them. Sara says that few of the other children wanted to come to Sara's house because they were afraid of her mother, and as a result she had few friends. She remembers her mother telling her that she didn't have any friends because she was a nasty, deceitful girl, and that it confirmed what she'd said all along, that Sara was a horrible child. Sara remembers feeling so awful that she wanted to die. 'I was ten years old and I was feeling suicidal. I never argued against Mummy's logic, she was a grown-up and grown-ups were always right, weren't they? So by the age of ten I was slowly getting used to the idea that I was worthless, that nobody loved me and that I should not expect love, I didn't deserve it.'

She did, however, make friends with a girl called Jackie. Her mother was a teacher who lived alone with her daughter not far from the Coopers. Jackie was the only friend Sara ever remembers coming to stay. She came for two weeks when her mother had to return to England. Sara remembers the time Jackie spent with them as a wonderful reprieve. 'Mummy didn't dare to be nasty to us, so we had two weeks of bliss.' When Jackie's mother finally came to pick her up Sara remembers crying in desperation. She ran out into the driveway and tried to puncture the tyre of the car by plunging a nail into it, in the hope that a flat tyre would mean Jackie could stay just one more day. As punishment Sara was made to spend the whole of the next day sitting in her room memorizing the names of all the prime ministers of England. Every half-hour her mother would call for her to recite them, and inevitably she failed to remember them. Her mother responded by shouting and telling her she was stupid and forbidding her to have any supper that evening.

Sara's life in the South Pacific was terminated abruptly when she was thirteen. The family had returned to England for a visit during which an aunt died, leaving the family a considerable inheritance. Richard Cooper returned to Fiji for a year, but Sara, Billi and their mother did not go back. Both Sara and Billi remember this period as particularly traumatic. Their father, whom they had always felt to be emotionally absent, was now physically absent, and both children lived in constant fear of their mother's anger. Their acute sense of insecurity was compounded by a feeling that they had been uprooted without the chance to say goodbye or prepare themselves for the loss of a home where, if things got too much, they had been able to escape by simply running outside to the freedom of the beach. They had left behind a language and a culture they understood and exchanged it for the cold austerity of a large rambling English country mansion.

Calder Abbey in Cumberland was a huge house attached to an old and crumbling monastery. Most of the rooms were closed off because it was impractical and far too expensive to keep them all heated. The girls and their mother rattled around in its vastness and set up home in one small section of the house. Their physical surroundings mirrored their inner feelings of isolation, and Sara and Billi increasingly relied on each other for support and companionship; they would spend the evenings together, Sara playing hymns on the organ and Billi singing. Sara loved music, her paternal grandmother was an accomplished pianist and from her she had inherited a talent for playing by ear.

Adapting to life in England was not easy. Sara went to the local secondary school where her accent denoted her privilege and her classmates soon began to taunt her. In self-defence Sara developed an air of superiority which did little to temper their jibes. She was small for her age and that too made her vulnerable to teasing. But she was vivacious, energetic and likeable, and after an initial period of antagonism she did manage to establish herself. Indeed, by the end of the academic year she felt quite comfortable at the school.

But just as Sara had settled in, her father returned from Fiji and the family moved again, this time to an old rectory in the Leicestershire countryside which was of slightly more manageable proportions than Calder Abbey. The process of adapting and trying to make new friends began again, and was again cut short. After just over a year there was another move – the third in as many years – to a Leicestershire farm in Carlton, a small country village fifteen minutes' drive, along winding country roads, from Atherstone, where Gerald and Luisa Austin lived. It was a big old house with stables and a small farm attached in an idyllic setting, surrounded by unadulterated countryside for as far as the eye could see.

Soon after the family's arrival in their new home, Sara was sent away to public school in Somerset. Boarding-school provided her with an escape from her mother, ironically perhaps, as Millfield had been chosen because Jane had been one of the first girls to go there. Co-educational and with an excellent reputation for sport, the school's buildings are scattered through the small Somerset village of Street. Throughout the day pupils can be seen making their way from class to class along the tree-lined pathways. As a boarder Sara lived in a neighbouring village, Meare Heath, and travelled in to school by bus. It was a set-up that gave her a lot of independence, not much of which was devoted to strictly academic pursuits. Sara's smallness and agility made her an excellent gymnast. She was intelligent and articulate, but her energies were poured largely into sports and she excelled in swimming and trampolining, winning a gold medal in the Somerset Schools championships.

Compared with home, the school's regime seemed very liberal. Sara experimented with her new freedom, frequently breaking rules and getting into trouble. She refused to wear a bra and smoked marijuana. A childhood of feeling rejected and just 'not good enough' made her crave attention, especially from men. Millfield was quite ahead of its time in being a mixed school, but Sara found it far easier to form friendships with her male classmates than female. She was loud, extrovert and flirtatious. She desperately wanted to be liked, but her behaviour had a tendency to alienate her from her own sex. Sara's relationship with her mother had left her mistrustful of women, whilst her father's apparent detachment had left her hankering for the affection she had not been able to secure from him. The attentions of her male classmates did not, of course, compensate for what she felt was a lack of love from her father, but they did go some way towards restoring her confidence. Even if her father did, as she saw it, disapprove of her, there were other men whom she could captivate and enthral. It was the beginning of a pattern of behaviour that was to recur throughout Sara's life.

At seventeen she was taken away from Millfield. The course of events that led up to her departure are not clear and Sara's recollections are not backed up by her father. Although the school records indicate no expulsion, Sara remembers being told by her parents that she had been asked to leave the school. She and Billi remember her failings and shortcomings being discussed but not being told definitively why she had to leave. The experience was a deeply shaming one for Sara and she convinced herself that she had failed, a feeling that was to haunt and undermine her confidence for many years to come. Billi remembers a series of family conversations in which Sara's behaviour at school took centre-stage and that these discussions had reinforced Sara's sense of shame.

Any seventeen-year-old might well have taken such failure badly, but despite repeated shows of bravado Sara was devastated by it. She wanted attention and approval; instead she felt she had got rejection and failure. It wasn't just that she thought she had left Millfield under a cloud; she had also left with very few qualifications. She was intelligent, but because of the disruptions to her education she never came close to achieving her full potential. Her school reports show that she was viewed as clearly having ability but neither the application nor the discipline to apply herself to developing it. Correspondence courses, disruptions to her Fijian education because of home leave and three switches of school when she came to England had left her with large gaps in her knowledge. As a result she sat five O Levels but passed only three. She was disappointed in herself, but more importantly she felt she had disappointed her father. She again felt the guilt and shame that had been with her since early childhood of not having lived up to what she believed were his expectations. Again she had failed to secure the approval and understanding she so desperately wanted. She had repeated the pattern she had developed as a child – she had attracted his attention by behaving badly but felt she had lost his respect. Rather than relive that sense of shame publicly, Sara resolved not to tell anyone she had failed her exams. The guilt of lying somehow seemed more bearable than the shame of repeatedly having to acknowledge that she had failed to meet what she thought were her father's expectations.

Shortly after Sara left Millfield, Billi was sent there. She too loved the freedom it gave her from their mother and spent a great deal of her time experimenting with it. As with Sara, school work was not a priority with her. She remembers eventually being told that she too had been asked to leave. The school records again do not indicate an expulsion, although they do note that after a discussion with Billi's teachers, who felt that she wasn't making enough of an effort and would do better at an all-girls' school, Richard Cooper withdrew his daughter. Both girls felt they had disappointed their father terribly. Billi's sense of shame was compounded by the fact that she learnt of her withdrawal from school from Sara, who warned her that she had better say goodbye to her friends as she had overheard her father saying Billi would not be going back that term. Billi then spoke to her teachers who confirmed that her father had told the school that she was going to be leaving at the end of that term. Family correspondence shows that her parents had told her she would have to leave if her work record did not improve.

Sara's departure from Millfield was a constant source of friction between her and her family. The sense of shame and failure that had been with Sara since childhood was compounded and built upon and she became increasingly depressed and difficult.

It is by no means clear why Sara experienced so many feelings of failure. Although she and Billi both remember her being told that she'd been asked to leave by the school, the records show she was in fact voluntarily withdrawn by her father. The school archives contain a letter from Richard Cooper saying that he wished to withdraw his daughter from the school as she was not working hard enough. The letter was, he says, written at Sara's request. Sara and Billi, however, are adamant that Sara was told she was leaving because of her poor behaviour. The school records do not reveal any serious misbehaviour on Sara's part; indeed, they contain a copy of a reference written for Sara by the headmaster when she later applied for a job working with children. That of course by no means indicates that Sara led a blameless existence at school, though it does suggest her departure from school was not quite as shaming as she remembers it being.

By then it was 1972. Donny Osmond was singing 'Puppy Love', and *Jesus Christ Superstar* was a hit. Flares were in fashion and Sara was not to be left out. She was still petite; her hair hung in thick brown waves. She liked going to parties and she liked boys. Her father tried to persuade her to take a pre-nursing training course, but she refused; she was searching for excitement and a feeling that she was special. There were rows about her future as well as about her failure at Millfield. One afternoon, when her mother and Billi were out buying shoes, Sara ran away. She told the housekeeper, Mrs Adams, where she was going but swore her to secrecy. She left behind a long and bitter letter for which her mother never forgave her.

Through a friend in London Sara was introduced to an agency for au pairs, which found her a job in Germany. What Sara had not realized was that she was pregnant: the father was a class-mate from Millfield. According to Sara, both sets of parents became involved and there were angry exchanges of letters. But these became academic: Sara miscarried.

Throughout her adolescence Sara seems to have been crying out for help. A highly intelligent girl underachieving at school and behaving in a provocative, extrovert way that alienated her peers, she was isolated and essentially very lonely. She was undeniably a difficult teenager to cope with. Her guilt and shame at feeling angry with her parents for not giving her the emotional support she felt she needed made her at one moment express love and remorse towards them and at the next anger, resentment and rejection. Perhaps not unusually, her parents were not the sort of couple to cope easily with the switchback of teenage emotions. While Jane Cooper was cerebral and strict in her approach, her husband seemed somewhat detached. Neither Sara nor Billi felt they could confide in either parent, something which only compounded Sara's sense of isolation.

Despite the abruptness of Sara's departure for Germany, the experience seemed to do her good. By the time she returned to England for Christmas she had fully recovered from her miscarriage. She had gained weight and was exuberant; she seemed to have found a new lease of confidence. Her father persuaded her not to go back to Germany, so she stayed at home and worked for a neighbour, looking after their children. Three months later she gave in to pressure from her mother and went to college in Manchester to train as a nanny.

While Sara was in Manchester, her mother had a brain haemorrhage. For a month she was looked after by a nurse, but then her husband and Billi took over the task of caring for her. That period gave Billi the chance to develop a closeness of sorts with both her mother and her father, an opportunity Sara never had. Even when paralysed and in a wheelchair, their mother remained a formidable force. They were safe from any physical assault, but she still dominated them.

For both sisters their grandparents' house in Atherstone provided a safe haven. They both remember the sense of freedom and liberation they experienced when they went there. Gerald Austin was still a keen Mason; he was also a Justice of the Peace, and he and his wife had run a counselling charity for servicemen together during the war. Luisa, too, was still very active in the local community and, like both Jane and Sara, was a fiercely independent, individualistic woman. Both Gerald and Luisa were sympathetic and indulgent; Sara and Billi found themselves cosseted and adored, which seemed to them to heighten their sense of emotional deprivation at home. Their grandparents' attentions irritated Sara's father, who felt with apparent justification that they undermined the discipline he had sought to impose. Both grandparents could see that Sara was emotionally quite needy, and they adopted a particularly protective role towards her. She in turn confided in them in a way she could never hope to with her parents. They would often collude with her against her parents and contrive to keep her out of trouble. Where her parents were judgmental they were compassionate; something which at one step removed was undoubtedly easier for them to be.

Despite her grandmother's support, however, Sara's moods were becoming increasingly erratic, and it was at this point, she says, that her mother got the family doctor to prescribe her some Valium. That summer things got too much for Sara. It was harvest-time, which was bad for Jane's asthma. A lot of dirt had been brought into the house by farmworkers coming into the kitchen for coffee. Sara put an attachment on the vacuum-cleaner to suck up the dust, but her mother was upset by the way she was doing it and accused her of trying to break the vacuum-cleaner. A row ensued. Jane telephoned her parents and they came over. According to Sara, her grandmother backed Sara's mother for once and told Sara she was a bitch. It was the only time Sara remembers ever being spoken to like that by her grandmother, and she felt terribly betrayed that the person on whom she had always previously been able to rely as an ally, had sided with her mother. She had also incurred her father's wrath; voices were raised and he took her mother out of the house. Gerald and Louisa also left. Sara felt desperate, alienated from both her parents and her grandparents. She decided she didn't want to live, and she took an overdose of Valium. She says that she took two tablets at a time over a fifteen-minute period. When her grandparents returned to the house, they found her curled up at the bottom of a wardrobe. They took her back to their house and she slept it off. The incident was not mentioned again, and Sara's parents were not told.

Jane Cooper's health gradually improved. She remained

slightly paralysed on her left side but managed to walk again and pursued her equine passions by driving a pony and trap. Sara returned to college in Manchester in the autumn.

That November, while Sara was visiting home, there was another row. The next day her mother had a second brain haemorrhage and was rushed to hospital. During the night Sara came into Billi's bedroom. She was in a hysterical state and Billi had to call the housekeeper for help. The following morning Sara answered the phone. It was the hospital calling to say her mother had died.

Both Sara and her father took the death very badly. Sara convinced herself that her father blamed her and the row she had had for her mother's death. She became very emotional. When Sara arrived back at college after the funeral, she found a letter waiting, which had been written and sent by her mother before her death. It was a very upsetting letter, in which her mother told Sara how disappointed she was with her and her performance at college. Sara was devastated. Even from beyond the grave, it seemed, her mother was expressing her disapproval. Sara dropped out of the college two months before the end of the course. She had only gone there to please her mother, and once again it was clear that she had failed.

Billi, who had remained at home, remembers this particularly upsetting time. Her father would become morose, Billi would retreat into herself, and Sara would become emotional.

Both girls were becoming increasingly independent and the following summer, they went on holiday to a Pontin's camp in Somerset. There Billi met her first boyfriend, and both sisters had such a good time that they decided to try to get a job with the company. They were taken on by a neighbouring camp, but Sara's behaviour, which was as usual extrovert, did not help their employment prospects. They were sacked after just one day after Sara joined a comedian on stage and threatened to take off her blouse. They managed to find work for the rest of the summer at another holiday camp in Devon, however, though Sara had problems with the other women who worked there, her flirtatious behaviour leading to jealousy and rivalry. The relationship between the sisters was also stormy. On one occasion a row developed over who was borrowing more clothes from whom. Sara was wearing clothes that belonged to Billi. She took them off in the main concert hall and then stormed to their chalet where she threw out all Billi's possessions. At the end of the season Billi returned home and Sara went on to work in a Pontin's camp in Blackpool. She fell out with some of the girls there and so Billi sent a telegram saying there had been a death in the family to enable her sister to make an early exit.

2 · Drifting

After that summer Sara's life became more turbulent. She was young, attractive and likeable but was beset by a sense of unease which prevented her from settling down and enjoying her life. A period of drift and depression ensued, a search for something or someone who would give her the security and affection she was lacking. Her father had become involved with a woman, Juliette, who was twenty years his junior and had two sons. A year after losing their mother, both sisters felt that they were now losing their father too. But at the same time they were glad he had found some comfort during this time of grieving.

Sara went back to Manchester where she got a job selling double glazing over the phone and fell into a relationship with a sales rep, Gordon. Feeling that her childhood home was no longer open to her, and desperate for some sort of security, she moved in with him. Her father had decided to marry Juliette and adopt her two sons. They sold the family home in Carlton and moved to a farm in Devon. When Sara went to visit them there she convinced herself that Gordon didn't match up to her father's expectations, and that her father seemed unimpressed by his Manchester accent and career in double glazing. Once again she felt she had failed to meet her father's standards. She became pregnant and Gordon paid for an abortion. Sara didn't feel that she had any option but to terminate the pregnancy but with that decision came tremendous guilt. Her relationship with Gordon broke down and she moved into a flat with a woman friend and her two children.

By now it was the long hot summer of 1976, complete with its drought and heatwave. Sara was still drifting. She was intelligent and articulate but was far from fulfilling her full potential. She drifted between casual jobs, finding it easy to meet people but difficult to develop or sustain friendships. She was physically attractive, open and generous, and her loud and extrovert manner gave her the appearance of being self-confident, but inside she was filled with a sense of self-hatred and despair which fuelled her insecurity. She was twenty-one and plagued by depression. During one particularly bad bout she took her second overdose, swallowing most of her flat-mate's anti-depressants. She was taken to hospital and had her stomach pumped but received no after-care.

Shortly after that incident Sara met a construction worker, Noel. He was part of a gang building a motorway and lived in a caravan on site. If Sara had perhaps been anxious about Gordon, it was clear that Noel was far less likely to secure her father's approval. But Sara, glad to have found affection and warmth, moved in with Noel and, believing they would stay together, became pregnant again. She started to bleed heavily, however, and was rushed to hospital. There she had her second abortion, again accompanied by guilt but also in the knowledge that the bleeding meant that the foetus would have been unlikely to survive. The relationship with Noel continued until one week-end he disappeared without telling Sara where he was going. That gave her the impetus to leave a relationship which had brought her a degree of emotional security but also feelings of shame and inadequacy because she felt that Noel could not match up to her father's standards. She got a place on her own back in Manchester, supporting herself by working nights in a hotel bar. It was there that she met her first husband.

Helmut Scharley was twenty years older than Sara, and German. He was in England working for a brewery. His English was poor but Sara spoke some German from her time as an au pair. She began to spend more and more time with Helmut. Sara remembers him telling her that his wife had been killed in a car crash and asked her if she would move to Germany with him. She telephoned her father to discuss the idea and was upset when she felt he didn't seem to be particularly interested in her dilemma, and convinced herself that he didn't mind if she left the country.

A couple of nights later Sara went to bed thinking about the family house that had been sold to enable her father to move to Devon with his new wife. Although she hadn't lived there for a number of years, she remembers going to sleep missing it and wishing she could go back there. The next thing she recalls is waking up in a police station. She had been found wandering the streets with no clothes on, clutching a teddy bear. Frightened and confused, she couldn't remember who she was, and when Helmut arrived at the police station to collect her, she didn't recognize him.

Helmut took her home, and the next morning she went to see the doctor. He found she had scratches all up her arm which he deduced had been made by a ring that Sara had been wearing. Sara had no recollection of that. She was admitted to the Withington Hospital for psychiatric treatment.

The doctors there considered her to be almost paranoiac. She was having trouble eating and sleeping, had lost a lot of weight, and was clearly in a highly distressed state. She told the doctors she was so convinced everybody hated her that she'd taken to going out only if she was wearing sunglasses so that nobody could recognize her and say anything nasty about her. She felt she should be happy because of her privileged upbringing but she found herself bursting into tears for no reason.

The only people who wanted her, she said, were men who could have her body. Crippled by feelings of guilt associated with her mother's death, she rationalized her loneliness by convincing herself that she must be lonely because she was bad. She felt locked into a constant struggle with a part of herself that wanted her to prove that that was the case and that she was indeed bad. It was that part of herself that she felt drove her into promiscuity and rebellious behaviour. It was that part, she said, which would spur her into asking a man she'd been having a drink with to go to bed with her, while her rational self would look on in amazement at how she was behaving. It was almost as if she was engaging in self-destructive behaviour to punish herself for having failed to live up to her own and what she thought were her parents' expectations. It was also clear that she had virtually no sense of self-worth or self-esteem. Casual relationships with men represented one of the only ways she knew to make herself feel wanted and valued. Although she was genuinely uninhibited and liberated in her approach to sex, promiscuity further undermined her own self-image because of her lack of emotional security, making her feel that it was only her sexuality that could attract people.

While she was in hospital, she also began to discuss her feelings about her parents for the first time. According to the hospital records, she told the doctors who counselled her that she felt she had been starved of affection as a child and that neither of her parents had really loved her but had always looked down on her. Now that her mother was dead there was never going to be the chance to form a loving relationship with her, and she felt that her father had betrayed her mother's memory by remarrying so quickly. Yet despite her apparent honesty with the doctors on those emotional issues, she still persisted with the lie she had carried with her from school. She told them she had succeeded academically and had three A Levels and one S Level.

The process of unravelling her feelings and her unhappiness was never completed, however. After four days she left the hospital for Germany with Helmut whom she had decided to marry. But it emerged that Helmut's wife was not in fact dead; instead she was living in his home with their children. Sara spent her first night in Germany in a field.

Sara was young and desperate for affection. Whatever doubts she may have had about Helmut were obscured by the life he seemed to be offering her: he did eventually divorce his wife. His work for various breweries meant that he travelled all over Europe, and Sara travelled with him. It was while they were in Marseille that she discovered she was pregnant. She was overjoyed and they married soon afterwards in a registry office in Denmark. Still on the move, Sara gave birth to a healthy baby girl in Belgium on 4 September 1978. She named her daughter Louisa after her grandmother, but when it came to registering the birth the Belgian official misspelt her name, ending it with an 'e' instead of an 'a' and omitting the 'o'. Sara stuck to her chosen pronunciation but accepted the official's spelling. The arrival of Luise increased her sense of security and well-being. Her relationship seemed to be going well and Sara felt she was very much in love. For the first time in her life she felt that things were as they should be and that all was well.

Helmut was offered a job in Venezuela designing and building beer tanks; both he and Sara enjoyed travelling and so he decided to take it. By March 1979 he had left for South America while Sara stayed with her grandfather in England where she got visas and malaria tablets for herself and Luise. On 1 July they left to join Helmut.

As she stepped off the plane at Caracas airport Sara was hit by a wave of heavy tropical heat. It was midway through Venezuela's rainy season and the atmosphere was hot and close. The airport had a threatening but exciting feel to it; Sara was quickly surrounded by people offering taxis, guides and hotels. She picked her way through the crowd and found Helmut. Luise had developed diarrhoea on the plane and Sara was exhausted.

Having travelled across the world to be with Helmut, Sara very quickly realized that her dream of a happy married life was not everything she thought it would be. She was confronted by a man who was very different from the one she believed she had married. During the five months they had been apart, Helmut had begun to drink heavily and was taking full advantage of Venezuela's seedy nightlife. He was buying and consuming vast quantities of rum and when drunk, Sara recalls that he would sometimes become violent. They lived in a small wooden chalet that was part of a hotel complex, where Sara coped with Helmut's drinking and violence as best she could until one night, about a month after her arrival in Venezuela, she decided she could stand it no longer. Sara took Luise and fled. On her return the hotel informed Sara that they had asked Helmut to leave but his bill was still outstanding. She had no money, only a diamond brooch that had belonged to her grandmother. In great distress she sold it, paid off Helmut's debts and flew home to England with Luise.

Perhaps other women would have seen Helmut for what he

was earlier – certainly those who met him while he was in England felt very uneasy about him. But for Sara, blinded by chronic need and loneliness, he had seemed the man of her dreams. Those dreams were now shattered, though, and her sense of loneliness and failure returned with a vengeance.

Driven from her marriage by fear and violence, Sara turned to her family for help. She felt ashamed of what had happened and did not want, once again, to feel that her father disapproved of her. So, as had been the pattern throughout her childhood, she turned not to her parents but to her grandparents for support. In fact her grandmother had died while Sara was in Venezuela, leaving her grandfather living alone in Atherstone, just 6 miles from where Sara had been born. He was old, frail and in need of help. Sara and Luise moved in with him.

Three Florence Close is a two-bedroomed bungalow on a small estate about twenty minutes' walk from the centre of Atherstone. At eighty-one Gerald Austin was in a quite dependent state. Two hip operations had left him barely mobile. Luise, who was still only ten months old, also needed constant attention. It was not an easy time for Sara. Her dreams of married life and a family of her own had been replaced with exhaustion and claustrophobia. Her grandfather had been a magistrate and a factory owner; now, trapped at home, he was often reluctant to let her go out. At the same time Sara's relationship with her father remained strained and volatile. When they spoke on the phone Sara would always feel that her failure to keep her marriage alive and to make a go of her life made her the subject of his disapproval.

Sara's sister Billi had by this time married an American and was living in California. She came to visit, bringing with her her two-year-old son. During her stay Sara's depression and resentment became overwhelming. She felt jealous of her sister who seemed to have made more of a success of her life; she felt trapped and drained. She telephoned her father in the hope that he might offer a way out and somewhere to live. Instead, she says, he seemed irritated by the fact that she was effectively living off her grandfather.

That Boxing Day Sara took a blade from her grandfather's razor and cut her left wrist. Her sister found her in bed, the sheets drenched in blood. Sara begged to be left to die, she said she didn't want to go on living. Billi woke her grandfather and called an ambulance. Sara refused to go in it but was eventually forced to. She was taken to hospital in Nuneaton where her wounds were stitched and bandaged, and she was back home within hours. It was clear to Billi that her sister needed help, but she was unable to convince her family that there was anything they could do. In the end she returned to the States and Sara stayed in Atherstone.

The following summer Sara started seeing a car-worker, Robert. As with her previous relationships it rapidly escalated in intensity. By the autumn Robert had moved into the house with Sara, her grandfather and her daughter. He had a son from a previous relationship whom he brought with him. Although there were only two bedrooms between the three adults and two children who were then living in Florence Close they all got on remarkably well.

The stresses and volatility in Sara's relationship with her father persisted, however. During one telephone conversation he asked her about the beautiful moon-shaped diamond pin brooch that had belonged to her grandmother, the one that Sara had been forced to sell to get back from Venezuela. Her father was furious: Sara's mother had lent it to her parents, and so as far as he was concerned the brooch belonged to him and should not have been sold. He was further irritated when he learned that Sara's grandfather had sold a painting. Sara inferred from this that he blamed her financial dependency on her grandfather for his decision to sell the heirloom.

The impact of that argument was compounded a few days later when a row developed over Luise. She had been sick in her cot and Sara decided to bathe her. Robert and her grandfather accused her of over-reacting. Sara felt as if she could please no one, not even the grandfather who had most often provided her with shelter from her parents' rage. She became very upset and told them she was going to bed. She had decided to kill herself.

Slitting her wrists last time hadn't worked. This time she cut her throat. Her grandfather found her.

Sara woke up in hospital unable to remember what she had done. Her local GP was not informed. Instead, she was seen by a junior registrar. Her neck was stitched up and she was kept in overnight. The following day she was allowed to go home without, as the hospital records confirm, receiving any counselling or psychiatric assessment. Her family was anxious to play down the incident and few people were told about what had happened.

Two weeks later, though, it became impossible to contain the situation. Sara had become hysterical, picked up a carving-knife and was threatening to kill herself. Her grandfather, unable to restrain her himself, called his GP, Dr Kenneth Farn. By the time he arrived Sara had locked herself in her bedroom with the knife. Dr Farn called for an ambulance and with the help of the team that arrived, coaxed Sara out of the bedroom. She was taken to the Walsgrave Hospital in Coventry. Dr Farn was convinced she was seriously ill and had her committed for immediate compulsory admission under Section 29 of the Mental Health Act.

Sara was diagnosed as suffering from reactive depression; in other words, the doctors thought her depression had been triggered by current events in her life rather than by any chemical or hormonal imbalance. The doctors found her intelligent, co-operative and pleasant, but at that stage she was unwilling to acknowledge that she had problems. She insisted that her childhood had been wonderful and again reiterated her lie about her O and A Level results. She told the doctors that she was not feeling suicidal and that despite her repeated bouts of depression she did not need any treatment. She was unwilling to remain in the hospital and less than a week later she was discharged.

Sara returned to live at her grandfather's. Her relationship with Robert continued for another year. When they split up she moved to Coventry where she shared a rented house with three friends. But the owner failed to keep up the mortgage payments and so the building society foreclosed. Sara went to a housing association for help and was allocated a small terraced house, 146 Kingfield Road. She moved in on 1 July 1983.

At twenty-eight Sara joined the horde of unemployed single mothers struggling to survive. She was lucky to have a relatively comfortable home, but she and Luise had to eke out an existence on £41 a week social security. There was no money for new clothes; no money for anything other than the barest of necessities. Sara was a good and ingenious cook, able to feed herself and Luise for very little, but her life became a perpetual struggle to meet the gas, electricity and telephone bills.

She supplemented her dole money with what work she could find, working on one occasion as a cook in a pub but mainly as a telephone salesgirl. But the jobs never lasted. She would get people's backs up virtually the first day she arrived anywhere. Her background and intelligence, combined with her seemingly arrogant manner, meant she did not fit in easily amongst those dependent on the black economy for income.

It was a lonely period for Sara. Although she longed for friendship, her erratic moods and uninhibited behaviour would often frighten and distance people. The friendships she did form tended to be intense and shortlived. Doris Foxwell and Veronica Costelloe were two friends who managed to ride out Sara's moods and maintain a long-term friendship. Doris lived across the street from Sara and became something of a surrogate mother to her and grandmother to Luise. When she could she looked after Luise so that Sara could go to work or have a night off. Gentle and older than Sara, Doris knew she could be volatile and accepted it as part of her personality. She felt her friendship gave Sara some stability. Veronica was Sara's contemporary. She too was a single mother, her daughter was just one year younger than Luise. Whereas others judged Sara, often quickly and harshly, she attempted to understand her. She found that Sara's provocative manner and strong temper were balanced by generosity, warmth and affection. Sara storming out and slamming the door one day would invariably be followed by Sara returning the next, giving Veronica a big hug and asking for everything to be forgotten. Whilst others thought Sara was spoilt and had

had it easy, Veronica believed Sara's transition from civil servant's daughter to single parent was in some ways harder to cope with than the steady material struggle that she had always known.

For the majority of those who knew Sara, though, the intensity and volatility of her moods were threatening and unacceptable. There were times when Veronica too became exhausted and drained by the friendship. When that happened she would pull away from Sara, sometimes for several months. After one such time, Veronica remembers Sara arriving on her doorstep wearing a headscarf and carrying a bottle of wine. She told Veronica that she realized she had been horrible and difficult and that she was sorry. To punish herself for being so awful to people, she said, she had shaved her head. Veronica looked under the scarf and saw that she was indeed bald. Once again Sara had damaged herself at a time of feeling tormented by a sense of rejection and despair.

Spurred on by a sense of inner emptiness and loneliness, Sara again turned to men to give her the affection that was missing from her life. As in her period of drift in Manchester, she lacked the confidence to believe that men could like her for herself. She was not inhibited about sex or her sexuality and her inner insecurity convinced her men would only want her for one thing. That being the case, she gave it in return for what was usually only temporary affection and closeness.

Financially as well as emotionally there was pressure on Sara to be with a man. A boyfriend with an income could fill in some of the gaps: shoes for Luise, a night on the town for Sara, small things that make the relentless grind of life on the dole a little more bearable. After a number of fleeting affairs Sara fell into a more serious relationship with an engineer called John. He was considerably younger than her and soon after they met he moved in with her. A year into their relationship she became pregnant again. She had been using contraception and was sure in her own mind that she didn't want another child. She told John she didn't want any fuss made and sent him to the pub to play pool, although secretly she had wanted his support and comfort. She coped with the trauma of her third abortion alone, and soon afterwards that relationship also ended.

During her relationship with John Sara had formed a strong platonic friendship with a man named Tim Haughton. He was physically disabled and with him Sara had what she felt was one of her only genuinely platonic relationships with a man. The friendship gave her confidence and security; because Tim made no physical advances towards her, she felt as if he wanted her for herself and not just for what she could give him. But he too was a depressive and on a visit to Scotland he committed suicide, leaving Sara a note apologizing for the pain he would cause her and £2000 in his will. Sara's depression worsened and her search for comfort intensified.

It was at about this time that Luise began to have serious difficulties at school. Sara had encouraged her to be independent from an early age. By the age of six she would travel by herself on the train to see her grandparents in Devon. But despite her maturity she could be difficult and disruptive. The insecurity in her mother's life was inevitably having its impact on her. In addition she was failing academically. Sara could not understand it, she knew Luise was intelligent yet her performance was well below average. She embarked on endless meetings with teachers to try to discover what was going wrong and was told that Luise was educationally sub-normal. That was a diagnosis Sara could not and would not accept. She took Luise to a string of specialists but to no avail. She suspected that Luise was dyslexic but no one would confirm it. It was not until they moved back to Atherstone some years later that Sara discovered her instinct had been correct – Luise was dyslexic. Sara's relationship with her daughter was strong but stormy. Each loved the other passionately but Luise was very like her mother, strong-willed and determined, and inevitably there were clashes. For Sara, her daughter was the only constant and secure feature of her existence.

Her next relationship was with a man called Frank whom Sara had known for some time before the relationship started. Sara says that one weekend when he was staying with her he suggested they get married. Sara took the offer seriously, but while she was contemplating it she discovered he had also asked her best friend Veronica for a date. She finished with him, feeling desperately hurt and rejected. Friends remember that Sara received a call telling her that Frank had been killed on a building site. Sara became hysterical and rang her sister in California and her father. Her father phoned a number of building sites but could find no trace of the accident. Sara later discovered that Frank was not dead at all and that the call had been a hoax. To her this was yet again evidence that she had let herself down by allowing herself to fall for someone who would treat her cruelly.

3 · 'Only When He Drinks'

Sara met Malcolm Thornton on 4 May 1987, appropriately enough, as it was to turn out, in a pub. She had travelled up to her home town, Atherstone, to visit the landlord of the Wheatsheaf, which stands at the end of Atherstone's main street and is the last in the string of eight pubs that line it. Locals say you either start or end the evening there, depending on which way you are travelling. Atherstone's pubs are perhaps the most remarkable thing about the town, which with a population of only 8000 boasts fifteen of them. They are the social epicentre of the town and drinking is the local pastime.

Sara remembers walking into the Wheatsheaf and seeing Malcolm there 'holding up the bar'. She had only to look at him to know he was something special. Immaculately dressed, his gentle bearing and distinguished air made him stand out from the crowd around the bar. He was tall, handsome, articulate and intelligent. He had grown up in Blackpool but his northern accent had been eroded by years spent in London and abroad. At forty-two he was ten years Sara's senior. They developed an instant rapport. He treated her with courtesy and respect, qualities which were all too often missing in the men she met. In Malcolm's company Sara immediately felt secure and relaxed. They left the pub and went for an Indian meal. From there they went to Sara's house in Coventry.

Over the next fortnight Malcolm called Sara at regular intervals. She was impressed by his humour, intelligence and worldliness and by the fact that he was behaving like a gentleman. He was the most conventionally eligible man she had fallen for. Unfortunately what she did not realize then was that despite his outward respectability, he would also prove to be the most dangerous. Malcolm Thornton was an alcoholic. The tell-tale signs were there from the very beginning of the relationship but Sara, herself a heavy drinker, either didn't see them or chose to ignore them.

Their second date also took place in a pub, this time the Stag and Pheasant in Coventry. It was the night of the FA Cup Final; Coventry had won and the atmosphere was electric. The evening went well until another man bought Sara a drink. Malcolm became very jealous and kept demanding to know why he hadn't also bought him a drink. Eventually, Sara poured her drink into his pocket in what she told him was an attempt to shut him up. Not surprisingly Malcolm left. But they spoke on the phone the following day and apologized profusely to each other. He invited Sara and Luise to come to Atherstone the next day.

They spent the day talking. Malcolm told Sara something of his past. He had grown up in Blackpool, the youngest of five children. As the son of strict Methodists he went to church three times every Sunday. His sisters had thought he might go into the church but instead, at sixteen, he left grammar school to become a policeman. Too young to be an officer, he served first as a cadet, becoming a constable three years later. During this time he met his first wife, Moyra Friend, who was a local girl and a friend of his sisters. They met when she was sixteen and he was nineteen and married four years later. After six years on the beat in Blackpool Malcolm transferred to London to join the Metropolitan Police. It was a big move for both him and Moyra, and his whole family turned out on the platform in Blackpool in the early hours of the morning to see them off.

Malcolm was ambitious and bright, and once he'd got himself settled he combined his job with courses in economics, law and politics at the local polytechnic. He became a lecturer at the Police Training School in Hendon and he also served on the streets in the Drugs and Vice Squad. But after his leg was injured in a car chase he decided that it was time to find a job that was a little more sedentary. By this time he and Moyra had two sons, Martin and Stuart. In 1975, after fifteen years as a police officer, he left the force to become a publican.

Running a pub was something Malcolm had wanted to do for a long time. But he soon found that he missed the freedom and constant variety that working for the police had given him. He managed two pubs, the first in Shepperton and the second in Staines, but less than two years later he quit to go back to security work. This time he chose the private sector, working first for British Airways, and then, lured by the prospect of a very large tax-free salary, he left England for Saudi Arabia. Moyra stayed in England with their two sons and the marriage gradually broke down. Malcolm enjoyed life in Saudi Arabia. He liked the freedom and the excitement of being away from home. He stayed there for six years and while he was there married again.

On his return to England with his second wife, Anne, Malcolm joined the international freight company, TNT, as a security manager in Leicester. When he was caught driving over the limit he lost his licence and nearly his job, because his work in Leicester necessitated driving. However, the company valued him and agreed to transfer him to a job where a driving licence was not a pre-requisite; the only snag was that it was in Atherstone and he had to live nearby in case there was an emergency. So he moved to a small house in Atherstone, seeing Anne only at weekends. By the time Sara met him his marriage had ended. She could empathize with his broken relationships, and just as he missed Saudi Arabia, she missed the Pacific.

Malcolm was a big man but he was also seemingly gentle. To Sara's delight, he was an excellent cook; one of his specialities was curry. He cooked for Sara and Luise the night he invited them to visit, and they arranged to spend the whole of the next weekend together. Luise and Sara travelled over to Atherstone on the bus the following Saturday morning. They arrived to find that Malcolm had made the house ready for them: he had laid lino in the kitchen and rearranged the attic so that it made a bedroom for Luise complete with television, radio and space for her toys and clothes.

Over the next few weeks their relationship continued to develop in the same vein, with each of them becoming more involved with the other. Malcolm offered Sara security, stability and the prospect of a more wholesome life. She had at last met someone who was her intellectual equal and who also, perhaps even more importantly, offered her a route back to the respectability she had not experienced since childhood. It was not respectability for respectability's sake that she wanted, but rather, it seemed to those who knew her, the chance at last to lead the sort of life which she felt had been expected of her since birth, and in so doing perhaps finally gain in her mind her father's approval. She didn't like Malcolm's heavy drinking but thought it was understandable, given the guilt and anger he felt at the breakdown of his second marriage. She felt gratified that Malcolm could let down his barriers and confide his pain to her. She felt it brought them closer.

Malcolm was by no means blind to the problems a relationship with Sara posed. Her reputation preceded her and his male friends tried hard to warn him off her. Atherstone is a conservative town and when it comes to what is considered acceptable female behaviour it is very backward. The men, according to one female resident, 'are somewhere back in the dark ages'. Sara was an outgoing, intelligent woman, she liked to discuss big issues and always seemed to have a cause to campaign for, whether it was seal-clubbing in the Arctic or Atherstone's litter problems. She would take on anyone in conversation at any time. Men in Atherstone were not used to being challenged by a woman and most of them didn't like it. Sara was also sexually promiscuous and dressed provocatively. During her childhood in Fiji she had grown accustomed to running around with few clothes on, but in Atherstone such behaviour was not acceptable. Sara viewed underwear as an unnecessary middle-class convention and she wasn't going to wear it. She liked male attention and dressed accordingly; uninhibited and confident about her body, she was certainly a very attractive woman. She had slept with a number of the men in Atherstone, but as is often the case, they did not respect her for it, indeed some of those who had themselves had sex with Sara tried to persuade Malcolm not to touch her. As far as they were concerned, casual sex was acceptable for men but not for women. Sadly, it wasn't just the men who were hostile towards Sara because of her sexuality. As often happens in small towns like Atherstone, the women tended to be as harsh, if not harsher, in their judgment and treatment of women like Sara. Many of the women in their social circle found Sara's behaviour and her attitudes threatening and they treated her accordingly. They too tried to warn Malcolm off her.

But Malcolm was anything but put off. Sara challenged him on every level: sexually, intellectually and emotionally. Whilst others warned him to steer clear of her flamboyant and often difficult behaviour, he was intrigued and stimulated by it. He sensed something underneath her outward displays of strength that her split-second critics missed: a deeper vulnerability and a desperate need to be loved and cared for. His two previous wives, Moyra and Anne, had been responsible adult women, but there was something of the child in Sara which when combined with her outward sophistication and liberation attracted him deeply.

There were serious problems, though, and they began to emerge quite quickly. That July TNT had their annual Open Day for staff and their relatives. Malcolm was actually on duty that day but he asked Sara to come along. She arrived with a friend and Luise but barely saw Malcolm all day. She left at five to go back and cook some supper at Malcolm's house but he didn't show up. Unbeknown to Sara he was getting drunk with his friends instead. Eventually one of those friends turned up at the house and told Sara that Malcolm wanted her to leave. She did, very quickly, but in the process she forgot important documents for a meeting at work the next day. The following morning her boss drove her round to pick them up. By that time, Malcolm was meant to be on his way to Blackpool to visit his sisters, but he was still at home, hung-over and full of remorse, when Sara arrived. He apologized profusely and that week sent her dozens of roses from Blackpool in an attempt to woo her back. And despite his behaviour Sara didn't want to lose him. He returned from Blackpool with a beautiful gold necklace and persuaded Sara to forgive him.

The relationship continued to develop. Later that summer, when Malcolm went on holiday to Spain, he sent Sara a postcard telling her he loved her. On his return they discussed living together. The only obstacle from Sara's point of view was Luise's education. Once she had found a school in Atherstone that would take her, she moved in with Malcolm. It was August 1987 and they had known each other for two and a half months.

To begin with, Malcolm would go out for a drink straight after work every night. He was a member of what he and his colleagues called the 601 Club, their name for the group that gathered at the pub the minute work was over. It upset Sara but she accepted it as a relic of his bachelor days and also as a pattern of behaviour he had developed to cope with the break-up of his second marriage. Gradually, though, he started coming home earlier, and they became happier and happier. They viewed each other as totally compatible and would laugh about the fact that even they, late in life though it was, had managed to find a 'PFL' as they called it, a partner for life.

Both Sara and Malcolm were naturally gregarious. They had an active social life, either going to the pub more often now together, or having people round. Malcolm's work as a security manager and his first career as a policeman meant that his close circle of friends were mainly police officers. He kept the house stocked with whisky for their visits.

Genuinely happy together, Sara and Malcolm began to look for a bigger house and found one at 73 Church Walk. Although Malcolm had insisted that their new home should not be more than three minutes' walking distance from a pub, this house lay towards the edge of the town in a quiet cul-de-sac and was a good fifteen minutes' walk from the nearest source of alcohol. They arranged to move in the week before Christmas.

Before that, though, an incident occurred that made Sara think seriously about her future with Malcolm. They had gone to one of Atherstone's many pubs, where Sara played pool with some of her friends and Malcolm stood at the bar talking shop with some of his. When Sara finished her game and went to find him, he'd gone. She took a taxi home but he wasn't there so she got

the taxi driver to take her on to the Wheatsheaf where she found
him in a drunken and abusive state. He refused to go home with
her so she left him and returned alone. About two hours later,
she says, he came in, and when she stood up to greet him, he
punched her on her left eye before proceeding upstairs to bed.
Shocked and terribly upset, Sara barely slept that night. Malcolm
left early the next morning to do a security search for TNT
and returned to the house for breakfast with a work colleague.
Apparently not remembering anything of the previous night,
Malcolm looked at Sara's eye and asked her what had happened.
Too ashamed to tell him what he'd done in front of a stranger,
she lied and said she had opened a cupboard door on it. Malcolm
chided her for her clumsiness, but when his workmate left Sara
told him the truth. She recalls that Malcolm was horrified. He
had no recollection of what had happened. The last thing he
remembered was leaving the first pub because, he said, he
couldn't stand seeing Sara playing pool with other men.

Research shows that 90 per cent of women who are hit by
their partners stay with them; Sara had now become one of
these. Assaults of this type can of course be isolated incidents,
but they can also mark the beginning of a dangerous pattern,
with the man losing respect for the woman because she has
apparently accepted his violence, making it easier for him to
become violent again in the future. For her part, the woman,
whose self-respect is severely diminished by the treatment, begins
to lose her confidence and her sense of perspective. She starts to
make excuses for his violence and try to find explanations. More
often than not, she ends up blaming herself, reasoning that she
must have done something to deserve it, otherwise why would
it have happened?

Malcolm was again filled with remorse. The following day he
bought Sara a pair of diamond and sapphire earrings which she
wore every day until her imprisonment. He promised faithfully
never to hit her again. It was a promise made to be broken.

Eight days before Christmas they moved into Church Walk.
Friends came over from Coventry and within a week it looked
as if they'd been living there for years. On Christmas Day Mal-

colm went to the pub before lunch. He was never abusive when sober, and Sara was beginning to identify a pattern to his drinking habits and the aggressive behaviour that could go with them. Lager alone was fairly safe – after drinking it Malcolm would usually just fall asleep on the couch; spirits generally spelled trouble. They made it through their first Christmas lunch together without a major incident. Malcolm retired soon afterwards to sleep it off, awakening only when more guests arrived that evening for a drink.

Sara soon learned that weekends and Bank Holidays were the trouble spots. Barely one would pass when Malcolm wasn't drunk. She recalls that one Sunday night, after a particularly boozy day, Malcolm fell asleep on his stomach on the floor in front of the television. Come bedtime, mindful of his habit of waking up, lighting a cigarette and then going to sleep again, Sara woke him up. Then, she says, he carefully stood up, emptied a large crystal ashtray on to the floor and smashed it down on her hand. He then went to bed. Sara spent the night crying, first downstairs and then beside Malcolm in bed. At four-thirty a.m. he woke up and asked her what he'd done. She turned on the light and showed him her hand which was by now swollen and very bruised. He went downstairs, made himself a cup of tea, and wept.

Despite his memory black-outs Malcolm still refused to admit he had a problem. Sara didn't really appreciate that he had either. She loved him, and for her, forgiving and trying to understand his violence was part of that process. When sober he was a gentle, kind man, full of remorse and full of love for Sara: it was only when he was drunk that he would become violent. Because it was possible to blame the violence on alcohol Sara could forgive Malcolm and blame the drink instead.

Sara was not alone in doing this. Few women feel they want to leave their husbands after the first few incidents of battering. Instead they look for an explanation for their partner's cruelty. If they can find one in the form of something like alcoholism it will give them a pretext to excuse, explain and attempt to understand their partner's violence.

Sara was a heavy drinker herself and her drinking increased as the stresses of her life overwhelmed her. Her own moods and volatility also contributed to the tensions in the relationship; she was not one to back away from confrontation, nor could she easily cope with feelings of hurt and rejection, which in many ways was what Malcolm's drinking and violence seemed to represent to her. Quite often, as an escape, she would go out to pubs and drink and play pool, trying to inject an air of normality into her fast-disintegrating life.

Any expert on addiction could have predicted that Sara's volatility and lack of self-esteem would have been increased by Malcolm's drinking, and similarly would have seen Malcolm's extraordinary swings between remorse and abuse as a clear symptom of the Jekyll and Hyde phenomenon, a classic indication of alcoholism, which is now, of course, a recognized disease. But they may well have questioned the attribution of Malcolm's violence to the drink. They may well have asked whether alcohol caused the violence or whether it merely enabled it. Alcohol's primary effect on behaviour is to disinhibit it. It defuses the conscience and in so doing enables the drinker to behave in a way that their conscience was previously stopping them from.

Neither Sara nor Malcolm realized they were being drawn into a dangerous and highly destructive cycle with both of them slowly but surely becoming enmeshed in a dependency on alcohol and violence. The cycle began to gather momentum. When sober, Malcolm was still the sparkling, funny, intelligent man Sara had fallen in love with. They shared the same sense of humour; they both loved to cook and to entertain. But once Malcolm started to drink, the dark side of his character would emerge. Sara saw it as a vicious circle, with Malcolm getting drunk to forget and then staying drunk to avoid the shame that inevitably accompanied sobriety. Once drunk, Malcolm would do anything he could to stay drunk.

When he did eventually come out of it Sara would nurse him. His hands would be shaking so much that she'd have to feed him; she'd massage his back and legs to ease the aching and she'd buy him cough mixture to help him sleep. He was always humble and grateful then, and Sara was forgiving, glad to have the non-violent side of Malcolm back again. Then, Sara says, he would insist on making love to show himself that he was forgiven. Although that would often make her feel resentful, she'd submit. She despised herself for it but she never found the confidence to say that she was too hurt to want to sleep with him. Instead she'd go through with it as convincingly as she could, knowing that to refuse his advances would give him an excuse to go on another bender.

July came round again and with it TNT's annual Open Day. Sara cooked a big picnic lunch while Malcolm went to the pub. Most of his afternoon was also spent drinking; something that wasn't altogether wise in view of the company's policy of forbidding the consumption of alcohol during working hours. Whereas the previous summer's Open Day had been very hot, this year it was raining. The adults took refuge in the beer tent while many of the children, Luise amongst them, played outside and got soaked. Sara asked Malcolm to take them home for a hot bath. Bad-tempered and clearly reluctant to leave his beer, he finally agreed. After a bath and a change of clothing he asked Sara to go back to the office with him to check that everything was secure. Thinking they'd only be half an hour, Sara left Luise to watch television. When they arrived at the office, however, there was a party in full swing. Sara was furious, she felt Malcolm had tricked her into going, and demanded he take her home to Luise. He did so in stony silence and left her there.

At about ten that night the phone rang. It was a security manager at TNT asking Sara to come and collect Malcolm from the Red Lion. She got there to find that he was quite far gone and drinking whisky. Sara began to cry and was chided for nagging by Malcolm's colleague, but, she says, she knew what she was in for. Malcolm took one look at her and left; she returned home alone. Two and a half hours later there was another call, this time from the warehouse at TNT.

Two of their employees had seen Malcolm in the car park outside the Red Lion. He was trying the doors on various cars.

One of the men, Steve Byard, knew Malcolm worked as a security manager for the company, with responsibility for preventing theft, and he concluded that it probably would not be a good idea for Malcolm or the company if he were to be caught apparently trying to steal cars. So he walked him away from the cars and up and down the road. Malcolm was very drunk and kept muttering, 'I know you, you bastard' under his breath, but after about three-quarters of an hour they managed to calm him down enough to get him into one of their cars. Their next problem, however, was that they didn't know where he lived. They drove to the police station to try to find out, but the police didn't want to know and wouldn't give them Malcolm's address. As a last resort they drove into work and got someone there to phone Sara. Less than happy at the prospect of him coming home in that state, but with little other option, she told them the address. Shortly afterwards he arrived home. Steve Byard and Stan Clarke got him out of the car and stood by the gate to make sure he didn't fall over as he walked in. As he was teetering along the path Sara came out of the front door to meet him. Malcolm greeted her with a very hard punch; the force of it lifted her off her feet and threw her backwards into a hedge. Luise stood at the doorway and screamed. Malcolm lumbered indoors and headed upstairs, at which point Steve Byard decided to intervene. He followed Malcolm in and grabbed hold of his leg as he started to climb the stairs. Malcolm lashed out and kicked him back down again. Steve pursued him up the stairs and after a prolonged struggle locked him into the bathroom. However, Malcolm managed to escape and attacked Steve, holding him in an arm-lock. Stan Clarke came to his aid and shouted for Sara to call the police.

When the police arrived Malcolm walked out looking as if nothing had happened and obviously heading for bed. When the police appeared to be about to leave it at that, Steve started to remonstrate, explaining what had happened, saying that he was not prepared to leave a woman and child alone with Malcolm and asking what the police were going to do about him. They told him it was 'only a domestic' and that he should leave it alone. He again explained what had happened, insisting that they take some sort of action to remove Malcolm from the house, at least until he was sober. He continued to argue and says he was then told that he was the one who would spend the night in the cells if he didn't leave the matter to the police. Stan also remembers the police getting very aggressive with Steve: 'It was all wrong, it looked like we were the ones who were going to end up getting arrested and he was going to be left where he was.' On that note they decided it was best for them to leave. The police did not charge Malcolm Thornton with assault, nor did they remove him from the house. They left him to sleep it off. The incident report records that in fact it was Sara and Luise who had to leave their home and spend the night in a hotel in Atherstone.

That was not the only time the police became involved, nor was it the only time they allowed Sara to be driven from her home by violence. In 1989 there was no national policy on domestic violence, only a series of recommendations from the Home Office. It was then, as it still is now, left very much to the discretion of individual police forces to decide how to deal with incidents of domestic violence. Few at that time had any cohesive policy for dealing with the problem, and so in practice officers were left to deal with situations as they saw fit, receiving little or no guidance from their Chief Constables on the special problems they might encounter in relation to the issue. The pattern generally was that they would try to calm the situation down and attempt some kind of reconciliation between the man and woman, and if that failed they would suggest the woman leave her home until her partner had had a chance to 'cool down'. It is generally accepted that officers rarely treated domestic assaults as seriously as they would ordinary assaults. The fact that women might be unwilling to press charges compounded officers' reluctance to arrest the man involved. So then, as often still happens, their most usual response if they were unable to calm the situation down was to suggest the woman left and spent the night somewhere else, regardless of the fact that she was the victim, not the perpetrator of the violence. One can imagine few

other crimes where it is left to the victim to leave their home
while the offender remains there unimpeded.

The Home Office at that time did not appear to be dealing
very effectively with an extremely serious problem. Over a third
of female victims of homicide are also battered wives, but in
1986 the Home Office guidance to chief police officers on violence against women was only three pages long and contained
just one paragraph on domestic violence. It was accompanied
by a report by the Women's National Commission which made
a number of recommendations regarding police training, police
willingness to arrest in a domestic situation, police knowledge
of and contact with Women's Aid and other organizations, and
the appropriateness of officers counselling reconciliation. To
almost all the Commission's statements the Home Office responded with a version of 'The Chief Officers will be asked to
consider' or 'Chief Officers will be asked to review' – not very
strong language from a body supposedly responsible for developing guidelines and policy. So the report did very little to
improve the situation, in that it was still left to individual Chief
Constables as to what if any guidance to give to officers dealing
with victims of domestic violence, leaving such victims dependent on the degree of enlightenment that existed in a particular
area. As a response to continued criticism of police procedure
in relation to domestic violence, the Home Office has since issued
a second circular, this time dealing directly with domestic violence. Much more comprehensive than the 1986 circular, it is
eleven pages long and goes into greater detail, using much
stronger language, stressing the use and value of arrest and the
dangers of seeking reconciliation. A number of police stations
now have special units which deal with domestic violence, but
the police's response now as then remains inconsistent and the
subject of sustained criticism.

The next morning the situation deteriorated still further. Malcolm got up, bathed and shaved without a word of apology.
After calling work to report sick he went to the garage to look
through some paperwork. He had been offered a job in Saudi
Arabia and his happy memories of the six years he had previously

spent there were more than enough to convince him that he'd be better off there than drunk and depressed in England. Sara was so dispirited that she encouraged him. Returning to her house in Coventry and withdrawing herself and her daughter from the current cycle of violence and despair seemed to be the only solution. At any rate a phone call was due from Saudi Arabia that morning to let them know whether Malcolm could go. When he emerged from the garage a few hours later he was drunk again: both he and Sara brewed home-made wine which was kept in the garage, and Malcolm had apparently consumed two bottles of it on an empty stomach. Sara got him to lie down and try to sober up for the phone call. At one o'clock it came but Malcolm was still drunk and his speech was heavily slurred; on Sara's advice he told them he'd had a local anaesthetic at the dentist's. They were unimpressed, and Malcolm did not hear from them again.

He lumbered upstairs to bed. Sara felt desperate, she knew he needed help but she didn't know who to turn to. The boost in self-esteem that her relationship with Malcolm had given her was fast being eroded and she needed to find help for herself as well as for Malcolm. Eventually she decided to ring Malcolm's boss, Ken Matthews, whom she knew as a friend of Malcolm's as well as his employer and so she felt she could tell him what was happening.

Ken Matthews was less than surprised. It was not the first time Malcolm's drinking had come to his attention. Eighteen months earlier, a month before Sara had met Malcolm, Malcolm had also called in sick. Within an hour of his call Ken had gone to visit him at home and discovered that he wasn't sick but drunk. He listened with some sympathy while Malcolm blamed his drinking on the breakdown of his second marriage and the fact that he was living in Atherstone rather than at home in Leicester. Although Malcolm had committed a sackable offence, Ken Matthews decided to let him off with a written warning. In the memo expressing his dissatisfaction that he sent to Malcolm the following week, he points out that this too was not the first time Malcolm's drinking had caused concern and affected his work; indeed it was earlier that year that Malcolm had been banned from driving for being over the limit. It was because of that, of course, that he was now living and working in Atherstone.

Atherstone's location, virtually smack-bang in the middle of England, singled it out as the ideal location for TNT's UK head-quarters. Birmingham was twenty-two miles away, Leicester twenty-three and Coventry fifteen. The company's headquarters dominates the industrial estate on the edge of the town. All the company's freight and parcels are sent to Atherstone to be sorted before being sent on to their destination, and that together with its geographical location has led the complex to be nicknamed 'the hub' – the centre from which routes to all over England emanate. The company's security operations were also based there. Malcolm's work as a security manager involved iden-tifying and tracking down fraud, which he had some consider-able success in doing. With millions of valuable items passing through the company's warehouse every year, the scope for par-cels to go missing, either through individual acts of theft or through organized fraudulent networks, was considerable. Working in tandem with the local police, Malcolm had suc-ceeded in uncovering a massive fraud operation which had resulted in a large number of arrests and had also secured his reputation. Malcolm had close links with the local police; indeed all but one of the security department's employees were former officers. The bond between them was strong and they would see each other in the pub as well as in the office.

Malcolm's charm and ability were to some extent both his saving grace and his downfall. Ken Matthews admits now that he might well have disciplined or sacked a lesser employee, but because he liked, respected and valued Malcolm he kept him on, making allowances for him and hoping the problem would resolve itself. Malcolm's colleagues also viewed him as a cut above the rest. Always immaculately presented, the half-moon glasses he often wore gave him a distinguished air. His handker-chieves and ties always matched, leading one colleague to call him the Burton man; he spoke a smattering of Arabic and he was comparatively well read. He was also great company and so his colleagues gladly covered up for him. Sometimes Malcolm would arrive at work smelling of booze; at other times he simply wouldn't turn up, but because he was liked and valued and because, ultimately, whatever his shortcomings he always managed to get his job done, nothing was said.

It is now a matter of regret to Ken Matthews that he did not take a firmer line with Malcolm. His nagging doubt is that perhaps through being understanding and sympathetic he may unwittingly have contributed to Malcolm's drinking getting totally out of control; that if perhaps he had offered ultimatums rather than sympathy, Malcolm would have pulled himself back from the brink. At the time, though, Ken and many of the others who knew Malcolm failed to realize he was anything more than a heavy social drinker.

By that Monday, however, when Sara had been driven to call Ken Matthews for assistance, Malcolm was clearly in need of help. When Ken arrived at Church Walk he was shocked by the decline in Malcolm's appearance. Unshaven and scruffy, he was barely recognizable. After trying to talk to Malcolm he agreed to run Sara over to Gateway's to get some food, but when they returned Malcolm had gone. Ken Matthews went back to work and Sara called their GP, Dr Farn. Dr Farn knew Malcolm and he knew the problem; he told Sara that Malcolm was very sick. Her best hope, he said, was to persuade Malcolm to seek treatment from a specialist in London, Dr Max Glatt. Sara needed little convincing, the problem was how to persuade Malcolm. The situation seemed to require more than persuasion. Malcolm was incapable of any sort of discussion. When he returned later that afternoon he was totally incoherent and went straight to sleep.

The following day while Sara was at work Malcolm again spent the day drinking. She persuaded a work friend of his, John Cole, to visit, to try to talk some sense into him. She arrived home with him to find Malcolm unwashed, unshaved and dressed like a scarecrow. John Cole's attempts fell on stony ground and while he was speaking to Sara in the kitchen,

Malcolm sneaked out to the pub, returning in a terrible state. Sara called Dr Farn again, but when he came round, Malcolm refused to co-operate and hid, like a small boy, behind a chair. Sara felt desperate; she could see his life, and with it hers, falling apart, and there seemed to be nothing she could do to stop it. He was not only drunk, he was also violent and aggressive. She says she spent the night with Luise barricaded for safety into the spare room.

When she went downstairs the following morning she found Malcolm sitting on the couch, dirty, smelly, unshaven and wearing the same clothes as the day before. Putting her arms around him she told him that she loved him. He started to weep. Both of them realized that he was indeed very ill. Dr Farn arranged for Malcolm to be seen in London by Dr Glatt at three o'clock that afternoon. Ken Matthews gave John Cole permission to take the day off work and he went with Sara to take Malcolm to London. When they got to Church Walk, however, Malcolm was nowhere to be seen: he had given them the slip again. Sara searched the house and then rang the local taxi company who confirmed that they had taken him to the Blue Boar. They eventually tracked him down, bundled him into the car and drove without stopping to Dr Glatt's home in Finchley.

They had picked the right man. Max Glatt was one of the world's leading experts on alcoholism. He was one of the pioneers who claimed the alcoholic was not someone who lacked moral fibre or self-restraint but rather someone who was sick. Just as a person diagnosed as having a heart condition could not be expected to cure him- or herself spontaneously, neither could an alcoholic. With Sara's support and a lot of coaxing and persuading, Dr Glatt eventually got Malcolm to admit to having blackouts and DTs and persuaded him to enter the Charter Nightingale Clinic in Lisson Grove, north London.

The clinic is a private one, as are most of those that exist to treat addictions. Although thousands of people die every year from alcohol-related illnesses, it is still very hard to find specialist treatment for it within the National Health Service, indeed there are only sixteen residential units in the whole country. Malcolm was fortunate in that he had health insurance, which paid for him to stay there for a month, sobering up, detoxifying and every night attending meetings with the nearest Alcoholics Anonymous group. He examined his past and his reasons for drinking, and accepted that alcoholism had three important characteristics.

It was, the Charter Clinic taught him, a primary disease. In other words, alcoholism was not an inability to cope with larger social, emotional or physical problems (though they might be a contributory cause) but a disease in its own right, like pneumonia. And, just as wrapping someone with pneumonia in a blanket or wiping their feverish brow might make them more comfortable, they would not be cured unless the disease itself rather than just the symptoms was treated. Alcoholism could not be cured simply by addressing the social and emotional problems that accompanied it.

Malcolm also learned that the disease was progressive, that it would not just find a status quo and stay there. Nor would it miraculously improve. Untreated, it would always get worse at some point. Alcoholics and their families might pin their hopes on an apparent decline in consumption, or indeed a period without any drinking at all, but ultimately the addiction would always re-emerge and progressively worsen.

Finally, the Charter programme, in line with Alcoholics Anonymous, explained that there was in fact no absolute cure; that alcoholism is, in a sense, a chronic illness. Thus the alcoholic, like the person who suffers from diabetes, must adapt his or her life to keep the chronic aspect of the disease at bay. In the case of alcoholism, that means never drinking again. While a few doctors do still advise alcoholics that they can drink if they keep it under control, Dr Glatt and his team at Charter made it clear that they believed any notion of 'controlled drinking' was nothing more than an exercise in self-deception; that the only path to recovery lay in total abstinence. Any consumption of alcohol at all would be enough to re-activate the disease.

The extent to which Malcolm accepted Charter's approach was made clear in a letter he wrote to Ken Matthews while he was at the clinic: 'I know I've let myself down, you, Sara and all sorts of people along the way. Facing up to my responsibilities in this respect and facing my guilt are all part of the process of getting better. And getting better I am. Physically I haven't felt as good as this in years – I'm eating like a horse and feel on top of it. The programme I'm on is hard and we are literally on the go from first thing till last thing at night. It is a good programme, though, and I've really thrown myself into it. It works and I can feel it working for me. The object of the course and the aftercare (through AA) is for it to work for life – and that is my ambition.'

Malcolm was transformed by the programme; he emerged healthy and positive. Dr Glatt would have liked him to stay on at the clinic for slightly longer, but his health insurance had run out and it appeared that the month he had spent there had more than done the trick. For Sara it seemed like the end of a terrible ordeal; her patience and perseverance had eventually paid off; she had managed to recover the man she had fallen in love with. TNT, too, were pleased with Malcolm's recovery; by this time he had got his driving licence back and they decided to allow him to return to his old job. Two weeks later Sara and Malcolm were married quietly at Atherstone's Registry Office.

Unfortunately the honeymoon was shortlived. Atherstone has an active Alcoholics Anonymous group, with all the members recovering alcoholics, all of them supporting each other through meetings akin to the group therapy Malcolm had attended while at Charter. But Malcolm attended only a handful of the meetings that should have been the mainstay of his continued recovery. A member of the Atherstone group, Patrick Hanlon, was worried about Malcolm from the first meeting he came to: 'He told the group he'd been cured. Now anyone who'd been to the Charter Clinic would know there's no such thing as a cure; that an ex-alcoholic is always a recovering alcoholic, that you're never over the addiction though you can be on top of it.' Patrick took this to be a bit of bravado but when he next saw Malcolm he knew it was more serious, that Malcolm had been bluffing. He and other members of the group suspected that he was slightly drunk: 'I could tell he'd been drinking. When you've worked for a long time with alcoholics, as I have, you can tell straight away when they've had a drink. Malcolm was bluffing, he was in a state of denial – denying that he had a problem and denying that he was drinking.'

There should be no underestimating how difficult it is for an alcoholic to stop drinking. Many addicts try again and again to give up, but even with the support of AA or private therapists a considerable number still fail. Malcolm and Sara lived in a town where heavy drinking was the norm for many. Local residents boast it has more pubs per square mile than anywhere else in England. Consumption of alcohol is so widespread in Britain anyway, that for most consumers, like Malcolm, it is easy to forget that it is actually a drug, which like narcotics and tranquillizers depresses the nervous system. The fact that alcohol has become a 'domesticated drug' doesn't, specialists believe, make it any less dangerous than illegal drugs like heroin or cocaine. On the contrary, its ready availability and social acceptance mean that people who wouldn't dream of misusing other potentially dangerous drugs will abuse alcohol.

There is no distinct line that an excessive drinker has to cross before he or she becomes an alcoholic. For many, the typical alcoholic is a 'skid-row' type character, someone who is constantly drunk and can't hold down a job, someone with whom the ordinary 'social' drinker has nothing in common. In reality, 'skid-row' drunks make up no more than a tiny proportion of problem drinkers and alcoholics. The vast majority are ordinary people living with their families, often still working and managing to a greater or lesser extent to conceal from the outside world the problems arising from their disease, and consequently remaining largely unrecognized, undiagnosed and untreated.

Only Sara and Malcolm's closest work colleagues would acknowledge his alcoholism. His family and many of his friends still deny it and insist that he just 'liked to have a drink'. For a community where heavy drinking is common, it is often hard to recognize where a friend or family member has a problem. From the moment that Sara recognized that Malcolm was an alcoholic she began a frenetic campaign to get him help, but apart from the support she got from Ken Matthews and John Cole at TNT, she did it alone. She contacted Dr Farn and through him Dr Glatt, she got him admitted to the Charter Clinic, she begged him to go to AA, and in desperation during the last months of her marriage she contacted a faith healer to try to help Malcolm find some peace of mind. It does not appear that any other member of Malcolm's undoubtedly loving family or his close friends in Atherstone did anything to help him solve his drinking problems. Rather than help Sara try to help him, they saw her attempts as over-reactions that would inflame rather than pacify the situation. To the extent that no alcoholic wants to be deprived of his or her fix, that in the short term may well have been the case, but something undoubtedly needed to be done. The fact that most of those around Malcolm refused to acknowledge he had a problem with drink must have made it easier for him to slip back into old habits. And with these came the well-known phenomenon associated with alcoholism — denial.

Malcolm convinced himself that the road to recovery did not lie with total abstinence. He told Ken Matthews that there are two types of alcoholic: one who is so addicted that he or she can never drink again, and a second type who can control it. Luckily for himself, he told Ken Matthews, he fell into the second category. Unfortunately Malcolm was deceiving himself. He told Sara the same lie. She believed it and on the strength of this would occasionally buy him alcohol as a special treat. Their lives still revolved around Atherstone's pubs. Sara herself drank quite heavily, which was something that many of their friends saw as counter-productive and dangerous; they felt she should have abstained from alcohol to help Malcolm. But at the Charter Clinic it had been made clear that recovering alcoholics should be able to cope with the reality that others around them would still be drinking without this weakening their own recovery, and so Malcolm encouraged Sara to continue drinking and they both continued to go to pubs.

In October the police were again called out to 73 Church Walk. Malcolm was drunk and had started to fight with Sara. Luise, terrified, ran next door to number 71, screaming hysterically. The neighbours called the police who once again arrived and made sure things had calmed down, but took no action.

Like many battered women, Sara was beginning to seek to rationalize and understand Malcolm's violence by reference to herself. She increasingly began to look for things she was doing that might contribute to his violence and his drinking. So that November, when she had to go into hospital for an eye operation and Malcolm arrived to pick her up smelling of booze, she privately blamed herself for leaving him alone. Previously she would take Luise away for the weekend if Malcolm had seemed set on an alcoholic binge; now she increasingly sent Luise away by herself while she remained at home.

Studies have found that even a single incident of physical violence in a relationship should not be underestimated. The balance of power can be dramatically altered, destroying a sense of openness and trust on the part of the woman and resulting in a permanent sense of inequality, threat and loss. Repeated assaults like the ones Sara was now being subjected to can have a cumulative effect. They build on the shock of the first assault and take the woman through a series of feelings and rationalizations as she seeks to reinterpret her life and her relationship in the light of continued attacks. Such attempts to rationalize and understand on the part of the woman are often seen as a sign of weakness by the man, which in turn can reinforce his sense of power and dominance. As he begins to lose respect for his partner he can become less and less remorseful after every beating, often even convincing himself that the woman deserves it.

In turn, the woman continues to lose respect for herself, partly because her partner's ability to beat her tells her she can't be worth very much, and partly because she is actually taking the beatings. As her self-esteem falls, it becomes more and more difficult for her to leave. She may have children and no money and believe that there is nowhere to go and that even if there were, how could she, by now a 'non-person' in her own eyes, survive? Or, as with Sara, the emotional ties may simply be too strong for her to want to leave. Whilst battered women may want the beatings to stop, they do not necessarily want their relationship to end. They may have endured what they have because they still love the man, and to walk away after having sacrificed so much of themselves may seem like throwing all they've suffered for away.

Although Sara fell prey to all the feelings of confusion that a battered woman typically experiences, she did not conform to the stereotype that many people hold as to how a battered woman should behave. She did not react to the battering by becoming withdrawn and submissive. She maintained a front for the outside world. She had always been flamboyant and confident, if not wild, and remained so throughout her marriage to Malcolm. When he hit her she sometimes fought back, although that in itself is by no means unusual. Women in the initial stages of a violent relationship do sometimes fight back. Indeed, many of those who observed Sara and Malcolm together at this stage describe Sara as 'giving as good as she got'. But although partners may 'trade punches', they rarely exchange injuries. Malcolm was a 6-foot, 13-stone ex-policeman. Sara was a 5-foot, 8-stone petite woman. Any attempt on her part to fight back bare-fisted was clearly going to be of no avail.

Rationally, she knew that only one person was responsible for Malcolm's drinking and aggression, and that person was Malcolm. On an emotional level, though, she tortured herself, convinced that there must be something more that she could do but unable to work out what it was. It was agony for her as she watched Malcolm behave in more and more self-destructive ways.

By then Sara had also started to work for TNT, as a telesales person. Those who worked with her remember her preoccupation with Malcolm's drinking. They thought of her as motivated and of above average intelligence; at times she could be great fun to work with, generous, warm and funny, but at other times her own emotional problems overwhelmed her and she became difficult and unpredictable.

At the Christmas round of office parties Sara noticed that Malcolm's Coca Cola was spiked with vodka, a clear breach of company rules and a clear breach of Malcolm's recovery programme. She tried to persuade him to rejoin Alcoholics Anonymous, but he refused, saying that 'controlled drinking' suited him. Unfortunately, it made life hell for everyone else.

In the meantime, though, Malcolm's career was taking off. He had a clear talent for computers and he found working with them challenging and fulfilling. TNT invited him to speak on computer security at their European conference in Holland. He wrote and rewrote his speech, practising long sections of it in front of Sara while she cooked and ironed. That preparation paid off and he returned home to Sara with the news that he had been promoted to head of computer security.

That February Sara had to go into hospital to have another operation on her eye. Two days afterwards she got a call from Ken Matthews. Malcolm had been stopped by the police and breathalyzed. He was over the limit.

4 · 'Only a Domestic'

Sara went upstairs and vomited. She felt it was the beginning of the end. Coolly and calmly she called a taxi, got Luise ready and collected up all the alcohol that was in the house. After dropping Luise and the bottles of drink off at a friend's for safe-keeping, she went to the pub. Malcolm, tearful and drunk, told her what had happened. He had been working in Nottingham and had stopped off for what turned out to be four vodkas and Coke on the way home. He knew that his job and his future were now on the line, and he was suicidal.

Dr Farn was called but with Malcolm drunk he could do nothing. His notes of the visit say he found Malcolm to be dazed, incoherent, tense, agitated and suffering from memory loss. He told him he needed immediate hospital admission but Malcolm refused all help. Dr Farn assessed that he was actively suicidal. Sara was in a state of shock; barely six months ago when they had married everything had seemed perfect but now, once again, their world was falling apart. It was not until the next day that she felt able to cry, she simply could not believe what Malcolm had done.

The following Monday Sara returned from a hospital appointment in Coventry to discover that Malcolm had resigned. His friends at TNT could not save him again. He told Sara that he felt as if he'd let everyone down. There was no point in Sara being angry, Malcolm was already too furious and upset with himself. They both feared that Malcolm was now unemployable. He rang Atherstone's other main employer, Lloyd's chemists, asking them if they could offer him anything. Sara rode round on her bike to deliver his CV, but they did not reply or even acknowledge receipt of it.

Malcolm went on what Sara could only describe as 'a bender

of heroic proportions'. Neighbours recall having to step across him when he was lying drunk in the street. On one occasion Sara found him face-down in an alley clutching a takeaway. She managed to get him home and into bed but it was clearly a losing battle. Every time she turned her back Malcolm would be drinking.

As there was nothing Sara could do to stop her husband drinking, she thought it might at least be safer if she could persuade him to do so at home. With that in mind, she went to Safeways later that week to buy him some whisky. She returned to find the kitchen covered in blood. Still feeling suicidal, Malcolm had decided to cook her and Luise what he called a 'farewell spaghetti bolognese' and in the process of so doing had cut his finger. Drunk, he'd failed to notice, and had smeared the blood everywhere. Leaving the onions frying on the stove, he took his whisky and lurched upstairs. She went to check on him and found he'd fallen asleep having barely drunk any. In a fit of frustration she filled his glass with whisky and woke him up, telling him that if he was going to be a drunk he should do it properly and finish the bottle. She couldn't rouse him, though, and in his semi-conscious state he had a fit. Terrified, she raced downstairs to call Dr Farn and an ambulance, returning to clean the blood and spittle from Malcolm's face. He had bitten his cheek and his mouth was bleeding. By the time Dr Farn arrived Malcolm had regained consciousness with devastating effect: Sara remembers he was rambling, aggressive, upset and threatening to kill her. He pulled the phone out of the wall and threw it at her and she fled in terror to her neighbour's house to call the police. The police arrived but they didn't intervene until Malcolm walked outside and collapsed. At that point, at Dr Farn's insistence, they took Malcolm to the police station for the night.

Sara was not just concerned for herself and Malcolm, she was also increasingly worried about the effect Malcolm's drinking was having on her daughter. Luise was becoming increasingly upset and although she clearly loved Malcolm she would become terrified of him when he was drunk. Whenever possible Sara would arrange for Luise to stay with friends while she attempted to look after Malcolm.

The following night Sara again had to call out Dr Farn and another ambulance: Malcolm had drunk a bottle of whisky and fallen unconscious. When the doctor arrived, Malcolm, who had come round by this time, staggered downstairs and threatened Sara in front of him. Earlier Sara had phoned Dr Glatt and begged him to help, and he had given her the name of a cheaper clinic she could try to persuade Malcolm to go to, and told her to call him at any time. Both Sara and Dr Farn tried everything to persuade Malcolm to follow that advice but he refused. There was nothing they could do as the law does not permit compulsory committal for drugs or alcohol abuse. Sara felt that she was being forced to watch her husband slowly but surely kill himself. She decided that if he was not going to give up drinking himself, the next best thing would be somehow to make it impossible for him to get any alcohol. She called his bank manager to try to persuade him to cut off Malcolm's flow of cash, but did not succeed.

The following morning Malcolm packed a small bag and said he was going and would never come back. He said he'd been an utter failure and hoped Sara would find someone decent when he'd gone. Sara remained unruffled, suspecting that he would merely book into the nearest pub to be able to carry on drinking without resistance. But when she checked the pubs she couldn't find him. She called every taxi company and hotel within a 10-mile radius but there was no sign of him. Fearing the worst, she called the police and reported him missing. At about midnight his brother Norman phoned to say that Malcolm had arrived in Blackpool.

Sara then thought very seriously about leaving. She was getting more and more damaged physically and emotionally; if she made the break she could start afresh. But it would mean leaving her home, her job and having to find another school for Luise that would be able to provide the special counselling she was now getting for dyslexia. It would also mean leaving Malcolm alone to drink and self-destruct; with her gone she feared there would be nothing to save him from himself. It was without doubt the lowest point in his life. He'd lost his driving licence, his job and any vestige of self-respect. Sara still loved him deeply and she could not justify walking out on him right at the time when she felt he needed her most. She did not believe Malcolm was naturally violent, she blamed alcohol for making the beast appear. While he was at the clinic, she too had attended counselling sessions and become convinced that alcoholism was an illness, and, she reasoned, you don't leave someone just because they're ill. Malcolm's vulnerability and sickness seemed to have bound her to him and to have prevented her from doing what undoubtedly would have been in her best interests: leaving.

Malcolm returned from Blackpool only to launch himself into another bout of drinking. Sara spent three days pulling him out of various pubs in Nuneaton. She had decided not to leave the relationship and she was going to fight to keep it and Malcolm alive. She tried everything she could to find Malcolm a job. She got him to type out his CV which she distributed to local employers. Employment, she believed, would provide him with the chance to regain his self-respect. The opportunity came not long afterwards.

Geoff Wilding was one of Malcolm's drinking companions and something of an entrepreneur. He had a small shop in Atherstone's shopping centre and had just taken out a franchise to sell Tandy electronic products. The recession was biting by now, and Geoff was by no means confident that the Tandy franchise would be a success. He offered Malcolm the chance to run it for him and see whether he could make it work. Initially the agreement was that Geoff would pay him a small wage and a percentage of the takings, but after a short while Malcolm, who had already opened a new section in the store to sell records, decided he wanted to take on the franchise himself. They reached a gentleman's agreement: Geoff would let Malcolm have the store at a peppercorn rent, he would just have to pay for the stock, and whenever he was able he would give Geoff £5000 for the goodwill that went with the business.

The deal gave Malcolm the autonomy and responsibility he

had wanted, but sadly he continued to slip further into his drink-ridden mire. On at least one occasion Geoff found him drunk in the shop. He warned him that he would call the deal off if Malcolm didn't stop. Malcolm said he would, but the next time Geoff saw Sara she had bruises around her eyes which she told him were the result of Malcolm hitting her.

Weekends were especially bad. Malcolm could be out of control for over forty-eight hours. When she could, Sara would take Luise away to stay with friends. Although by this stage her house in Coventry had been rented out she still had friends there with whom she could stay for the occasional night. The first weekend in April was Malcolm's birthday weekend. He made it clear on the Friday night that he intended to spend it in a stupor. Sara could either stay around and get hit or she could go. She decided that self-protection was the best course of action and she took Luise to Coventry for the weekend. Sara was still in touch with her old neighbour, Veronica Costelloe, and they met up for lunch on the Sunday. Veronica offered to give Sara a lift home. Sara said she needed to go home at six but Veronica said she would have to take her earlier because she had work to do.

The front door to 73 Church Walk opens on to a corridor, at the end of which, on the right-hand side, is the kitchen. Sara left her bags there and went on with Veronica into the living-room, which is at the rear of the house. There they found Malcolm, face-down and fast asleep on the sofa. Sara walked over to wake him up and say she was home. Once awake he was annoyed with her for coming back early and accused her of doing so to try to trick him. He went into the kitchen where Sara had left the bags. Next, when they heard the sound of things being thrown out of the back door, Sara went into the kitchen and Veronica heard her ask him not to throw her things out. Veronica then went to see what was happening and found Malcolm hitting Sara on the back of her head as she bent over to put the bags down. He called her a whore and asked her who she'd slept with over the weekend. Veronica grabbed his arm and pulled him away. He pushed past her and thumped up the stairs muttering 'Big, bad Malcolm'.

Sara's nose was bleeding and she was shaking badly. She was clearly embarrassed by what Veronica had seen, and apologized profusely to her for Malcolm's behaviour. She put the kettle on and made three cups of tea, calling Malcolm down to drink the third. When Luise came in from the park where she had been playing with Veronica's daughter she kept asking, 'What's wrong, Mummy?' Malcolm started copying her, saying, 'What's wrong, Mummy?' Worried that both children were getting frightened, Veronica sent them back to the park. Sara took her bags upstairs and Malcolm followed. From the lounge Veronica heard arguing and then Sara saying, 'Stop it, Malcolm, please stop it.' She was crying and there was a loud thump, so Veronica went upstairs. They were in the spare bedroom: Malcolm was hitting Sara while she was trying to cuddle him, saying, 'I love you, stop it.' Veronica screamed at them and Malcolm went back downstairs. She tried to get Sara to leave, terrified of what would happen if she left her in the house. But Sara refused, saying she had to work the next day and that she needed to keep an eye on Malcolm as he was suicidal at times.

Veronica stayed long enough to make sure the situation had calmed down. Before she left she asked Malcolm what had happened, why he was behaving so differently from the man she knew. He held his head in his hands and said only that he didn't know why they'd come back so early.

Not long after the deal on the Tandy shop was agreed, Malcolm announced he would spend the following Sunday stocktaking. He had spent the previous day drinking, and when Sara and Luise went round to the shop to see how his stocktaking was going, they found it empty and locked up. They went on to the pub where they'd all agreed to have lunch; there was no sign of Malcolm there either. They ate alone and then got a taxi back via the shop to see if Malcolm had appeared. He had. They found him drunk and in the toilet with blood and faeces running down his legs. He was embarrassed, and Sara decided she'd better take Luise home. She then rode back on her bike to find the shop door open and Malcolm lying on his back, fast asleep. There were tools scattered around the shop; he had obviously fallen down several times. Sara woke him up but he refused to go home. He tried to throw Sara out, saying, 'Choose a window, you're leaving.' In the ensuing struggle he hit her on the back of the head. Sara ran to a nearby taxi rank for help, but there was nobody there. She returned to the store and tried to get Malcolm to come home. He threatened her again and physically tried to throw her out of the shop. Then, as suddenly as his anger had come it left, and he staggered off, leaving Sara to lock up the shop. When she got home Malcolm was in the spare room which was where Sara had taken to sleeping when he was drunk. He was half-asleep, slumped in a chair with a burning cigarette in one hand. Partners of alcoholics often become obsessed by the fear that they are going to burn themselves or the family to death by falling asleep with a lit cigarette or by forgetting to turn off the stove, and so on. Their fears are well founded for an estimated 20 per cent of deaths by fire are alcohol-related. Sara asked Malcolm to go to bed and he started shouting at her, calling her a whore and a slag. She told him to leave and he started to throw her clothes over the banister. When she tried to stop him, she says, he tried to throw her over as well. The police were called and he was taken away for a few hours. By eleven o'clock, though, Sara says, he was back home.

Sara did not know who to turn to for help. She had tried the police, she had tried her doctor, and none of her friends wanted to get directly involved. In desperation she turned to the church. Her local Methodist minister suggested she ring a local faith healer, Keith Lee. At that time Malcolm was undergoing what he described as a 'religious awakening' and decided that the whole family should start going to church. Sara remembers: 'We togged up for church every Sunday but the reality was that Malcolm actually went to the pub earlier. . . . I'm ashamed to say I usually agreed. To say no usually meant a row.' For Sara too, of course, the pub was a familiar and welcoming place. As Malcolm's drinking got worse, so hers increased. Her mood-swings, which had always been erratic, became more pronounced, and friends noted that during this period she seemed to behave even more flamboyantly than usual. Those who knew what she was going through took her behaviour to be a response to the stress she was under. Others judged her less charitably and said she exacerbated Malcolm's drinking through her loud and often stormy moods.

For several weeks Sara rang Keith Lee whenever there was trouble, to talk to him about what she was going through and to seek advice. One evening she asked him to come round. Keith sat on the patio and talked to Malcolm. Malcolm admitted he had a problem with drink, he said it had started when he had had problems in his first marriage; he kept going back to that as his reason for drinking. He was not, however, prepared to talk about his violence towards Sara. Keith left hoping that things were really as calm and reasonable as they seemed. But they were not. Sara tried contacting Alcoholics Anonymous again, and Patrick Hanlon, who had first seen Malcolm when he came out of the Charter Clinic, called round. The first thing he noticed was the appalling decline in Malcolm's appearance. The once immaculately turned out security manager was now wearing flip-flops and a pair of old and very dishevelled shorts. He spent an hour talking to Malcolm and found him to be in a state of deep self-pity. Suffering from what Patrick could only describe as the 'poor me' syndrome, Malcolm catalogued the woes in his life, mentioning in particular that he was jealous of the fact that Sara still worked at TNT whereas he did not. Patrick listened and extracted a promise from Malcolm to stop drinking and start going to AA again. But this was a promise Patrick could not believe, for as he was going home he spotted Malcolm heading for the pub.

As Malcolm's humiliation, shame and self-pity increased, so did his violence. By the third weekend in May things had reached crisis-point. It was hot and Sara had bought Luise a paddling-pool. Luise spent the afternoon christening it with the help of two friends. That evening Sara cooked supper on the barbecue. When Malcolm arrived home she explained that they would have to eat early as Luise's friends were to be collected soon by their grandmother. The prospect of company provided Malcolm with a convenient pretext to go to the off-licence to get some wine. He returned with 1½ litres of wine and a bottle of Bailey's Irish Cream which he said was a present for Sara. Her heart sank. He kept pouring her glasses of it which she kept surreptitiously tipping away. Malcolm, however, became drunker and more abusive and agitated. He started swearing in front of the children. Not surprisingly, Luise's friends' grandmother decided it was time for them to go.

Furious that Malcolm had humiliated Luise in front of her friends, Sara started to argue with him. Malcolm said he was going to the pub to get away from his nagging wife. As he started to leave Sara tried to stop him. She reached out and grabbed hold of his T-shirt, which tore. She saw Malcolm raise his clenched fist and within seconds was knocked unconscious.

Luise, who was just ten years old, had witnessed the whole incident. She later told the police how she had seen Malcolm return from the off-licence drunk. She said she could tell when he had been drinking because he went 'all wobbly', his eyes tended to half-close and he would get angry with everyone. After her friends had gone she'd tried to watch TV while her parents argued in the kitchen. She saw Malcolm try to go and her mother reach out to stop him. As his clothing tore, she saw him thump her mother on the back of the head. She jumped up to try to intervene, but Malcolm then pushed Sara backwards on to a chair and punched her very hard with a clenched fist three times in the face. As he did so he was repeatedly shouting, 'I hate you' and swearing.

By this stage Luise was screaming and she eventually got Malcolm to go upstairs. She saw that her mother was unconscious, with both her nose and lip bleeding. Luise thought she was dying. Remembering the first aid she had been taught in school, she tried to give her mother the kiss of life. As soon as Sara started to come round, Luise dialled 999 and asked for the police and an ambulance to come quickly. Malcolm came downstairs. When he discovered that the police were on their way he announced he was off to the pub as he didn't want to be arrested. Soon after that the ambulance arrived and took Sara and Luise to the hospital. There Sara was treated for bruising and swelling to the bridge of her nose and both cheek-bones. Her lip was cut, she was dizzy, sore and disorientated. This time she asked the police to press charges.

Malcolm went to ground. The police didn't find him for another three days. He said he had acted in self-defence. In the meantime Sara had taken Luise and gone to her father's house in Devon. At first he was cautious about taking her in and even called the police to make sure her claims of having been battered were true. They confirmed there was cause for concern, indeed it was as a result of their advice that it would be wise for her to stay out of Malcolm's way that Sara arranged to take time off work and fled to Devon. Her respite, however, was short-lived. As usual there were tensions between her, her father and her stepmother. Her stepbrother, Tim, was doing his A Levels, and a row developed between him and his parents. Sara took Tim's side and things became so fraught that Sara, Tim and Luise left for Atherstone.

In Sara's absence Malcolm had telephoned the elder of his two sons, Martin, for help. Martin, who was twenty, was living in London with his mother. He agreed to come up the same day, although he had seen his father only four or five times in the previous four years. The last occasion had been in December when he had come to stay at Church Walk with a friend. It was the first time he had met Sara; he liked her and thought she got on really well with his father; it was also the first time he had noticed that his father liked to drink. When he came up to Atherstone that May he realized that his father had a serious problem. The afternoon he arrived was the only time he worked in the shop with his father's help, after that he was left to run it alone. Malcolm would come in occasionally, sometimes to take money out of the till, and then disappear. He was drinking heavily. He would be drunk when Martin got home and did not seem to eat anything except the occasional Chinese takeaway.

Sara arrived back in Atherstone from Devon late on 26 May to find Malcolm asleep on the couch. He seemed surprised and happy to see her, making every effort to appear sober and telling her how much he loved her. She gently persuaded him to go upstairs to bed and he spent the night asleep in her arms. The following morning he announced that, as she'd come home, he was going to stop drinking for good. The following afternoon she called to see Martin in the shop, told him the good news and also warned him not to bring any alcohol back to the house so that his father would not be tempted. When she got home she found Malcolm going through quite severe withdrawal symptoms. She phoned their doctor who prescribed him some Valium to help him through.

That Sunday they had a barbecue. Malcolm didn't touch a drop of alcohol all weekend or indeed for the next two weeks. Tim stayed with them for a week before heading off to meet up with his girlfriend. Martin, who had started seeing a woman in Atherstone, Jill, decided to stay on for another three weeks. The atmosphere in the house was good; both Malcolm and Sara were avoiding pubs and instead would stay in and play games like Scrabble to keep Malcolm's mind off alcohol. Malcolm even contacted Alcoholics Anonymous again and went along to two meetings where he participated in group therapy. He was drinking nothing but apple juice and Sara's hopes rose as once again she allowed herself to believe they were going to win the fight.

Sara had been asked to attend a TNT conference, grandly entitled 'Same Day into The Nineties', in the second weekend in June. Malcolm, as Sara's husband, had also been invited but he'd declined – he couldn't face seeing all his old colleagues, he would have felt too embarrassed. Initially Sara had qualms about going but was persuaded by her work colleagues to take part. On the Friday before she left, Malcolm asked her whether, given that he'd now stopped drinking, she would consider withdrawing the charge of assault (he was due to appear in court in three weeks' time). Sara agreed, there seemed little point as everything now seemed to be fine. She said she would have a word about it with an officer, Martin Langley, who was a friend of theirs. As she packed that evening Malcolm got her to try on the clothes she would be wearing for the 'evening do': feeling jealous, he said he wanted to know how she would look in front of the men who would be there. She offered to cancel the trip if it was going to upset him but he wouldn't hear of it. She had reservations about leaving him, though, and before going she had a quiet chat with Martin in which she asked him not to leave his father alone, especially not with Luise. When she spoke to her daughter about going, Luise said she didn't want to stay at Church Walk for the night Sara would be away. When Sara told Malcolm she was going to arrange for her to stay with friends he was hurt. He asked Sara when she was going to start trusting him again. So she decided to put him to the test.

The conference was taking place in the De Vere Hotel in Coventry. Sara and the women she worked with had arranged to travel together. They organized the journey in stages. One of them, Judy Thomson, drove with her husband to pick up Helen Thomas. They then continued on to Atherstone to collect Sara, ending up in Nuneaton at the home of the fourth woman, Diane Davies. They then swapped cars and Diane drove the four women to Coventry.

The De Vere Hotel is in the centre of town. Catering mainly for large tour parties and business conferences, it is not much to look at from the outside but inside is quite plush with a good restaurant, smart bar and very comfortable rooms. There must have been a general buzz of excitement surrounding the conference. About two hundred TNT employees were attending it and most of them were staying at the hotel. Sara was feeling good about her work and for the first time in a long time she was also feeling good about her marriage. The excitement and fun of the conference provided some much-needed light relief from all that she had gone through over the previous months. At six o'clock, before the main evening dinner got underway, Sara phoned home as arranged. Luise was out playing with friends and she presumed Martin was busy closing up the shop. She spoke to Malcolm and felt a little uneasy as she thought he might have been drinking. He assured her he had not, but her feeling of unease increased. At nine o'clock she left the dinner to call him again. This time Luise answered the phone. She was hysterical and told Sara that Malcolm was drunk and had spilled Chinese food everywhere.

This confirmed Sara's intuition, and she was furious. She called Ella Thompstone, who ran the local taxi firm, and arranged for her to collect Luise and take her to stay with some friends, Dave and Jane Baxter. Ella sent a driver to pick Luise up and bring her to the taxi rank. She arrived in her pyjamas and dressing-gown, very upset and crying. Martin, who was on his way home from the pub, saw her, and she ran to him. Ella then came out to take Luise to the Baxters herself. Martin asked her where she was taking Luise but she refused to tell him and they drove off. Sara called the house again twenty minutes later by which time Martin had returned. He told Sara his father was not drunk but she didn't believe him. She felt bitterly disappointed and angry with him for leaving Malcolm alone for long enough for him to get drunk. Martin later told the police that his father had been drinking when he got back, though he wouldn't say he was drunk. Malcolm wanted to know where Luise was, and when Martin told him he got angry and went out. About forty-five minutes later he returned with eight cans of beer. He put them in the fridge and then took Martin to the pub. When they got back Martin hid the beers his father had put in the fridge and went to bed, leaving Malcolm on the sofa.

When Luise arrived at the Baxters she was still very distraught. She told them Malcolm had been drunk and that she was scared as her mother was away. Shortly after Jane Baxter had settled her in bed Sara rang back, angry and upset that Martin hadn't stayed in to look after Luise and to make sure Malcolm wouldn't drink. She said she had promised Luise she would never have to see Malcolm drunk again, and now that promise had been broken. Jane told her not to worry as Luise was all right and had settled down for the night. She said they would return her to Church Walk the next day.

Sara stayed at the conference overnight. It seemed pointless to make the journey back home. Luise was safe and it was useless to try to deal with Malcolm while he was drunk, and anyway Martin was now back there to make sure he was all right. She shared a room with Helen Thomas, and the following morning they shared a taxi back to Atherstone. Martin was in the kitchen to greet them and also to warn them that Malcolm was very drunk. It appeared that early that morning he had found the cans that Martin had hidden. Soon afterwards Malcolm himself came downstairs, dressed only in a pair of silk boxer shorts. Martin had not underestimated his condition; he was clearly very drunk, with spittle all over his face. Sara was very angry, both with Malcolm and with Martin. She lost her temper, kicked over a chair and stormed out of the room. Embarrassed, Helen left.

To Sara it was obvious that Malcolm must have been drunk the night before when she had phoned him from Coventry; she was angry with Martin for denying it. Together they searched the bins and elsewhere in the house but could find no empty cans. Eventually they found the evidence they'd been looking for – some empty cans and an empty bottle of vodka – in a litter-bin outside the house. With the characteristic guile of a dedicated alcoholic, Malcolm had taken the trouble to remove the evidence of his drinking from the house. In the bin Sara also found a receipt for the vodka which he had bought the day before in the Co-op. That told her that Malcolm had gone out and bought alcohol with the deliberate intention of getting drunk as soon as her back was turned.

There was no ignoring the severity of the problem. After two weeks dry, Malcolm had deliberately sabotaged his own recovery: he was chronically involved with alcohol. Sara was desolate and furious. She began to suspect his dry spell might only have been an attempt to get her to withdraw the police action against him. Malcolm had arranged for his friend Detective Constable Martin Langley to come round that morning so that she could withdraw the assault charge. She rang the police station and left a message for him telling him not to come.

Sara was going to try everything she could to stop Malcolm drinking. She called Patrick Hanlon from Alcoholics Anonymous again and he promised to come round as soon as he could, but he warned her that if Malcolm was drunk there would be little he could do. In the meantime Malcolm was in a very ugly mood, threatening Sara and 'her bloody daughter', seemingly furious that she had caught him out. She was genuinely scared and when Patrick arrived she ran out of the house to greet him in floods of tears.

Patrick's arrival seemed to make Malcolm even worse, however, perhaps because he felt it was a confirmation of his guilt. Patrick took him outside to have a talk. Although Malcolm claimed to have had only one and a half pints of lager, it was clear to Patrick that he was very drunk. At one point Luise came out to ask Malcolm something about the washing-machine, and he became very aggressive and shouted, 'I'll break your fucking legs when I get hold of you.' Once Luise had gone, Malcolm told Patrick he was angry with her for running out in her pyjamas the night before. He said he had got drunk that weekend because Sara had gone to the conference in Coventry. Patrick calmed him down and Malcolm continued talking. He said his grandfather had been an alcoholic and had died young. He also said he was consumed by jealousy. He was jealous of Sara both sexually and professionally. She was still working at the company he'd been sacked from and he told Patrick that losing his driving licence for the second time had made his life not worth living. What's more, he said, the conference in Coventry was really no more than an orgy.

Jealousy was a recurring feature of Malcolm's drunken rages. He would often taunt Sara about her promiscuity and about imagined sexual relationships. In fact this form of jealousy, often called the 'Othello Syndrome', is a very common feature of alcoholism; the taunts and constant accusations which Malcolm levelled at Sara would have been familiar to many partners of alcoholics.

After twenty minutes of Malcolm venting his spleen Patrick came into the kitchen to talk to Sara and Martin. They heard Malcolm go upstairs to look for his wallet which, unbeknown to him, Sara and Martin had hidden earlier along with the key to the shop in case Malcolm decided to raid the till for money to buy drink. He came down fuming. Sara was attempting to prepare Sunday lunch, stuffing cloves of garlic into the skin of a chicken with a sharp knife. Malcolm demanded to know where his money was and according to Sara threatened her and Luise, saying Luise would be 'dead meat' if she wasn't careful. Sara explained that in his own best interests they had confiscated his money. Patrick, who witnessed the assault, says Malcolm grabbed Sara by her neck with one hand and slapped her across the face with the other. Sara recalls that she was still holding the knife with which she'd been preparing the chicken and waved it at Malcolm threateningly. At one point in the argument Malcolm also threatened Sara with a guitar. Patrick felt driven to intervene. He shouted at them to grow up and Malcolm stormed out of the house in the direction of the pub. As he left Patrick heard him threaten to break Luise's neck. Luise began to cry, and Patrick told Sara she would really be better off leaving the house when Malcolm was like that. She replied that she didn't see why she should have to leave her home so that he could smash it up. Patrick left, irritated by Sara's defiance and saddened by Malcolm's condition. In his opinion Malcolm had surrendered himself to his disease and had no real intention of giving up the bottle.

Sara took Martin out to play a game of pool. She felt devastated but wanted to appear in control for Martin's sake. They went to the New Swan. Sure enough, there in the lounge, was Malcolm perched over a pint. They went to the other bar and played four games of pool. Sara liked Martin, they discussed the future and talked about the idea of buying a house in Atherstone which they could rent out to pay for the mortgage. They both agreed, though, that their first priority was to save the business and that that would be impossible unless Malcolm sobered up. On their way home they dropped round at Jill's, Martin's girlfriend's, house. While they were there they saw Malcolm lurch past, clearly on his way home. Martin and Jill went back to look after him. Sara stayed on to talk to Jill's mother, Mary.

By the time Sara got home she had decided that the only way to save Malcolm from himself was somehow to get him into hospital. She decided to put into action a scheme which in retrospect would seem crazy, but at the time, to two people desperate to stop a third person, whom they loved, from destroying himself, it seemed to make sense. Malcolm was asleep when Sara got back. He woke up with a severe headache. She took him upstairs for a bath and hand-fed him bits of chicken and two Mogadon tablets. After his bath she fed him more. Then, about half an hour later, she gave him two more Mogadons. All in all she gave him six Mogadons interspersed with chicken.

If Malcolm would not go to hospital voluntarily they would have to get him admitted some other way. Sara called her doctor and told him that Malcolm had taken an overdose. He advised her to dial 999. By the time the ambulance arrived, Malcolm had fallen asleep in a chair. He awoke to be confronted by two ambulance workers intent upon carrying him off. He was furious. Barely affected by the pills, he refused to go with them, and once they'd gone he exploded with rage, threatening to kill Sara and Luise. Sara went to join the others in the kitchen and together they leaned against the door to prevent him coming in. She had known that six pills would not harm him in any way but she could not believe they had not even pacified him. Undeterred, Malcolm went outside and round to the back door which also led into the kitchen. The top half of it was glass and he threw a chair through it. By this point Sara and Luise were absolutely terrified. They ran with Jill to a neighbour's house and called the police.

A number of police cars and another ambulance duly arrived. Police Constables Woollaston and Belcher found Malcolm outside the house. He told them he had been locked out of the kitchen and so had smashed a window to try to gain entry. He also explained that his wife had called an ambulance because she claimed that he had taken a large quantity of sleeping pills, but that this was not the case. Martin then appeared and explained that in fact Malcolm had unwittingly taken six. By this time Sara and Luise had gone back inside the house. PC Woollaston asked Malcolm if he had somewhere to stay that night and he said he would take a room at the Three Tuns Hotel in Atherstone, but looking in his pockets he realized that he still did not have his wallet. PC Woollaston agreed to go inside and get some money for him. He found Sara and Luise in the kitchen with two other officers. He told Sara, who was clearly angry and upset, that to solve the immediate problem Malcolm would stay in town overnight but that he needed his cheque-cards and wallet. Knowing only too well what he would do with the money once he had it, Sara became more upset, shouting and screaming that he was a bastard and had spent all their money on drink. However, she pulled his wallet down from its hiding-place on top of the kitchen cupboard, selected one card and gave it to the officer.

Martin and Jill then took Malcolm off to the pub to calm down. There was no further police action despite the damage to the window and the clear state of fear Sara and Luise had been put into. It is unlikely that the police would have taken the same non-interventionist attitude had the incident happened between strangers. An insight into how they viewed the situation is given in the incident report which records that the officers involved had told their controller that it was 'only a domestic'.

5 · Losing Control

From the moment Sara had got back from the sales conference to find Malcolm drunk she felt that she was losing control. But the more out of control she felt inside, the more she tried to appear in control externally. Desperate to maintain a pretence of normality, she was going to work with a smile on her face as if everything in her life was fine, all the while knowing that her world was falling apart and that her insides were being eaten away by fear, anxiety and pain.

As agreed, Malcolm did not come home that night. But for safety's sake Sara had spent the night barricaded into the spare bedroom with Luise, who had been terribly upset, telling Sara that they should just go, that they should forget the cats, forget the house and leave because otherwise Malcolm would kill them.

The next morning Sara got Luise ready for school and on her way to work stopped by at Jill's house. To her surprise Malcolm was there. Still furious with her, he rejected her apology for the Mogadon incident, saying that he wanted her and Luise to leave the house – abuse had now become their normal currency of exchange. Sara left and went with Martin to the shop. She decided to leave her bicycle outside in the hope that, if he came, Malcolm would see it and be deterred from coming in. Both Sara and Martin were worried that Geoff Wilding would see him drunk and throw them out of the shop. Once her shift had finished at lunch-time, Sara returned to the shop where Martin confessed that Malcolm had been in and that he'd given him his wallet back. A little later Malcolm reappeared, very drunk; on seeing Sara he left immediately and Martin went after him. Sara was left to mind the shop. Worried about Luise coming home from school and having to confront Malcolm, she ran to the taxi company and asked Ella Thompstone to pick her up. Ella told her that Malcolm had been in to try to get a taxi to take him to Blackpool. She'd told him to go home and sleep it off as no one would want to see him in that state. It was by no means the first time that Malcolm had tried to run home to Blackpool when the going got tough; even if he had gone Sara doubted it would have been for very long.

After Sara returned to the shop she received a visit from a police officer about the pending assault charge against Malcolm. He told her that Luise would need to give a statement to corroborate Sara's. He predicted that Malcolm would get a hefty fine and a community service order. Sara knew only too well who would have to find the money to pay any fine. She told the officer he might just as well give Malcolm a couple of hundred pounds and ask him to beat her up.

Martin returned to tell Sara that Malcolm had said he wasn't coming home, which in view of what Ella had told her did not surprise her. They both took Luise to the pub for supper and returned home just after seven to tackle the mess Malcolm had left in his wake. Martin used the truncheon Malcolm had kept from his days in the force to break the remaining splinters of glass out of the door and then went out with Jill.

Sara remained at home, anxious that Malcolm might appear at any moment. She called his old boss, Ken Matthews, to talk through her concerns about Luise having to give evidence in the court case. She was worried that at ten years old her daughter was too young. Ken Matthews reassured her that the police would handle it sensitively.

By eleven that night there was still no sign of Malcolm so Sara again locked herself and Luise into the spare room to try to get some sleep. That morning she had telephoned her solicitor and made an appointment to see him about getting an official separation from Malcolm. The appointment was not until 22 June, the day after the court case – she had been advised, she says, to wait to see what happened with that first. She also telephoned her colleague from TNT, Helen Thomas, at regular intervals, sharing with her her fears and anxieties.

Sara and Luise woke the next morning to find Malcolm downstairs asleep on the sofa. He had been sick in the kitchen and
there was a large cigarette-burn on a chair in the lounge. It was
by no means the first time he had got dangerously close to setting
the whole house on fire; the furniture was foam-filled and Sara
lived in a perpetual fear of everything going up in smoke. She
and Luise, in a by now familiar routine, crept round the house
trying to get ready for school and work without waking him.
Sara once again took his wallet as a precaution. She also found
some emergency cheques which she hid, again fearing he might
be tempted to use them on alcohol.

Stemming Malcolm's supply of liquor had become an increasingly compelling imperative for Sara. She went round to Jill's to
try to enlist Martin's support. He agreed that Sara should ring
the bank from work to try to find a way of stopping Malcolm
spending the business's remaining assets on drink. As on the
previous day, she left her bike outside the shop to try to deter
Malcolm from entering and then went on to TNT. She spoke to
the bank manager and he suggested that the business account
be frozen and a new one opened with just Martin and Sara as
signatories. Sara didn't think to ask him what the balance of the
account was – she discovered that when she went to see Martin
at lunch-time. They had acted too late; the day before, Malcolm
had emptied the business account of everything except £100.

Martin went off to meet his father for lunch. He returned in
under an hour with the news that Malcolm was drinking double
vodkas and had withdrawn Sara's power of signature at the
bank. Sara was close to tears; instead of fighting his alcoholism
Malcolm was fighting her. They had sent cheques to suppliers
that could not now be met because there were no funds, and she
did not see how the business could survive. She told Martin not
to worry, she would raise some money somehow. First she went
to the jewellers to try to sell her engagement ring but all they
would offer her was £100 – it was worth close to £1000. She
then went to the bank and pleaded with her own bank manager
to increase her personal overdraft limit. He refused.

By now Sara was in tears. She bumped into a taxi driver she

knew called Alex Patrick and asked him if he could lend them £500. Alex didn't have that sort of money, but seeing that she was clearly very distressed, he took her to the pub, bought her a drink and listened to her as she talked and cried for a couple of hours. She told him that everything she tried to do to improve their predicament was foiled by Malcolm. She was being forced to watch him engage in slow-motion suicide and she was at the end of her tether. She told him she couldn't go on any longer.

Talking to Alex helped Sara to calm down sufficiently to remember that she had to take Luise to the police station to make her statement about the assault. She waited outside the interview-room as Luise recounted to a police officer the events of 21 May; she told him how she'd seen her stepfather punch her mother until she was unconscious, shouting as he did so that he hated her. Her statement ended: 'Malcolm and my mum argue quite a lot. It always happens when Malcolm drinks a lot. He gets very angry and he has hit my mum before. I don't think my mum loves him any more.' Sara wished that that last line had been true; it would have made what she was going through now a lot easier to bear.

They arrived home to find Malcolm drunk on the patio. Sara arranged for Luise to go and stay the night with an elderly relative who lived in Atherstone, as she was worried that Malcolm would find out from one of his friends in the force that she had just made a statement against him to the police. Once Luise was safely despatched in a taxi she relaxed a little and tried to do some normal household chores. As she was bringing in the washing Malcolm kept trying to pick a fight. He asked her where her wedding ring was; she had taken it off earlier because her eczema was bad, but exasperated with her husband and in a typically defiant mood, she replied that she didn't think they had that much of a marriage. At that Malcolm took off his own wedding ring and threw it into the garden. Sara tried to remain calm, but inside she was terribly upset, desperate for Malcolm to realize how much his jibes and accusations were hurting her. They seemed to have a cumulative effect on her with each one reigniting the pain from the ones that had gone before.

She needed to go out and asked Martin if he would come with her for a game of pool. They decided to stagger their departures, because in Malcolm's current frame of mind he often became irrationally jealous and was capable of accusing her of anything. Being accused of having a relationship with her stepson was not something Sara felt able to cope with at that point.

Martin went out first, arranging to meet Sara further up the road. Knowing all too well the potency of his father's jealousy, he told him that he was going to visit Jill. Sara went up to change, selecting a skimpy boob-tube as an act of defiance. It had been in her wardrobe for ages but Malcolm wouldn't let her wear it; putting it on felt like an expression of her anger and frustration. Before leaving the bedroom she noticed that the bottles on her dressing-table had been knocked over; she reached over, picked up a lipstick and wrote on the dressing-table mirror: 'I hate you, Malcolm Thornton.' No matter how bitter their rows had got before, she had never ever said she hated him before. Throughout their relationship they would often write each other notes and letters saying how they felt about the other's behaviour. It seemed to Sara at that point that only the most blunt of messages would get through to Malcolm. What she wanted more than anything else was for him to realize what he was putting her through and to stop.

When Sara left to meet Martin, Malcolm was asleep on the couch. It was now shortly before closing-time, so Sara and Martin had to try various pubs before they found one willing to serve them. The Three Tuns obliged and Martin bought a vodka and tonic for Sara and a pint of lager for himself. While he sat down to drink his pint Sara remained at the bar, chatting to four men about TNT and trying to persuade them to use the company for their business. After about five minutes of that Martin decided to go, and he told Sara it would make more sense if, having left separately, they arrived home separately. He kissed her goodbye, jokingly calling her 'Mum' as he did so.

Before going to bed Martin poked his head into the lounge. His father was lying spread-eagled across the sofa. He called 'Dad' but getting only a mumble for a reply went upstairs. It was about ten past twelve. He lay in bed dozing and after a while heard Sara's key in the front door.

When she got in Sara went straight upstairs and changed into her white dressing-gown. She didn't want Malcolm to see how she'd been dressed in case it provoked him. Now suitably attired she went into the lounge to try to persuade him to come up to sleep. He was lying awake on the couch and as she walked in he looked her up and down and tutted his disapproval. He knew she had been out and to her he seemed to lie there festering with hate. He accused her of being a whore and of having been out to sell her body. He said he wanted her and her damned daughter out of the house. Sara tried to calm him down. She explained that Luise had already gone and that she had tried to sell her engagement ring that day to raise some money. He replied that the business had plenty of money but only he and Martin knew where it was. Trying not to rise to his bait, she again asked him to come to bed. If she left him he might fall asleep again with a lit cigarette in his hand. She was also getting frightened, knowing that at any moment he could just explode into violence without warning.

Living with Malcolm when he was drunk was like living on the edge of a live volcano; he would seem peaceful and calm enough one moment and then the next, without any warning at all, he would erupt into violence. Sara was exhausted from living under the constant threat and fear of violence and from having to absorb so much emotional pain and disappointment. Her own reserves of emotional stability and strength had not been that strong to begin with, but the relationship had by now almost totally depleted them. The strain and stress of never knowing what Malcolm would do next, never knowing when his threats were idle and when they were all too serious, had substantially eroded her judgment, leaving her feeling as if she constantly had to be in a state of readiness to defend herself. And for someone like Sara, whose life had always been highly charged emotionally, it felt as if there was nothing she could cling on to for stability.

Part of Sara felt anger and self-loathing that she had tolerated so much violence and abuse without leaving, but another part of her still loved Malcolm in spite of everything and was unwilling to let go of the hope that one day things would get better. She felt she had invested so much love, energy and emotion in the relationship that to walk away now would be impossible. Just as the gambler who keeps losing stays glued to the roulette wheel, so Sara was unable to detach herself and go.

And if she did go it would be back to a life that she remembered only with misery; back to a life of single parenthood and loneliness; and perhaps even more depressingly, back to a life where she felt she would once again have to face her father's disapproval. Her father and stepmother had met Malcolm only once but they had left her in no doubt that they approved of the match, it was the first time in her life that she felt she had won their endorsement. She had failed too many times in life to let go of this relationship. She might threaten to leave and want to leave but on a deep emotional level she simply was not able to.

Sara knew that if Malcolm's temper didn't cool there would be violence that night. Alcoholics Anonymous had taught her to leave a situation if it was becoming fraught, so she walked into the kitchen, praying. She knew she had to get him to go to bed and that she couldn't leave him downstairs. She couldn't sleep knowing that he could either set the house on fire or erupt into a furious rage.

She decided she needed to arm herself just in case, and looked for Malcolm's truncheon in the kitchen, but could not find it in its usual drawer. She expected him to burst in on her at any moment and so, when she couldn't find the truncheon, picked up a knife that was lying on the sideboard. Feeling at least Malcolm's equal she went back into the living-room. She wanted to frighten him and by doing so forestall any violence.

Malcolm didn't need any weapon to frighten Sara, just his fist and his tongue. He started to goad her again, calling her a whore and accusing her of being after his money. As far as Sara was aware he had by that time spent everything on drink, but she recognized the paranoia. He was forever telling her that his first two wives had taken him for his money, and when drunk he would accuse her of trying to do the same. There was no foundation for any of this; just as with his sexual jealousy, it was a classic, textbook alcoholic paranoia.

He told Sara that she wouldn't get him to move, but she asked him again to come to bed; at one point she sat down on the sofa beside him. He taunted her with his inaction, saying 'Come on, yeah.' She felt he was goading her into striking him as if a bit of him, in his self-destructive stupor, wanted her to lash out at him.

Calmly and deliberately she held the knife over him. One part of her was thinking that if he saw her apparently prepared to use the knife she might shock him just enough for him to stop her and to say, 'Enough is enough, I'm sorry.' That had happened once before when he had been on a bender like this. She had heard him on the phone saying insulting things about her, about how she couldn't cook or wash, and so she had opened the fridge, taken out a large bottle of wine that Malcolm had put there, and slowly and deliberately poured it down the sink. She says he then put down the phone and started to move towards her. She grabbed the empty bottle, smashed it and held it out in front of her. Completely taken by surprise, he grabbed the bottle and in the process cut her face. But she felt that was a small price to pay as the severity of the conflict shocked him enough to stop him drinking for over a month.

This time, as Sara brought the knife down towards Malcolm's stomach, she recalls that she wasn't thinking of hurting him or allowing the knife to go in, just of getting him to stop drinking so that they could love each other again. She was convinced he would grab her arm or knock it away. But she was deluding herself.

As she lowered the knife she was looking at Malcolm's face, waiting for him to react. She didn't feel the knife go in and didn't realize what had happened until he let out what she described as a low noise but what Martin believes was a scream. She looked down and saw the knife sticking out of Malcolm's stomach.

6 · The Aftermath

The events that followed were a haze to Sara. She remembers thinking she must get help but she does not remember calling the ambulance. She remembers seeing Malcolm lying on the floor and not being able to believe he was really hurt. She thought he must be faking it, pretending that it was worse than it was to gain sympathy and attention or to get back at her for bringing a prosecution against him. At no point did she allow herself to think that he might actually die, that she might really have killed him. In her shocked state it seemed like an extraordinary and absurd situation. The man she loved was lying on the couch with a knife in his stomach that she had put there. It seemed to her to be beyond belief.

Martin, however, does remember the details of that night. He heard Sara rummaging through a drawer in the kitchen. He heard what he says was a loud scream from his father. He jumped out of bed and ran downstairs to be greeted by Sara who looked him straight in the eye and said, 'Martin, I've killed your father.' He remembers her saying it calmly and matter-of-factly, as if she was talking about some mildly unpleasant household chore. He brushed past her and into the lounge.

By now his father was on the floor, the knife lying between his slightly open legs. It was about eight inches long and smooth, the bottom half was covered in his father's blood. Martin shook Malcolm and called his name but there was no response. He ran into the kitchen where Sara was already on the phone telling someone that she had just stabbed her husband. She gave her name and address and details of the incident. After putting down the phone she went to the freezer, took out some curry and put it into the microwave. She looked calm, as if she hadn't done anything. She then gathered up some clothes from the floor, opened up the washing-machine and put the clothes in. As she picked up a woolly jumper she looked at Martin and said, 'I think the leather bits on this might shrink in the machine.'

Martin couldn't believe what he was seeing. The psychiatrists who were later to examine Sara diagnosed her as having been in a state of disassociation, of complete and utter shock; unable to cope, she had completely detached herself from the reality of what was happening. To Martin, standing there in the kitchen, while his father was dying next door, Sara must have seemed like a cold and callous murderess.

Police Constables Peter Harwood and David Gill arrived to find Sara standing in the kitchen with a floor-mop in her hand. They rushed past her into the lounge where they found Malcolm. His body was cool and sweaty; his breathing was irregular and they could find only a faint pulse.

Sara told PC Gill that she had stabbed Malcolm and pulled up Malcolm's shirt to show him a puncture-wound in the left-hand side of his stomach. There was surprisingly little blood. PC Gill says he then asked Sara whether she had tried to kill him to which he says Sara replied: 'Yes, I wanted to kill him.' PC Gill then went to look for the ambulance. The ambulance workers arrived and assessed Malcolm's condition as critical. PC Gill told Sara that he was arresting her for the attempted murder of her husband and asked her to go into the kitchen while they attended to him. He cautioned her that she did not have to say anything unless she wanted to but that anything she did say might be used in evidence.

After helping the ambulance workers, PC Gill returned to Sara who at this point was standing in the hallway near the kitchen door trying to take a photograph of Malcolm. She still could not take in what was happening. PC Gill took the camera from her and watched as she crouched down beside Malcolm and called his name. He had to remove her forcibly to the kitchen and in his notebook afterwards recorded having the following conversation:

PC GILL: You cannot leave this kitchen, do you understand?
   We are trying to save the life of your husband.
SARA: I don't know why you're bothering, let him die.
PC GILL: Do you understand what you are saying?
SARA: Yes, I know exactly what I'm saying. I sharpened up the
   knife so I could kill him. Do you want to know what he's
   done to me in the past?
PC GILL: When did you sharpen the bread-knife?
SARA: After I went to see him in there. I said, 'Are you coming
   to bed, love?' and he told me to fuck off out and fuck some
   blokes to get some money, so I just walked into the kitchen,
   got the knife, sharpened it up and stuck it in his belly.
PC GILL: Did he beat you up tonight?
SARA: No.
PC GILL: Did he threaten to?
SARA: He would have.

Martin then walked past and Sara, taking his arm, told PC
Gill that it was all her fault and nothing to do with anyone else.
As PC Gill helped the ambulance men to put Malcolm on a
stretcher, Martin said he wanted to see Sara locked up for what
she had done.

The ambulance men needed to know in what direction the
knife had gone into Malcolm's body. Sara demonstrated it for
them, making a downwards motion with her right arm.

After Malcolm was carried out of the house Sara was seen
eating the curry she had got out of the freezer earlier. She asked
repeatedly whether she could have her guitar to tune up. As she
attempted to find it PC Gill restrained her, warning her that he
would handcuff her if she did not behave. She replied, 'OK, you
only have to say please, that's all. This sort of thing has never
happened to me before.'

Sara then called the taxi firm in Atherstone to ask them
whether she had left her white handbag in the cab that had
brought her home that night. Twenty minutes later she called
them back and asked them to bring her a packet of cigarettes.
She was in a state of deep shock and behaving more and more

bizarrely. PC Harwood thought she appeared quite casual and unconcerned, while PC Gill described her as being 'blasé and unaffected by the situation'. Just as before she had sought to hide her feelings behind a façade of self-control, now she was clinging to any action that would make her feel vaguely normal, as if by denying the reality of what had happened it would cease to exist. Something was clearly wrong with her; PC Gill thought she might be drunk but there was no strong smell of alcohol on her breath and she did not appear to be unsteady on her feet.

As an officer led her up the stairs to collect some belongings she reached out and squeezed PC Gill's bottom and told him he'd got a lovely bum.

Malcolm had a heart attack within seconds of being placed in the ambulance. The ambulance men struggled to revive him; as well as a steadily weakening heart he had substantial internal bleeding in the intestine and liver. He was taken to Nuneaton Manor Hospital, the same hospital where thirty-four years earlier Sara had been born, and was rushed into the emergency bay. Half an hour later he was rushed into the operating theatre for emergency surgery. At 3.24 a.m., on the morning of 14 June 1989, he was pronounced dead. The post mortem gave the cause of death as shock and haemorrhage from the stab-wound to his abdomen.

By that time, Sara was in Nuneaton Police station where she had arrived at 1.30 a.m. An hour later she was allowed to make two telephone calls. She used one to call her friend Jane Baxter to tell her what had happened and to ask her to look after Luise; she used the other to call her solicitor, Leslie Abell.

According to the Home Office, anyone detained in a police station should be allowed to speak to their solicitor on the phone in private. Calls should not be monitored and they should not, as a matter of course, be overheard. That guidance was not followed in Sara's case. In many police stations, Nuneaton included, facilities do not exist for such calls to be made in private; instead they have to be made from the charge-room, where there is usually at least one officer present. Normal practice in that situation is for the officer to keep a discreet distance to allow the caller some privacy. In Sara's case not only did she have no privacy, but a police officer, PC Guy Hawthorne, was ordered to listen to her end of the call and make a note of what she said. Such monitoring, whilst not illegal, was clearly less than desirable police practice. Furthermore, the notes PC Hawthorne made of Sara's supposedly private call were to be influential later on when it was time to decide what she should be charged with.

PC Hawthorne also watched Sara as she was waiting to be questioned. He noted that her mood seemed to swing from being very upset and emotional to being very calm; at times she wept openly and at others she sat quietly as if nothing had happened.

At 4.15 a.m. Sara's interrogation began. Despite the clear evidence of her bizarre behaviour that her mental state was not normal, no psychiatric assessment of whether she was capable of giving a meaningful interview was made. Accompanied by her solicitor, Sara went into the interview-room where she saw Malcolm's friend, Detective Constable Martin Langley. She recalls hugging him and being told to sit down. Once she was seated she was told that she was now under arrest for murder as Malcolm was dead.

Sara's interview was tape-recorded. Her sobs can be heard on the recording as she responded, 'Oh God, I loved him so much. . . . I want to die too . . . Oh God, Malcolm, oh no. . . . I can't believe he's dead, oh what a waste, oh my darling . . .' And a few minutes later: 'I can't believe I've done it. Are you sure? I always thought he'd kill me.'

Also present in the interview-room was Detective Sergeant Stephen Richardson. He too was known to Sara as an associate of Malcolm's. Not only had she just learned that she had killed the man she loved, she was also confronted by two people who knew him personally as her interrogators. While there is absolutely no indication that either officer behaved less than professionally, it seems wrong that Sara should have been interviewed by people she knew to be sympathetic to the person she had killed. Similarly, it must be of concern that no professional attempt was made to find out whether her mental state was sufficiently stable to sustain prolonged questioning.

The interview lasted for two hours and eighteen minutes. In it Sara recounted the history of their relationship, her attempts to get help for Malcolm and the constant fear and stress under which she had lived. She explained how she was afraid to go to sleep when Malcolm was drunk in case he accidentally started a fire, and described the times she and Luise had had to sleep barricaded into the spare bedroom for safety. She told her interrogators of Malcolm's accusations and goading that night and how it had affected her: 'I wanted to frighten him, I was angry, I was hurt, I wanted to frighten him. I didn't expect it to go into him. . . . I was crying, he'd called me a whore when I'd been out that afternoon trying to sell my engagement ring so he could pay the bills for the shop. Yes, I was angry. But I didn't want to kill him, I didn't mean to kill him. It's like the time he threw the coffee table at me. He didn't mean to do my knee in.'

Sara was told that she had said she sharpened the knife. She denied having done that absolutely and said she had no recollection of having said that she did.

She was then put into a police cell until the early evening. It was dirty and uncomfortable but, deeply exhausted, she managed to sleep. At about 5 p.m. she remembers being given a pill by a police doctor which she says made her feel calm and detached. By this stage it had become apparent to more senior officers that Martin Langley had a personal interest in the case and so should not have been interviewing Sara. Detective Sergeant Steve Richardson, who was a less close friend of Malcolm's, was allowed to remain in the room, but Detective Inspector Steven Hussey, who had not known Malcolm, was asked to take over the questioning. Before the interview started Leslie Abell explained that Sara had taken an Emilevine tablet at about five o'clock. It had made her mouth dry and made her feel slightly divorced from reality but she said she felt fit to be interviewed. No independent medical advice was sought to confirm that she actually was in a fit state to respond to questioning. Detective Inspector Hussey took her through the events which had immediately preceded Malcolm's death. Throughout the interview she seemed to be in a peculiarly detached state.

Whereas in the earlier interview she had been clearly distressed and quite emotional, by the time of the second interview she seemed to have cut herself off almost completely from the reality of her situation.

She described how she had felt when she saw that the knife had entered Malcolm's stomach: 'It sent me into total shock. It was like as if everything was moving as a video would when it's being played fast forward. It's disjointed, it doesn't make sense, you're trying to comprehend.' She again denied having sharpened the knife.

DETECTIVE INSPECTOR HUSSEY: Why did you say to the police officer that you'd sharpened the knife?

SARA: I've been trying to think of that all day. The absurdity of the situation. I couldn't believe it. Can you understand what I'm saying? I couldn't believe I'd stuck a knife in my husband. I still at that stage did not realize the seriousness of his injury . . . and I said I've killed my husband . . . it was like an exaggeration because it seemed such an absurd, improbable situation. I didn't mean it literally.

At 10.35 p.m., half an hour after the interview finished, Sara was formally charged. The police had a choice and a discretion: they could charge her with either manslaughter or murder. If they chose the former, it would indicate that they believed that there were clear extenuating circumstances; if they chose the latter, it would indicate that they believed she had intended to kill Malcolm and that she had done so knowingly and in cold blood. The decision was taken to charge Sara with murder.

It was Detective Inspector Colin Port who made that decision. He had only arrived in Warwickshire the day before the killing, prior to that he had been working in Manchester. An officer of a new breed, he was unusually aware of the issues surrounding domestic violence and has since tried to reform the area's policies on the crime. He had not interviewed Sara himself and he relied on what he was told by his officers. In reaching his decision he took a number of factors into consideration.

He was concerned by Sara's bizarre behaviour and her seemingly blasé manner. This could, it seemed to him, indicate that Sara was under the influence of drink or drugs or that she was mentally unstable. He also had to consider whether she was acting in self-defence or had lost control as a result of Malcolm's threats. If that was clearly the case, then she should only have been charged with manslaughter.

But there were other factors that outweighed those concerns and which seemed to indicate a definite intention to kill on Sara's part. Sara had seemingly contradicted herself on a number of points. During both interviews she had maintained that she had not intended to stab Malcolm, let alone kill him, that she had only wanted to frighten him. But Colin Port's officers told him they had heard her say a number of things immediately after the stabbing that undermined that claim. PC Gill had noted that she'd said, 'I wanted to kill him.' And while attempts were being made to save Malcolm's life she'd been heard to say, 'I don't know why you're bothering, let him die.'

Further, PC Hawthorne had recorded something in his notebook while listening to Sara's phone call which the police believed strengthened the case for murder. He had overheard her saying to her solicitor, 'He said, "I'll fucking kill you," so I went to get a knife and I stabbed him.' That, they believed, indicated that Sara had deliberately got the knife to stab Malcolm. When this was put to Sara in her interview she had protested that she was simply summarizing what had happened so that she could explain events as quickly as possible to Lesley Abell. But it was decided that there were too many factors weighing the balance in favour of murder, and in a case of this gravity it was sound police practice to charge the suspect initially with the most serious offence. What is not clear, however, is whether when that decision was made Sara was really in a fit state to be interviewed at all and what the effect of being confronted by two of Malcolm's friends, rather than officers who would have appeared to her to have been more impartial, had on the answers she gave in the interview.

Colin Port did bear in mind, though, that ultimately it would be for the Crown Prosecution Service to decide what Sara should stand accused of at trial; and that, if it wished, it could reduce the murder charge to one of manslaughter. Until the mid-1980s the police were responsible both for investigating crimes and for prosecuting those accused of them. In 1986, however, the Crown Prosecution Service (CPS) was introduced, its role being to act as an independent prosecutor. Part of its function was to ensure that where appropriate, charges could be reduced or dropped, something which officers who had invested a lot of time, resources and energy in a case might be reluctant to do themselves. It was also meant to leave the police free to investigate a case without having to be too preoccupied with whether or not a conviction was secured as a result of their efforts. The idea was that any pressure that existed on police to collect only evidence that supported the subsequent prosecution would be removed. In practice, however, many of those pressures can still be seen to weigh down on the police. The measure of a successful investigation is still by and large whether or not the prosecution has resulted in a conviction.

Similarly, the extent to which the CPS is really independent is often questioned. Whereas in other countries, like France, the independent prosecutor regularly makes use of his powers to investigate crimes, in England the 'independent' prosecutor is still actually dependent upon the police to carry out all its investigations. And as it is the police who have interviewed the witnesses and been able to assess their credibility at first hand, understandably the CPS often merely endorses the police's view of a case. In many cases that is of minimal significance as the correct charge is usually apparent, but in cases like Sara's, where there is a choice between two courses, the influence of the police officers involved can be crucial. If the police, at that stage, had perceived Sara in a more sympathetic light, she might ultimately not have had to answer a murder charge.

Sara was granted bail and moved back to Coventry. Over the next two months the police collected evidence; scores of people were interviewed and their statements taken. Detective Constable Martin Langley was clearly intimately involved in this process; his name appears on the bottom of at least ten of the witnesses' statements collected by the police, indicating that, despite his personal involvement in the case, he had conducted interviews with potential witnesses. Again, there is no indication at all that he personally acted improperly, but there must be grave doubts over how appropriate it was for him to be so closely involved with the case.

Among those Martin Langley interviewed was a woman who was to emerge as one of the prosecution's main witnesses: Helen Thomas. She was the friend with whom Sara had shared a bedroom at the TNT conference the weekend before Malcolm's death. In her statement to Detective Constable Langley she made it clear that she did not approve of Sara's often outrageous behaviour. She described their relationship as strained and she made it clear that while Sara often turned to her for friendship and support, she felt uncomfortable about her as a person. She confirmed that Sara had frequently complained of being beaten by Malcolm and that occasionally she had seen marks on Sara's legs and face.

Helen Thomas freely describes herself as having led a quiet and sheltered life. In her statement to the police she described how Sara had embarrassed her on a number of occasions by taking off items of clothing; in particular she recalled Sara wandering naked around their hotel room before taking her bath while they were at the TNT conference. She also told Martin Langley that Sara had lain on the bed and scratched her vagina, something which Helen clearly found disturbing and threatening. Even now Helen Thomas speaks of Sara with fear and finds it impossible to talk in any detail about how she felt Sara behaved while she was getting ready for her bath and later for bed. Even recalling Sara wandering naked around the room still unnerves her. But it was not her account of Sara's explicit behaviour which directly concerned the police but rather something which she remembered Sara saying to her while they were at the TNT conference.

Helen Thomas had spoken to Sara immediately after her phone call to Luise in which Luise had told her mother that

Malcolm was drunk and frightening her. She recalled the conversation that had taken place directly after that call. Their colleague Diane Davies had turned to Sara and told her that she had to sort the situation out. Sara, Helen says, replied: 'The only way to sort this out is to kill him.' Helen says she did not think about that remark at the time but remembered it after Malcolm was dead. She told Martin Langley that she was convinced Sara meant it. If that was the case the police had found, in Helen Thomas's testimony, their only strong piece of evidence so far to suggest that they were dealing with a clear case of premeditated murder.

Talking to Helen Thomas now, it seems clear that her interpretation of events, while undoubtedly genuine, may well have been coloured by her shock and embarrassment at Sara's explicit behaviour that night in Coventry. It is also apparent that Sara's remark appeared to be of little significance until after Malcolm's death. As is often the case, the words seemed to take on a greater significance when examined with reference to the events that followed than they had at the time. At that point, though, Helen Thomas was one of the police's only witnesses to suggest that Sara was indeed guilty of premeditation and therefore of murder.

For the next eight months Sara juggled her life, trying to lead a relatively normal existence in the knowledge that she had killed the man she loved and would soon be standing trial for his murder. Not surprisingly, it was an incredibly difficult and troubled period for her. The weekend after Malcolm died, when the relief of being on bail had subsided, she remembers awaking on the Sunday morning feeling totally bereft. 'I wandered off and eventually found myself in a church. The service was nearly over and as I waited, a man of the cloth asked me if I was all right. I told him I had just murdered my husband, and started to cry. He backed away, looked at me for a minute, then whispered harshly, "Have you told anyone else?" I realized he was frightened and unable to help at all.'

Fortunately for Sara, though, there were two people who were able to help and support her during that time: her old friend

Veronica Costelloe and her probation officer, Aevril Kennedy. Two months before her long wait to go to trial came to an end, Sara met someone else who was going to be able to offer her support, Clive Wright, a local businessman whose small business was in the same street as Sara's house. They developed a close friendship although Clive remembers it as a very sad period for both of them, since his marriage had just broken down and Sara was still grieving for Malcolm. But they were at least able to offer each other some comfort and support at a time when they were both frightened and alone. One month before the trial Sara's sister, Billi, travelled from America to be with Sara and to try to help her. Acknowledging the need to be prepared for the worst, they agreed that if Sara was imprisoned Billi would take Luise back to the States with her.

During this period Sara seemed to veer between two extremes, her moods alternating between periods of near-suicidal remorse and depression and a state of almost complete denial. Sometimes she would be so distraught that those around her feared for her sanity, yet at other times she would go out and behave as if nothing had happened.

Aevril Kennedy remembers Sara breaking down on countless occasions, saying she couldn't believe what she'd done, that Malcolm didn't deserve it, that she loved him and that she couldn't live without him. She was desperately sorry and so apparently desperate somehow to gain Malcolm's forgiveness that on a number of occasions Aevril Kennedy feared she might kill herself in an attempt to bring herself close to Malcolm again. One of Sara's bail conditions prevented her from going back to 73 Church Walk, so she had to ask Aevril to go there to collect what she needed. Although Sara was missing many practical things from her home, there seemed to be only one thing she really desperately wanted: a video of Malcolm taken during a barbecue which Sara described as the last happy time they had together. Malcolm was sober and at that point in their lives it seemed that everything was possible. Sara would sit and watch the video again and again for hours on end.

Often it seemed that Sara could not actually accept the fact of Malcolm's death. She would often say 'we' rather than 'I' as if by preserving a linguistic fiction she could keep him alive. Similarly, it was difficult for her to grieve and go through the normal process of bereavement. For while mourning his loss, she knew that ultimately she was responsible for it.

At other times, however, Sara would appear cocky and full of life. She would attend the probation centre provocatively dressed and, as usual, knickerless. Her self-assured demeanour marked her out from all the other clients there. She would act with confidence and arrogance and many outsiders presumed she must be a member of staff rather than a client. When Aevril Kennedy challenged her over her sexually provocative behaviour Sara would tell her not to be so mean and to stop fussing.

Aevril deeply respected Sara's spirit but interpreted her behaviour as in the main stemming from her insecurity. She felt that Sara had not learned fully how to relate to people in an appropriate adult fashion. She viewed her as desperately craving a lasting, meaningful relationship and yet lacking the skills to develop one. Her need for closeness to people and for drama would often drive her into situations that were less than desirable and into relationships with people who would only damage her further. Malcolm had offered her the respectability and the security she had craved; he had also given her the status of a respectable, middle-class wife. Now she was back to square one.

It seemed to those who were close to Sara during that period that there was an obvious connection between her difficulty in forming and maintaining lasting, healthy relationships and her troubled relationship with her father. It was a relationship that haunted Sara terribly at that time. When she had first been granted bail she actively tried to avoid talking to her father, telling him on the telephone that he had never helped her before so she didn't want him to help her now. But that was shame, hurt and despair talking. On a number of occasions Aevril Kennedy found her distraught, sobbing desperately and calling out for her father. There was one afternoon when Aevril received a number of phone calls from both Veronica and Sara. Veronica called initially to say that Sara was out of control, then Sara called, so upset that she couldn't speak properly, she was just whimpering and calling out, like a baby, for her father. When Aevril managed to leave work to visit Sara she found her curled up in a foetal position in a corner of a room saying over and over again that she wanted her father. In her distressed state she was calling out to him, 'Daddy, daddy, please forgive me, I need you, please help me.'

Aevril called Sara's father to ask for his help. She explained to him that his daughter desperately needed his support and that she feared for Sara's sanity. Richard Cooper was reluctant to become involved, particularly as Sara herself had said she didn't want anything to do with him. Aevril says he told her that he had been let down by Sara too often in the past. Aevril was persistent, reminding him that Sara was his daughter; that she loved him and needed him and that although she may have caused him pain he was the only person who could help her at that stage. But her entreaties were to no avail; Sara's father felt he had been hurt too many times before. Indeed, when Billi made it plain that she intended to do everything she could to help her sister, her father wrote to her advising her not to get involved. He warned her that Sara had 'brought nothing but misery and tragedy to everyone who has been closely involved with her over the past ten years'.

Richard Cooper was not remaining totally detached from the proceedings. He was in contact with the Atherstone police and according to them he offered his assistance. They viewed him as a potential witness against his daughter although that is something he said he most definitely wanted to avoid. Sara had no idea of this at the time.

Despite her constant battle with her emotions and her anxiety about the trial, Sara managed to visit the drop-in centre run by the probation service every Monday and before very long she was organizing activities for everyone else. She cooked and taught others how to cook, ran the crèche and threw a party for everyone at Christmas. Just as some remember her for her inappropriate and oversexualized behaviour, others were struck by her warmth, kindness and generosity.

Her strengths as a mother were also apparent during this period. Those who knew her and Luise remember them as having an extremely close relationship, offering each other mutual support. When Sara was low Luise would support her, telling her that everything would be all right. In many ways Luise had been forced to assume a maturity well beyond her years, and Sara for her part treated her very much as a young adult. Aevril Kennedy saw Sara and Luise as inseparable and had no doubt that if Sara were to go to prison Luise would be severely disturbed and damaged by it.

7 · Trial by Gender

Birmingham Crown Court is a modern red-brick building ten minutes' walk from the city centre. Built in the 1980s, it is fronted with glass which in turn is overhung by brown awning. Visitors are searched on entry and any electrical equipment like cameras and walkmans removed. Inside, the walls are an institutional yellowish-beige; the floor is covered by a green cigarette-stubbed carpet. For a court building, though, it is light and airy. Skylights and large plants bolster its architect's attempts to create a modern and functional building, attempts which are undermined only by the trails of habitation left by those who have to use it. The green seating banks are heavily scuffed and the walls patterned with the stains of too many cigarettes smoked by those waiting in nervous anxiety for justice to be done.

Court Nine is on the third floor and it was there, on Tuesday, 13 February 1990, that Sara was to stand trial. It was not a particularly big court, and nobody at that stage had any reason to expect that Sara's fate would be of interest to anyone other than those who knew her or Malcolm. Indeed, only three people accompanied her, her sister Billi, Clive Wright and Veronica Costelloe. The rest of the small public gallery was filled with Malcolm's relatives, led principally by his first wife, Moyra.

Moyra had undoubtedly loved her former husband very deeply and on learning of his death she made it her business to represent what she perceived would have been her former husband's best interests. She had remained close to Malcolm and their relationship could possibly have enjoyed a revival had Sara not come along. On learning of Malcolm's death Moyra travelled to Atherstone to supervise the winding-up of his estate. She went to the Tandy store where her son Martin had been helping Malcolm, and asked that any cash in the till was handed over to her for safekeeping. This Malcolm's business partner refused to do and similarly he resisted her attempts to carry out a stock-take. Moyra's concern for ensuring that her former husband's affairs were properly wound up was matched by her utter contempt for the woman who had killed him.

Moyra is a bold, strong and handsome woman. When she attended Sara's first bail hearing, she wore around her neck a chain that had belonged to Malcolm, making it plain where her allegiances lay. She made sure, too, that she attended every subsequent hearing, accompanied by a group of friends. When Malcolm's estate yielded no money for the two sons she had had with him (73 Church Walk was repossessed and the proceeds from selling the furniture went to cover the funeral costs), she became convinced that money must have gone astray. She found it hard to believe that a man who had spent six years working tax-free in Saudi Arabia and who was always careful with money could have died leaving next to nothing. As her conviction that money that was rightly her sons' was missing grew, so did her enmity towards Sara. Although Moyra had never met her, she believed vehemently that she was devious and evil, 'another Myra Hindley', and that she must have killed Malcolm for his money. Having grown up in Blackpool with Malcolm she knew his family well, and they too became convinced that this was not an unpremeditated domestic homicide. They had never liked Sara and, like many of his friends, denied that Malcolm was an alcoholic. To them, Malcolm had always been gentle, supportive, warm and kind.

Malcolm had wanted to be buried in Blackpool and Moyra and Martin made sure that happened. The funeral took place in the driving rain but it was well attended; Malcolm had been a very popular man. Among the friends who gathered around the graveside to pay their last respects was Detective Sergeant Steve Richardson, the very same officer who had questioned Sara on the night of Malcolm's death and who had been closely involved in investigating the case against Sara. His presence at the funeral could have been a mark of normal police courtesy or it could, as it seemed to some of those who met him at the funeral, have been a sign of genuine friendship. If the latter was the case it must, as with his colleague, Detective Constable Martin Langley, increase concern about the propriety of his being involved in the investigation. Steve Richardson, together with his senior officer, Detective Inspector Steven Hussey, was also present at Sara's trial.

In the eight months leading up to the trial Sara's solicitor, Lesley Abell, had been working hard to prepare her defence. Murder was a far cry from the usual work of an Atherstone lawyer. Lesley Abell's practice saw the occasional attempted rape or burglary, and he had even had to deal with an attempted buggery, but that was as serious as crime got in the town. As with any small country practice, there wasn't enough of any one kind of work, except perhaps conveyancing, for a solicitor to specialize exclusively in a single area of law, and although Lesley Abell did a fair amount of criminal work, the bulk of his workload consisted of matrimonial cases. He was not, however, a man to take chances. Cautious, meticulous and sympathetic to Sara from the outset of the case and at every stage thereafter, he consulted a Leicestershire barrister, Graham Buchanan, who specialized in criminal law, for advice to ensure that everything was done correctly.

Again, because of the severity of the charge, a more senior barrister, David Barker, a Queen's Council (QC), was also instructed to act for Sara. She says she met him only once before her trial and remembers being terrified of him. In her distressed state she felt she was a powerless, bad child who must rely on an adult to sort her predicament out.

Sara was advised by this triumvirate of legal expertise that she had a number of possible defences which they could try to argue on her behalf. She herself pointed out that as she had not intended to kill Malcolm but had only wanted to frighten him, the stabbing was in a sense an accident. Her lawyers, however, did not feel that they could convincingly argue accident on behalf of a client who had stood with a knife over her husband's body and then plunged it at least four inches in. Similarly, they could see difficulties in pleading self-defence, which would also have been a complete defence to the charge of murder. If they could prove that Sara had acted only to defend herself, she could walk free. That, however, they advised her, would not be possible. To succeed, she would have to show that she was under imminent threat of attack. In view of the fact that Malcolm was lying down and, by her own evidence, had not done anything to attack her physically that evening, her lawyers advised her that pleading self-defence would not be the right course.

The two other defences she could consider using would both have reduced murder to manslaughter. Because murder, the deliberate taking of another's life, is viewed as the most heinous of offences, it carries the harshest penalty – an automatic life sentence. Manslaughter, on the other hand, does not have any mandatory sentence attached to it – the judge may pass whatever sentence seems appropriate in all the circumstances. It was therefore vital, from Sara's point of view, to show that she was guilty only of manslaughter. To do this she could either argue that she was provoked or that her responsibility was diminished.

Her lawyers considered the defence of provocation. For this to work, Sara would need to show that she had suffered a sudden and temporary loss of self-control, in other words that she had acted in the heat of the moment. They would have to prove that that loss of self-control was a result of words or actions on Malcolm's part and that those words or actions would have been enough to make a reasonable person in Sara's position and with her characteristics do what she did. Her lawyers advised her that this defence, too, was unlikely to succeed. They pointed out that on her own account of events she had gone into the kitchen to fetch a knife, which did not make her response very 'sudden', and she had brought the knife down into Malcolm's stomach slowly, which did not indicate – as a more frenzied attack might have done – that she had 'lost control' in her distressed state. As a result they judged that such a defence would have been exceptionally difficult to argue persuasively. Sara did not understand the full meaning of this line of defence: 'I thought they meant, had he hit me on the day, to which the answer was no. But he did tell me he was going to kill me, and I believed him.'

It was the degree of diminished responsibility that immediately struck Sara's lawyers as the more appropriate course. To succeed, they would need to show that she was suffering from an abnormality of mind that was serious enough to impair her mental responsibility for the killing. The phrase 'abnormality of mind', which sounds pretty serious, in fact covers the full ambit of mental incapacity, ranging from fairly mild neurosis to psychopathy. As far as legal terms usually go, it is an extremely broad one. The classic definition of 'abnormality of mind' was given by Lord Justice Parker in a case in 1960. He said it was 'a state of mind so different from that of ordinary human beings that a man with a normal mind would term it abnormal'. Sara's lawyers commissioned reports from two consultant psychiatrists, Dr Henrietta Bullard from the Wallingford Clinic in Oxfordshire and Professor Sydney Brandon from the University of Leicester.

Sara herself was not entirely comfortable with this defence. Because of her experiences she disliked and mistrusted psychiatry and had a natural hostility towards practitioners of the science. Foolishly in hindsight, she gave the doctors only a sketchy outline of her past, mentioning the incident in which she had cut her throat but missing out on other important parts of her psychiatric history. Even without the benefit of full disclosure on Sara's part, however, both psychiatrists concluded that she was suffering from a personality disorder that was sufficiently serious to substantially diminish her responsibility for the killing.

Given the existing state of the law, Sara's lawyers' advice on the various defences open to her was in no way negligent or incompetent. However, it would later come in for much criticism.

Dr Bullard interviewed Sara on 2 February, just eleven days before her trial was due to begin. She found her friendly and co-operative but also restless and unable to concentrate. That she felt remorse about Malcolm's death was, Dr Bullard believed, clear, as was the fact that Sara had obviously suffered a great deal during her marriage to Malcolm and that his repeated alcoholic relapses, in the face of Sara's attempts to get him help, had had a very debilitating effect on her. She concluded that Sara was suffering from a hysterical personality disorder, the symptoms of which included rapidly changing moods, inappropriate and histrionic behaviour, impulsive, self-destructive acts and an excessive dependence on others for attention and affection. She also diagnosed Sara as having a propensity for dissociative states, in other words periods when she would become dissociated from reality and behave in an unusual way of which she had little recollection afterwards. One obvious example of this was her bizarre behaviour immediately after she stabbed Malcolm.

Professor Brandon saw Sara on a couple of occasions. He related her behaviour to what he described as her 'emotional, social and possibly educational deprivation in early life'. Alternating periods of neglect and harsh control had, he said, led to her becoming attention- and affection-seeking, experiencing difficulty in establishing close and lasting relationships. He too found evidence that Sara suffered from dissociated states after which she could not remember anything, and concluded that Sara displayed the symptoms of someone suffering from a histrionic personality disorder. The disorder, he said, was characterized by a marked pattern of excessive emotionality and attention-seeking which had been established by early adulthood. He too listed a variety of classic symptoms from which Sara was suffering, including constantly seeking or demanding reassurance, approval or praise; inappropriately sexually seductive behaviour; inappropriate expressions of emotion; rapidly shifting expressions of emotion and a style of speech that is excessively impressionistic and lacking in detail.

Professor Brandon also found evidence that Sara was suffering from post-traumatic stress disorder – the same condition that victims of tragedies like the Hillsborough Football Stadium disaster have been found to suffer from. He believed that if it was explained to the jury that such a condition was a medically recognized illness, they might be more sympathetic to Sara, despite her peculiar and seemingly callous behaviour.

For her part, though, Sara felt she had killed not because there was something wrong with her mentally but because she had been put in an intolerable position. She believed that her actions should have been seen as a reaction to Malcolm's violence and alcoholism, not as a psychological defect on her part. But along with many other women who have found themselves in the same terrible predicament, she was told that her best defence lay in pleading an abnormality of mind.

Sara says she never really felt she fully understood what her lawyers were doing on her behalf, despite their endeavours, and she does not remember being allowed to see the psychiatric reports that had been commissioned for her and written about her. Indeed it is still normal practice amongst many lawyers not to let their clients see the details of their psychiatric reports lest the bluntness of the opinions expressed in them upset them. They, as lawyers, would take care of Sara's defence, and they believed that the evidence of diminished responsibility was strong. Indeed, right up until the beginning of the trial, they were hopeful that the prosecution would be prepared to accept a plea of guilty to manslaughter on the grounds of diminished responsibility and not push them into going through a full-blown murder trial.

Prosecutors are sometimes prepared to accept such a plea; it saves the expense of a massive trial which, if there is strong evidence of diminished responsibility, there is often little justification in incurring. The prosecution team in Sara's trial was headed by a senior QC, Brian Escott-Cox. Acting on behalf of the Crown, as in all criminal cases, he took his instructions from members of the Crown Prosecution Service in a series of meetings which were also attended by the investigating police officers – in this case Detective Inspector Steven Hussey and Detective Sergeant Stephen Richardson. Brian Escott-Cox says he would never have accepted a plea rather than go to a full trial. The prosecution was determined that Sara should stand trial for murder.

That being the case, Sara was led into Court 9 on the morning of Tuesday, 13 February. Whereas in American courts the accused, who is, of course, meant to be presumed innocent until proven guilty, is allowed to sit beside his or her legal representatives, in English courts the accused is marked out physically from

the beginning of the trial by being forced to sit in the dock. Sara
sat dwarfed within the confines of a stand built for suspects
larger and more threatening than herself. The dock occupied
almost a quarter of the entire court-room and could have accommodated up to fifteen defendants. To her right were the seats
where the jury would sit in judgment of her, and in front of her,
on a raised bench stretching almost the width of the court-room
and built from the same light pine as the dock, sat the red-robed
judge, the appropriately named Mr Justice Igor Judge. Described
by those who come before him as a fair, humane although at
times slightly conservative judge, he had had a swift and successful career. Clearly very bright, at forty-eight he was young for
a High Court judge and had already risen quite high up the
judicial hierarchy, chairing the Criminal Committee of the
Judicial Studies Board, the body that supervises the training of
judges. He had been a successful prosecutor for the West Midlands Police and the year before being made a High Court judge
he had successfully rebutted the first appeal by the Birmingham
Six – an appeal which was, of course, eventually overturned
nearly four years later. Facing him in the centre of the court sat
the lawyers for both the prosecution and the defence, with their
backs towards Sara.

Sara stood as she was charged with the murder of Malcolm
Thornton, to which she pleaded not guilty. Twelve jurors were
sworn in, four of whom were women.

Brian Escott-Cox rose to begin his opening statement, an outline of the prosecution case. He is known to those who practise
with him as a tenacious, old-style prosecutor, robust and traditional in approach. He was not a man to lose a case if this could
be avoided and he had at his disposal an array of techniques that
would prove very useful in a case like this. Beside him sat his
so-called 'junior', which in the idiosyncratic and anachronistic
language of the Bar means any barrister who has not yet had
bestowed on him or her the lofty title of Queen's Counsel. In
this case it was Stephen Campbell, a barrister with some eight
years' experience. Behind them sat the lawyers from the Crown
Prosecution Service who, once they had given evidence, would

be joined by the police officers who were supervising the case.

In many respects the prosecution had an easier task in front of them than in most murder trials. They had an accused who had undoubtedly killed the victim and who, to make life even easier for them, admitted having done so. Later on, if the defence (as the prosecution had been warned they would) raised the defence of diminished responsibility, they would have to disprove it, but at this stage all they had to show was that Sara had killed Malcolm and that she had done so deliberately. They would obviously be assisted in persuading the jury that Sara had acted with intent if they could provide a motive. That is just what Brian Escott-Cox attempted to do in his opening speech.

After explaining to the jury that the accused had been assaulted by the deceased in May, and that court proceedings had been started against him for which he was due to appear in court the week after his death, Brian Escott-Cox began to construct a picture of Sara's alleged motive. She had, he claimed, become obsessed with the idea that if she left her husband she would get nothing. Her motive for killing him was by implication therefore mercenary, in that she believed she would lose out financially if she simply ended the relationship. Although there was no evidence that Sara could gain financially from openly killing her virtually impecunious husband, the allegation was asserted and the seed of suspicion planted.

The first witness for the prosecution was then called and Martin Thornton took his place in the witness-box. Tall, handsome and well-built, he cut a sympathetic figure. Giving his evidence quietly and revealing little of the emotion and pain he must have felt inside, he described how he had met Sara for the first time with his father in December 1988 and thought that they got on well as a couple; how when he had come to help his father in the Tandy shop he had discovered for the first time that his father had a considerable drink problem; and how Sara had secretly fed his father Mogadon, to try to get him admitted to hospital.

At one point Martin's evidence became unclear, not surprising, perhaps, in view of the stress of the trial and the horror of the events he was describing. When asked about the incident during which Sara had been preparing a chicken and had threatened his father with a knife, he told Brian Escott-Cox that Sara had grabbed a knife and threatened Malcolm after his father had smashed the glass in the kitchen door; he said he had had to take hold of her to make her drop the knife. However, when cross-examined he agreed that the incident had in fact taken place much earlier in the day while Sara had been preparing the lunch and while Patrick Hanlon, from Alcoholics Anonymous, was there.

Martin said he had never seen his father being violent, but again under questioning from the defence he said that on the evening before Malcolm's death Sara had been edgy in case he took a violent swing at her and that his father had thrown her clothes out of a bedroom window, saying he didn't want her. He also admitted that on the Sunday when Sara had threatened Malcolm with the knife he saw his father threaten her with a guitar and later that day break the glass in the back door.

Martin confirmed that he had told Sara that Malcolm had withdrawn her power of signature on the business account and then described how later that day he had found his father dying and how Sara had seemed so calm and unaffected. He said she had told him that she had just killed his father in the same matter-of-fact way as she might say she was putting out the rubbish.

As the son of the man Sara had killed, Martin obviously commanded considerable sympathy from the jury. He had spoken calmly and impassively and had given evidence that was potentially useful to both sides. From the defence's point of view he had confirmed the image Sara would later paint of Malcolm as someone who drank and was capable of violence. But from the prosecution's perspective Martin had shown that Sara had threatened her husband with a knife and drugged him with Mogadon three days before eventually killing him.

While there may have been some ambiguity about just how

damaging Martin's evidence was to Sara's case, there was absolutely no doubt that what the jury heard next could not but
devastatingly undermine any sympathy Sara would later try to
evoke. After she had killed Malcolm she had, as Martin confirmed, called for an ambulance. That telephone conversation
had been taped by the ambulance service and that tape-recording
was played to the court. At that point the jury had of course
heard no evidence about the symptoms of shock and post-
traumatic stress disorder. But even for someone with full knowledge of the psychiatric effects of trauma, the tape would have
made chilling listening:

OPERATOR: Ambulance Emergency.
SARA: Hello, good afternoon, I've just killed my husband. I
    have stuck a six-inch carving knife in his belly on the left-hand
    side.
OPERATOR: Where are you, love?
SARA: Bring an ambulance and the police around straight away.
OPERATOR: Where are you?
SARA: I'm at 73 Church Walk, Atherstone, Warwickshire. My
    name is Mrs Sara Thornton, my husband is called Mr
    Malcolm Thornton and I think he's dead.
OPERATOR: 73 Church Walk, Atherstone.
SARA: Warwickshire.
OPERATOR: Yes, darling, your name is, again, Mrs Thornton?
SARA: Thornton, shall I pull the knife out or leave it in?
OPERATOR: Leave it where it is, darling.
SARA: Leave the knife in.
OPERATOR: That's right.

Sara finished the call with a composed 'Thank you, good night',
as if nothing had happened.

The court-room fell totally silent while the recording was
played. Sara sounded cold, callous and completely in control.
The impact of that tape-recording was undoubtedly immense
and it was built upon the next day by the prosecution's other
main witness, Helen Thomas. Whilst Martin Thornton had

provided what could, at a stretch, be interpreted as earlier attempts on Malcolm's life in his description of the Mogadon incident and Sara's waving of a knife the previous Sunday, Helen would, again at a stretch, provide evidence of apparently clear premeditation.

Helen Thomas was a woman the jury would undoubtedly have felt they could rely upon; softly-spoken, respectable, well-dressed and sincere. It was also obvious that she was taking no pleasure in having to give evidence, appearing particularly reluctant when it was something that could be damaging to Sara. Guided by Brian Escott-Cox, she described how she had attended the TNT conference with Sara; how Sara had become upset after a phone-call to Luise and how in front of herself and their colleague, Diane Davies, she had clearly said she was going to kill him. Helen claimed that Sara was not emotional although she was very angry, and in what must have seemed to Sara like a final twist of the knife, said, 'She did point out that she was not prepared to lose everything. She was not going to let Malcolm make her lose everything which she had got.'

Helen also went on to describe a phone call she had received from Sara the evening after their return from the conference. In it, she said, Sara had talked about money; in particular about money that might be coming from Saudi Arabia and about wanting to divorce Malcolm but not thinking that she could as they had not been married for twelve months. She also said that Sara had talked to her about the house in Church Walk, saying that she was not prepared to give it up; that she was not prepared to give up everything for Malcolm.

No explanation was given in court as to what sum of money was expected from Saudi Arabia and whether it had ever actually arrived. In fact the only suggestion that there ever was any money due from Saudi Arabia was that Sara had read an advertisement in the newspaper placed by a company which claimed to be able to recoup any health and pension contributions paid to the Saudi Government by foreign workers. At her suggestion, Malcolm had written off to them, more in hope than expectation, to see whether they could retrieve any funds. Any financial windfall would obviously have been extremely welcome at that time but she had never heard anything back.

On one interpretation Helen had described the words of a woman trapped in a violent relationship with an alcoholic man, revealing, in an everyday expression, the frustration and pain she felt when her partner continually abused her trust; desperate to leave but at the same time not wanting to lose everything by doing so. On the prosecution's interpretation, however, Helen had painted a picture of an angry woman who was determined not to lose out financially. As if to bolster the latter interpretation, the prosecution then resorted to a tactic they were to repeat later in the trial; they introduced evidence which seemed to observers to bear no obvious or direct relation to the crime in question but which could considerably damage Sara's standing in the jury's eyes.

Brian Escott-Cox prompted Helen to describe Sara's drinking habits. Helen responded that whilst she would not say that Sara had a drink problem, she did remember one occasion when Sara was upset and had offered Helen and a friend a big bottle of wine at just five-thirty in the afternoon. This, Helen said, did not seem reasonable in her opinion; she also described how Sara had on one occasion offered her a joint and on another had said she had smoked one while at work, although she was careful to point out that she had not herself seen Sara smoke one. Neither Sara's drinking habits nor her attitude to marijuana seemed relevant to the case, but they both served to bolster the prosecution's picture of Sara as a 'bad' woman: a woman who drank and smoked drugs, a woman who didn't conform to the stereotype of a clean-living, respectable and trustworthy person. Further, by getting Helen Thomas to reveal her views on too much drink and illegal drugs, the prosecution had subtly provided the jury with a 'respectable' comparison against which to measure Sara – a softly-spoken, gentle, conservative woman who would never do the things the accused did.

Whilst Brian Escott-Cox adopted a rumbustious, lively and at times almost bullish approach to his task, his opponent, David Barker, Sara's QC, had a somewhat more gentle demeanour. If

Brian Escott-Cox was a streetfighter, David Barker was a gentleman. In the rough-and-tumble atmosphere that Brian Escott-Cox
had created in the court-room, David Barker, while appearing
educated and calm, seemed to some of those watching the proceedings to lack his opponent's vigour and sparkle. Whilst the
job of the jury is, of course, to decide the case which it is
empanelled to judge on its facts, it would be naïve to suggest
that the personalities of those presenting the arguments on both
sides play no part.

In his cross-examination of Helen Thomas David Barker got
her to undermine her own evidence significantly. She admitted
that she had not taken what Sara had said at the conference
seriously and that although Helen said she was worried by the
remark she had not told anyone in authority about it or indeed
informed the police. In fact its significance did not appear to
have struck Helen until after Sara had killed Malcolm. Brian
Escott-Cox did not re-examine Helen Thomas, but before she
sat down the judge himself decided to ask her a question. It was
a question which seemed to point to Sara's abilities as a mother
and which again undoubtedly contributed to the picture the
prosecution were painting of her as a less than perfect woman.

JUDGE: On the night when she came and spoke to you . . .
    about her upset at what had been going on between Luise and
    Malcolm . . . did she suggest that she should go home?
HELEN: No.
JUDGE: Did you suggest that she should go home?
HELEN: Yes, I did.
JUDGE: Do you know how old Luise is?
HELEN: I believe that she is ten.

Again, the good woman, indeed the good mother, as personified
by Helen Thomas, would have gone home to her child. It was
left to David Barker to defuse as best he could the impact of the
judge's interjection. He did not mention the fact that Sara had
been told by the Baxters, with whom Luise had gone to stay,
that she was in bed and therefore quite settled and safe, he merely

suggested that Sara might have been happier about staying at the conference because she knew Luise was no longer at home. Helen agreed, but the judge's interjection may well have still sown a seed of doubt in the jury's mind about Sara's capabilities as a mother.

The prosecution also called Reg Kimberley to the stand. He was a taxi driver who on the evening of 13 June had driven Sara home from the pub. He was in fact the last person to have seen Sara before she confronted and killed Malcolm. His evidence was relatively brief – he described Sara as having been very short with him and in an arrogant mood.

In the same way as the personality of those who argue on behalf of either side in court can affect the jury's view of a case, so – obviously, and perhaps far more crucially – can the witnesses who are called. Martin Thornton and Helen Thomas were undoubtedly helpful to the prosecution's case. The presentation of the defence's case did not, however, go so smoothly.

The main witness for the defence was the accused herself. Sara had watched quietly from the dock as the prosecution witnesses had given their evidence against her. It was Friday, 16 February, the fourth day of the trial, and she was to give evidence for most of the day.

Just as she had refused to conform to the stereotype of the model wife, so Sara refused to conform to the image of the contrite, submissive woman, cowed with shame and desperate for the jury's mercy. Most of those who watched Sara felt she did nothing to help her own case and that in fact she damaged it irreparably. Her energetic mixture of bluster and apparent confidence did little to help her in Court 9. She was intelligent rather than helpless and apparently in full control of her mental and emotional faculties.

David Barker led Sara through her early life. In answer to his questions she briefly described her childhood in the South Pacific, describing her father as 'very stiff upper lip' and unable to show emotion; and saying that she felt neither parent had been capable of showing her affection. When it came to describing her time at Millfield she perpetuated the deception she had begun in her late teens: she said she had passed seven O Levels and three A Levels.

She mentioned only two details relating to her mental health: that at seventeen she had been prescribed Valium and that at twenty-six she had cut her throat. She described the period leading up to her attempted suicide, when she had been looking after her grandfather, as a happy though stressful time that ended when 'my father told me I should not be sponging off my grandfather, but on the other hand my grandfather did not want me to leave him and I felt torn, that I could not satisfy anybody, and I got, I suppose, very depressed and eventually I cut my throat'. Sara was then asked to leave the dock and show the court the two scars that still disfigure her neck, a process she found demeaning and humiliating. She felt dehumanized, like an animal in a zoo being asked to perform and display herself. David Barker then guided her on to her admission to the Walsgrave Hospital which she said she had convinced the doctors to let her leave.

David Barker did not ask Sara to go into the details of her marriage to Helmut but when it came to Malcolm he led her through the whole relationship. Sara catalogued in detail the incidents of violence and the devastating impact his alcoholism had had on her. She described the attempts she had made to save him from the disease and the failure with which they had ultimately always been met. She explained how he was only ever violent when he was drunk and how he had hit her most frequently with his fist on the back of her neck so that the bruising would not show.

She denied having said she was going to kill Malcolm at the TNT conference but admitted to being very angry on that occasion. She described how Malcolm had taunted her on the night of the killing, and as she spoke there were tears on her face.

SARA: He called me a whore and said I had been out selling my body, and that he wanted me out of the house, and I was not going to get his money; things like that.

Sara as a baby with her mother and grandmother;
right her grandfather; 1955

Sara and her parents

Sara in the early seventies; *right* Sara and Billi, a few years later

Malcolm Thornton at work at TNT

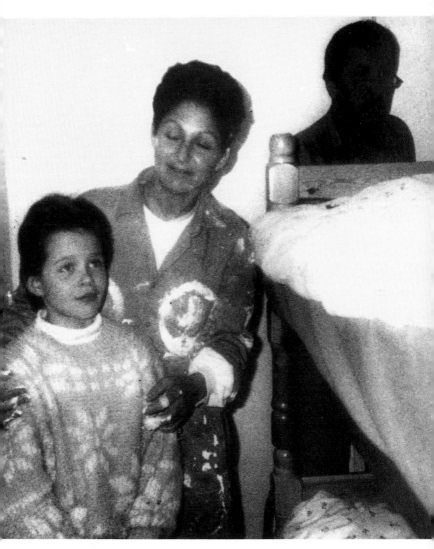

Luise, Sara and Malcolm

Sara leaving the Court of Appeal to return to prison
(Graham Turner/Guardian)

Sara's supporters mount vigils outside Holloway Prison in
1991 while inside Sara is on hunger strike
(Graham Turner/Guardian)

BARKER: What money had he got for you to have?

SARA: He did not have any . . . I asked him to stop all this, please, come to bed . . . he continued in the same vein, saying horrible things to me . . . the ones that hurt me so much, calling me a whore, saying he was going to kill me.

Sara said she then went into the kitchen 'to calm down, to calm the situation down', feeling 'terrible . . . terribly hurt'. Once in the kitchen she said she thought: 'I know, I will get the truncheon out of the drawer and if he has a go at me I can clock him with it . . .' When she couldn't find it in its usual drawer she picked up the knife that was lying on the sideboard. She said she saw it as an alternative to the truncheon.

BARKER: So what had you in your mind when you picked that knife up?

SARA: I did not want to be hurt by him any more.

BARKER: But what were you going to do with the knife?

SARA: Frighten him and show him he could not hurt me . . . I went back into the lounge.

BARKER: Why not just call it a day and go upstairs?

SARA: I wish I had. I wanted to get him to come to bed . . .

BARKER: Why not go upstairs rather than going back into the sitting-room?

SARA: I do not know.

Then, Sara said, she had stood at the edge of the couch and started talking to him again, trying to get him to come to bed. She described how Malcolm just sort of looked at her in defiance: 'He told me he would kill me when I was asleep. He was goading me.' She then described how she had sat on the edge of the couch 'just to get closer to him . . . just to say, "Look, please stop it. Come to bed."' When he refused to move, she said, she stood up again and shifted her hand so that he could see the knife: 'I held it there for a second.' At that point David Barker asked her to stand up so that the jury could see her demonstrate how she had held the knife over Malcolm's stomach.

BARKER: And you held it there for a second?
SARA: Yes.
BARKER: And then?
SARA: I put it down.
BARKER: 'Put it down' with what sort of force?
SARA: I do not remember exactly. It was not a stabbing, swift jerk.

David Barker then asked her to demonstrate what she meant and she showed the court how she had brought the knife down slowly into Malcolm's stomach.

BARKER: Why did you do that?
SARA: I thought he was going to push it away.
BARKER: Did you want to kill him?
SARA: No.
BARKER: Or hurt him?
SARA: No, I did not mean to at all. I did not want to hurt him.
BARKER: Were you thinking clearly at the time?
SARA: No, I do not think so. I was not thinking anything . . .
   I was upset, a little confused. I was angry. There is no doubt
   I was angry . . . I just wanted him to come to bed, and I
   wanted him to see how much he was hurting me and
   destroying everything.

Sara could not recall anything after that. She could not remember cooking a meal, asking for her guitar, squeezing PC Gill's bottom or saying 'I hope he dies', or even going to the police station.

David Barker had just one more question: 'So you obviously did stab him?' Sara replied: 'I did not mean to stab him at all. I did not mean to hurt him. I loved him.'

David Barker sat down and Brian Escott-Cox rose to his feet. It was now his turn to question Sara. Some of Brian Escott-Cox's friends tell him that he is unkind to witnesses during cross-examination; others would merely say that he is tough. He had been unhappy about the way Sara had described her time at

Millfield, sensing that something was not right. He asked her how old she was when she went there and how old she was when she left. She seemed unsure about the dates and whether she was seventeen or eighteen when she left. She lied again and said she had passed three A Levels.

Brian Escott-Cox then announced that he had unearthed the records from the Walsgrave Hospital where Sara had been admitted soon after cutting her throat. He pointed out to her that she had told the doctors there that her childhood was 'wonderful'. He said she had also told the doctors that she had not been to school at all until she was fourteen, something which was untrue. And he pounced upon one further discrepancy – the records showed not that Sara had persuaded the hospital into letting her go but that she had expressed the desire to stay on there until the day of her release. Those inconsistencies, Brian Escott-Cox proclaimed to Sara, show that 'You tend to recount things as you think people want to hear them rather than what actually happened.'

Then he took her through her time in Coventry jibing that with seven O Levels and three A Levels she seemed rather over-qualified for her job as a cook in the City Arms pub. However, it was when it came to the history of violence in her relationship with Malcolm that Brian Escott-Cox's sense of irony really came into its own.

He asked Sara to describe the first time she had really realized Malcolm needed help and so, called their GP, Dr Farn. It was the period after the TNT Open Day when Malcolm had got very drunk and called work to say he was sick. The Open Day had been on a Sunday. Sara could not remember when she had called Dr Farn, whether it was on the Monday evening or the Tuesday. Brian Escott-Cox then asked her whether she could remember anything else that had led her to call Dr Farn.

SARA: I think Malcolm was abusive towards me on the Monday night.
ESCOTT-COX: What do you mean by that?
SARA: Threatening me. I do not know if he hit me or was

threatening to hit me . . . but I tried to talk to him and I remember Malcolm was very belligerent at this stage.

ESCOTT-COX: Anything else?

SARA: When Dr Farn actually came to the house Malcolm was still angry.

ESCOTT-COX: Mrs Thornton, I am going to put a very different version of these events to you and I want you to tell me whether this version is right or not, that after a heavy drinking session he assaulted you, the police were called and you told the police he had tried to kill you and that that was what prompted you to ring Dr Farn. Is that right or wrong?

SARA: Yes, it could well be right.

Brian Escott-Cox then asked Sara to reconcile that with the version she had just given him. Sara appeared confused and unsure of herself. It did not emerge in court that that was in fact totally understandable as the description Escott-Cox had put to her was not connected with the incident she had been describing at all, which involved calling out Dr Farn following the TNT conference, but referred to a very similar incident that had occurred some eighteen months later when Sara called out Dr Farn after Malcolm had lost his licence. Whether deliberately or unintentionally, she had been made to look unreliable.

Then came a moment no one who attended the trial will ever forget. After an hour's adjournment for lunch Sara was to continue being cross-examined by Brian Escott-Cox. She had spent the lunch-time period alone in the cells, not allowed to talk to anyone as she was only part of the way through giving her evidence. When she returned to the court, before Brian Escott-Cox had a chance to continue his cross-examination of her, she said she had something she wanted to say to him. During the lunch-break she had been thinking about her evidence. She knew it was vitally important to be truthful but she also knew that she had lied. She wanted now to be honest, so she stood up in court and made an admission: 'I would like to admit and apologize, I lied about my O Levels and A Levels.' The court fell totally silent; members of the jury, obviously shocked, looked glum. Sara's own lawyers could not believe what she had done. She was on trial for murder and she had jeopardized her entire credibility by lying about something as seemingly trivial as exam results. Not only had she lied about it but she had then admitted to having lied about it, and they were not sure which was worse. It would of course be a gift to the prosecution: if she was prepared to lie about her A Level results then no doubt, they would imply, she was capable of lying about anything.

Sara, of course, had not seen it like that. Observers saw what she had done as at best naïve and foolish and at worst a complete sabotaging of her own case, but she viewed it as her first attempt in more than sixteen years to confront the truth of her childhood. For her, standing up and being honest about her failure was a brave first step towards accepting who she really was; for her case, though, it was a potential disaster.

Naturally Brian Escott-Cox did not waste a moment. He had in fact been making inquiries of the school, and although he had not discovered what Sara had told him, he made it seem as if Sara had only spoken out because she feared she would be exposed. There was in fact no way Sara could have known that the prosecution had rung her school – she had been locked in a cell for the whole period. That was not to be the end of the matter, though. Brian Escott-Cox then asked her whether she had been expelled. Sara replied that she had been asked to leave, which at that stage she believed to be the truth, although she was never clear as to why it had happened. She had always assumed that it was a result of her not wearing a bra or of smoking marijuana. In retrospect, of course, her confusion can be seen as the natural result of the fact that she was unclear about why she was withdrawn from Millfield. She did not know at that time that rather than being asked to leave by the school she had in fact been withdrawn. Sara could just feel herself sounding less and less convincing and becoming more and more confused.

Brian Escott-Cox then moved on to ask Sara why, if Malcolm

was so violent, she had not left him. Again her reputation as a mother was impugned.

ESCOTT-COX: Why did you not leave then?
SARA: Because I loved him.
ESCOTT-COX: Did you not love your daughter?
SARA: Yes.
ESCOTT-COX: Was the fact that you might be killed or injured by this man in a drunken rage and leave your daughter an orphan not a greater consideration than your own affection for him?
SARA: No . . . I just loved him. I think, too, I neglected my daughter. I agree.

Having got Sara to admit to inadequacies as a mother, Brian Escott-Cox moved back to his favoured motive. 'You hung on in that house because you were frightened that you would lose out if you left?' he challenged. Sara denied this, and before long the questioning had changed tack again and was back on the night of the TNT Conference. Again it was implied that Sara was a bad mother for not leaving the conference that night, but this time the implications went further.

ESCOTT-COX: You had a very good time at that party at the hotel, did you not?
SARA: I enjoyed myself, yes.
ESCOTT-COX: Including having a little fling with one or two young men who were there?
SARA: No.

The prosecutor then went on to suggest that Sara had left the main area where the party was taking place with one young man in particular, for more than a few minutes. Sara again said this was not true. Nor did it seem relevant. The prosecution produced no evidence to back up the allegation, they did not need to; the mere fact of making it would ensure that Sara's character was once again further undermined. Sara's lawyer could have objected but did not do so, doubtless not wanting to draw further attention to a damaging remark.

Sara, it seemed to some, was not just on trial for killing her husband but also for failing to conform to society's notions of what constitutes a 'good' woman. She was either a madonna or a whore; the former could not be guilty of murdering her husband, whereas the latter, of course, could. By suggesting that Sara was a bad wife and a bad mother, the prosecution were gradually defeminizing her, making it easier for her to be perceived as bad (which is one step closer to actually being so) and for her to be ultimately convicted.

Brian Escott-Cox then returned to the question of why Sara did not leave her husband. He pointed out how scared Luise appeared to have become of Malcolm and challenged Sara as to why she had not gone with her daughter to safety. The presumption was the same as that seemingly made by the police: if the man is violent, it is up to the woman to get out. Sara said her reasons were twofold: 'I had nowhere to go, first of all. And, secondly, I did not want to leave my home and my husband and my family. My whole life was there, my job, Luise. She is dyslexic, she has special education in Atherstone and was doing very well.' Brian Escott-Cox did not suggest Sara should have run for safety to her house in Coventry as it had already come out in questioning that she had let it.

Sara confirmed that on the Monday before the stabbing she had rung her solicitor to make an appointment to talk about getting a divorce. Malcolm had also attempted to contact his solicitor. Brian Escott-Cox then wanted to know why Sara had decided to send Luise to stay away from home on the night she killed Malcolm. He implied this was suspicious. But it was in fact something she had done quite regularly when Malcolm was drunk and she replied that on this occasion in particular she had wanted her daughter away from Malcolm in case he learned from his friends in the police force that Luise had just made a statement against him.

Next there was the phone-call Sara had made to Helen Thomas on the evening of the killing. Sara said she could well have called her but did not remember for sure. Helen Thomas had told the court that during the conversation Sara had said, 'I'm going to do what I said I would do', or words to that effect – words which Helen Thomas had taken to mean that Sara was going to kill Malcolm. Sara disputed that, saying that if she had used those words she would only have meant that she was going to have to leave Malcolm, not that she was going to kill him. Helen, she reminded the court, knew that she had arranged to see a solicitor to discuss that very possibility.

Brian Escott-Cox was not just tenacious and vigorous, he was also extremely thorough. He wanted to know why Sara had not been able to find the truncheon which Martin said he had returned to the drawer, implying that she had lied about looking for it and was always going to get a knife. Sara again denied this, and after the trial the police did in fact accept that the truncheon had not been returned to its usual drawer. Similarly, Sara categorically denied having sharpened the knife, and indeed no evidence was adduced to prove that she actually had. Martin had told the court and earlier the police that although he heard Sara rummaging in a cutlery drawer he had not heard any sharpening of a knife.

Sara had maintained persistently throughout her interviews with the police that she had not intended to stab Malcolm and that it had been an accident. Her lawyers were convinced that this was not a fruitful line of defence but Sara stuck to it as she felt it to be the truth. Brian Escott-Cox similarly doubted it, but he needed to confront and disprove it. He pointed out that Sara had stuck the knife some five to six inches into Malcolm's body. Similarly, although the defence had decided not to raise the defence of provocation, he needed to dismiss it. He asked Sara, 'Can we get this crystal-clear: you are not saying you did it deliberately because he provoked you into it?' Sara, who had been told by her lawyers that according to the legal definition, which required a 'sudden and temporary loss of self-control', it would be very difficult to argue that she had been provoked, replied, 'No.' A few minutes later Brian Escott-Cox, sat down: he had more than lived up to his reputation.

If he had wanted to, David Barker could have re-examined Sara on any of the points raised by his opponent; he could have attempted to redress some of the prejudice that had been created or to dispel some of the confusion. Doubtless for good reasons, he declined, and Sara was not re-examined.

Things were not going too well for Sara. Her lawyers believed their job had been made a lot harder by their client's decision to admit she had lied about her exam results. They did not see it as an example of how honest Sara was striving to be but as foolish and potentially very undermining of her credibility. They still felt, however, that the case was winnable. That was until the next bombshell dropped.

Billi had been sitting in court, dismayed by the way the trial was going. She had noticed that during much of her sister's evidence that morning a juror appeared to keep falling asleep: his head was resting on his hands and every few minutes it would slip off, waking the juror with a jolt. (This juror was later to be discharged because of illness.) It was her first close contact with the criminal justice system and she was appalled to see that her sister's life was being decided by people who could not even stay awake to hear her side of the story. The lawyers dismayed her too; to them it was, naturally enough, 'just another murder trial', and she would see them outside the court laughing and joking with each other, but to her it was the process that would decide her sister's fate. Sara's liberty was hanging in the balance and it seemed preposterous to Billi that the process that would decide her future should depend on such a pompous and anachronistic system. The lawyers did not speak in plain English, and the judge was dressed in robes which seemed better suited to a historical tragedy than a modern court-room. Her sister, whom she knew to be a strong and intelligent woman, seemed to be swamped and dwarfed by a process that appeared to ignore the realities of the human beings with which it dealt. The questions that were being asked of Sara seemed to show that there was no comprehension of her personality and experiences; even when she firmly denied the false accusations that were put to her it seemed that just the very making of them would be enough to damn her. The eloquence and confidence of the prosecuting counsel had certainly made Sara seem at best confused and at worst dishonest.

But more importantly than all that, she felt the truth was not coming out. That was not just something Billi thought, it was something she knew. Her sister's defence depended upon proving that she suffered from some sort of mental abnormality and yet evidence that would have proved that that was the case was not being presented. Billi knew her sister had attempted to kill herself when she was living with their grandfather; she knew Sara had had a troubled and very difficult emotional past; what she did not know was why more of it was not being brought up in court.

Sara's QC, David Barker, seemed to her to be so lofty as to be almost unapproachable: indeed, the rituals and conventions upon which the legal system depends deliberately foster that impression. Clients instruct solicitors and solicitors instruct barristers. An ordinary member of the public cannot employ a barrister directly, they must first employ a solicitor. This, the Bar believes, preserves its members' status as independent expert advisers, a status it has enjoyed since the thirteenth century. But equally, a sceptical lay-person may feel prompted to observe, this ensures that two people are always employed to work on one job. Clients, once a barrister has been instructed on their behalf, are not even allowed to contact him or her directly. Indeed, although the barrister is ultimately being paid by the member of the public (or by the Legal Aid Fund on their behalf) the barrister's Code of Conduct forbids him or her from seeing their client alone; the solicitor must always be present to act as a chaperone, again ensuring that both branches of the profession are paid for each meeting. Solicitors deal with people; barristers with the law. The fact that the law is meant to serve and administer to people seems for a large part of the legal system's history to have been overlooked.

And then, of course, there is the accompanying and much-cited concept of professionalism. Naturally, according to the Bar, it might be unprofessional for a barrister to deal directly with his or her client; the barrister might become too involved with the client and lose sight of his or her objectivity and independent role. It is for solicitors to become intimately involved in the case; the barrister's role is to advise. But, of course, when the case comes to trial it is the barrister who will be arguing it; it is the barrister upon whom the client will ultimately depend. Outsiders might wonder – naïvely as many barristers would have it – whether getting more involved in their case is not exactly what their legal representative should be doing. However, that distance between the client and the barrister is felt to be best for the client and does, as one of the counsel in Sara's case later explained, 'make it easier to go home and sleep at night'.

Feeling unable to approach her sister's leading counsel, but knowing she had to tell someone, Billi decided to speak to David Barker's junior, Graham Buchanan, whom both Billi and Sara viewed as more accessible: indeed, his bouncy, jovial character had inspired the sisters to nickname him Tigger. Billi went up to Graham Buchanan during a recess and asked why her sister's attempt to kill herself previous to the throat-cutting incident had not been brought out. For a short but unique moment, he was rendered speechless. What Billi was telling him about her sister's past was, as she was pointing out, highly relevant to Sara's case, but neither he nor any other member of the legal team knew about it. Sara simply hadn't told them.

Never, in his not inconsiderable twenty years at the Bar, had Graham Buchanan encountered a client who deliberately withheld evidence that was so apparently vital to the case. It is by no means clear why Sara had not revealed this. She herself was to say that she didn't consider it to be relevant, that what should have been important was not the intimate details of her psychiatric history but the pressures Malcolm's violence and alcoholism had put her under. That in turn ties in with her feeling that she did not really understand the defence that was being mounted on her behalf. She also says she cannot remember being specifically asked about earlier details by the psychiatrists, though even if she had been, she might well have felt reluctant to reveal them. Despite her openness in matters sexual and

emotional, Sara still bore a deep sense of shame about her past.
Just as she was ashamed of revealing her poor exam performance, so she was also undoubtedly ashamed of revealing the true
level of emotional turbulence and pain she had been through.
Her friend Clive Wright, who was present for the trial, found
that despite Sara's explicitness in certain areas she had a strong
sense of pride and would become very embarrassed about the
depression she was going through. He remembers her begging
him not to reveal to anyone that she had been sobbing; she
wanted outsiders to think that she was all right. That, he
believed, also fitted in with her propensity to appear calm and
cool when inside everything was completely chaotic. During the
twelve or so years of their friendship, Veronica Costelloe had
also noticed that Sara would always appear to be most 'on top'
and bubbly when in fact she was crumbling and racked with
pain inside.

As soon as the court broke for lunch Sara was told that she
must come clean. As best she could, she told her lawyers the
most painful moments of her past, many of which she had not
even told Billi about. It took until well into that evening for her
to disgorge the most intimate parts of her emotional history. At
one point her counsel felt she might break down; there seemed
to be experiences that seemed too painful for her to acknowledge. She felt humiliated and invaded but understood now that
it was an essential process. It was difficult for her to remember
many parts; she had buried them so deeply to shield herself from
the pain they caused her. Her tendency to deny things as a form
of self-protection made it a very difficult process. Eventually,
though, she came out with a statement from which her lawyers
could work. In it she detailed her suicide attempts, her broken
and painful relationships, her disastrous marriage to Helmut and
the sequence of events that had led to her admission to the
Withington Hospital in Manchester.

For her lawyers this was a double-edged sword. They felt that
if the medical history had come out before the beginning of the
trial, they might well have been able to persuade the prosecution
to accept a plea of guilty to diminished responsibility. The fact

that it had only come out now still strengthened the case: it revealed more evidence to bolster their defence of diminished responsibility, as did the fact that, in their view, Sara had not acted in her own best interests. However, balanced against that they were concerned that it might appear that, as with the A Level results, Sara had not told the whole truth. And, again as with the lie about the exam results, it was unlikely that Sara's reasons for being less than honest would come across as convincing to the court.

That afternoon Billi herself was called to the witness-box. Strongly, calmly and, as always, dependably, she told the court that she had come forward to give evidence as important things had been missed out. She described Boxing Day eleven years earlier when she had been visiting Sara and her grandfather in Atherstone; she described going into the bedroom, turning on the light and finding her sister lying in a pool of blood with her wrist cut.

That weekend, the psychiatrists who had been instructed to report on Sara did their best to fill in the missing gaps. They contacted the Withington Hospital and managed to get hold of a copy of her records. The court was adjourned on Monday to allow the defence to acquaint themselves with the evidence that had now emerged.

On Tuesday morning Sara was recalled to the witness-stand to give evidence. For the first time in the trial she cried outright. She described how she had taken an overdose at eighteen; become pregnant and had an abortion three years later; taken another overdose the following year while living in Manchester; become pregnant again and had to have a second abortion because of heavy bleeding; and then how, after she'd met Helmut, she had been found naked wandering through the streets of Manchester, clutching a teddy bear.

Sara talked about her brief admission to the Withington Hospital, recalling only a sketchy outline of what had happened: 'I remember talking to a psychiatrist. I wanted to tell them about how I felt about Mummy and how I felt about Daddy, but I could never really bring it all out . . . I was ashamed of it. I have always known really there is something wrong with me, but I never told anybody and I never discussed it.'

David Barker asked her why she had not told the court these details during her main evidence the previous week. Sara again replied, 'Because I am ashamed of it. Normal people do not go around cutting their wrists and finding themselves naked in a police station in the middle of the night. I have never really talked about it to anybody. Not even my best friends knew before this case started.'

Then Sara went through her traumatic marriage to Helmut; her third pregnancy and abortion; and the suicide attempt that her sister Billi had described to the court a few days earlier. As when she had told the court she had cut her throat, she was asked to parade the evidence of her injury in front of the court. Feeling humiliated beyond belief, Sara showed her wrist to the judge, the jury and the prosecuting lawyers in turn.

David Barker then asked her whether there was anything else that the court should hear about. Sara replied: 'Only that every time I do this it is when I have an argument with my father or a call with my father, a discussion with my father. You notice he is not here today. He has never wanted to know.'

What neither Sara nor the jury knew was that her parents and the police had again been in touch. Sara's stepmother told them she was prepared if necesary to give evidence to disprove the unpleasant and, as she saw it, 'untruthful' things Sara had said about her childhood. Even though Juliette Cooper had not become involved in Sara's family until Sara was seventeen, she felt very strongly that Sara had no justification for speaking ill of her childhood. She felt that it was relevant that when Sara had come to stay with her father's family after being assaulted by Malcolm in the month prior to his death, she had displayed no signs of being a battered woman. Sara's father had said the same, in a letter to Billi, in which he told her that Sara was certainly not a 'battered wife'. Indeed, before agreeing that Sara could come and stay with them in Devon, he had rung the police to check whether his daughter was really in danger. The police told him that there was 'cause for concern'; indeed, the incident had been viewed as serious enough for the police to bring a prosecution and for her doctor, who had examined her, to give her a certificate of sickness – Sara had after all been knocked unconscious and treated in hospital. But Sara's parents, no doubt because of their first-hand experience of her often emotional behaviour, appeared to be far more sympathetic to Malcolm's position. As far as they could see, the only evidence of any possible injury to Sara was a cut on her lip, which was not enough in their view to make her the victim of battering. Although Sara's father had met Malcolm only once, he wrote to Billi before the trial telling her that Malcolm was a very nice man and that neither he nor his wife could understand why Sara had not mentioned him or telephoned him to see how he was when she was staying with them. The fact that she had just been assaulted by him obviously did not appear enough of a reason for his daughter not to be behaving like a 'good wife', and a 'good wife' would have telephoned her husband.

In spite of the hurt, pain and disruption Sara had caused her parents, lawyers and senior police officers involved in the case were surprised by her parents' apparent hostility towards her.

Back in the court-room it was again Brian Escott-Cox's turn to question Sara. He immediately spotted an apparent contradiction in the defence that was being run for her. It was the same apparent contradiction that had made Sara believe her medical history was not truly relevant.

ESCOTT-COX: Are you still saying that what happened was in effect an accident in the sense that you intended him no harm whatsoever?

SARA: I did not mean to hurt him at all, sir.

ESCOTT-COX: Let us have this absolutely crystal-clear. You are not saying to my Lord and the jury, 'Yes, I murdered my husband, but I am not guilty of murder, because there is something wrong with me.' You are not saying that, are you?

SARA: No, I am not.

Sara was saying, as she had all along, that she had not intended
even to wound Malcolm, just to frighten him as a response to
his behaviour – in other words, that her actions had been provoked by him – but that was not the defence that was being put
forward by her lawyers. They were, of course, seeking to prove
she had been suffering from diminished responsibility.

Brian Escott-Cox led Sara briskly through the details of her
suicide attempts and then fastened skilfully upon something that
he was sure the jury would find much more interesting. It was,
again, something that seemed irrelevant and potentially highly
prejudicial. Sara had told the court that initially she had been
too ashamed to reveal the full details of her psychiatric problems.
However, Brian Escott-Cox knew that she was not ashamed
about her body.

ESCOTT-COX: You are hardly a modest person about your
   body, are you?
SARA: No . . .
ESCOTT-COX: You have a habit of going out in public or going
   out of your house without wearing any knickers or
   underclothes?
SARA: Yes, I stopped wearing pants, because I got thrush so
   badly.

It did not seem remotely relevant but the damage had been
done. Sara was the sort of person who didn't wear knickers, and
every good juror would know what implication to draw from
that. And it was the sort of detail which the prosecution must
have known would damage Sara's reputation still further in the
eyes of the jury. At this point, as when Sara's drinking and
possible drug habits were raised, along with her alleged brief
absence with a man from the TNT party, there was no objection
from the defence. Maybe they felt it would draw still more attention to them if they did; or maybe this just appeared to be the
normal sort of exchange that takes place in an English court-
room. In any event, such tactics are old court-room tricks: some
would call them cheap but they are often effective and can assist

anyone who is willing to use them in promoting their side of the case. They also seem, of course, chauvinistic; no man, standing accused of a non-sex-related crime, would have been as likely to have his sexual reputation alluded to and besmirched in the way Sara's was. But then, when men stand trial the proceedings are usually restricted to the offence of which they stand accused, not their whole history and life-style. For women, it is often still the case that just as throughout history they have been punished for failing to conform to society's expectations, so today their sexual promiscuity or their non-conformist life-styles are all too often viewed as relevant to those who stand in judgment of them.

Indeed, following Sara's case, one of the lawyers involved in it was heard to remark that she was to a certain extent unlucky to have been convicted but that he felt no sympathy about the fact that she had been imprisoned for life. When questioned further he replied, 'She's not just promiscuous, she's aggressively sexual. She goes about seducing all classes of people . . . a very undesirable lady.'

8 · Mad or Bad?

Sara's ordeal was not over yet. Although she would not address the court again, the process of sifting through the revelation of the most intimate details of her life was to continue. It was now time for the so-called 'expert' witnesses to be called to analyse and assess her state of mind.

If her defence of diminished responsibility was to succeed, her lawyers had to be able to prove two elements required by the law. First, they had to show that she had been suffering from 'an abnormality of mind', and second, they had to prove that whatever abnormality she had been suffering from was serious enough substantially to impair her mental responsibility for killing Malcolm. Ultimately it was an issue which the jury would have to assess and decide, but to aid them in their deliberations psychiatrists were called to support both sides of the case.

First the defence called Dr Henrietta Bullard to the witness-box. She repeated her view that Sara's responsibility was definitely diminished at the time that she killed Malcolm. The more recent revelations about Sara's past had, she said, 'just gilded the lily in psychiatric terms'. She told the jury that Sara could be 'a charming, soft-spoken, sensitive woman', but that she had another side which was 'unable to cope with the stresses of life, who flies into rages, harms herself, brandishes weapons, behaves in a sort of way which most people would consider abnormal'.

Asked to explain Sara's cold and callous voice when on the telephone to the ambulance service, she pointed out that although Sara had sounded totally in control she had actually said 'Good afternoon' to the operator when it was quarter to one in the morning. It was a clear example of the kind of dis-associated behaviour that people with the sort of hysterical personality disorder that she'd identified in Sara display. Dr

Bullard also provided evidence which, had Sara's lawyers decided to argue provocation as a defence, would have come in very useful. She said that the act had occurred not just because of instability on Sara's part but also because of her relationship with Malcolm; and that Sara was demonstrably coming to the end of her tether in the weeks leading up to the incident.

Dr Bullard had sat in court and watched as Sara gave her evidence. Indeed she had been in court for all but the first two days of the trial. She told the jury that the evidence pointed to Sara 'being very over-involved with her husband's problems. She would not let him go. She kept on and on at him about the drink; the hiding of the beer and other drink; preventing him having his money; interfering in his business. She could not accept that you cannot control other people and if they are going downhill they will have to go.'

Under fire from Brian Escott-Cox, Dr Bullard acknowledged that there was some evidence that Sara was slowly maturing, the last major bout of obvious psychiatric disorder occurring in 1981 when Sara had cut her throat and been admitted to the Walsgrave Hospital. Brian Escott-Cox then led her into a corner he had especially prepared for her. Again, it was one of the techniques in which he was very accomplished; it was a way of legitimately getting a witness to say something that would in practice have a highly prejudicial effect.

He asked Dr Bullard whether, in her opinion, if events had been sufficiently stressful, Sara could have killed at any point since 1981. Henrietta Bullard replied that if an identical situation had arisen, which was obviously in practice very difficult to envisage, it might have been possible that she would have behaved in a similar way and that because of the abnormality of mind she was suffering from she would not have been guilty of murder.

Brian Escott-Cox pounced on this, pointing out that it was effectively granting Sara a licence to kill. Dr Bullard, of course, denied that anyone at all should have such a licence and said that that was not what she was saying. Brian Escott-Cox then rammed home his point, suggesting that if Sara had killed once in stressful circumstances, she could kill again. Dr Bullard countered that that was not likely and that the statistics showed that domestic killings very rarely repeated themselves. But the seed had been sown in the jury's mind. If they let Sara off the murder charge and found her guilty only of manslaughter, would they effectively be granting her a licence to kill?

That was a piece of potential prejudice that David Barker could not allow to remain. He rose to his feet and told Mr Justice Judge that he needed to discuss a matter of law. In legal terms that meant he needed to discuss something in the jury's absence and so Mr Justice Judge asked them to leave the court-room for a short while.

Once they had filed out, David Barker stood up again and addressed the bench. He was wondering, he said, whether he ought to apply for a new trial: 'What my learned friend has in effect been suggesting . . . to the jury is that if they let this defendant go she may do it again . . . that is so prejudicial that this jury really cannot contemplate this case now with any degree of objectivity.' Juries are not meant to be asked to contemplate what will happen to the defendant as a result of their decision to acquit or convict, as deciding on sentence is a question for the judge alone. The jury's job is only to decide on guilt or innocence without referring to the potential consequences of either verdict.

After discussing the issue with Graham Buchanan and Sara, David Barker decided he would apply for a re-trial. He reminded Mr Justice Judge that in a recent case the Court of Appeal had expressed disapproval of the line of questioning that had been used: 'What we object to particularly is the emotive words and thoroughly prejudicial words "licence to kill", they add a headline . . . that can only remain in the jury's minds from the beginning to end of their deliberations.'

Mr Justice Judge did not agree. He roundly rejected the application, saying that he did not think there was the 'slightest risk' of the jury, if properly directed by him in his summing-up, reaching any adverse conclusion about the defendant on an improper basis.

The jury were invited to return and sit through the evidence of the two remaining witnesses. First, it was the defence's turn to call their second expert witness – Professor Sydney Brandon. He had examined Sara twice, the first time two weeks after she had killed Malcolm. He too backed up the view he had expressed in the report he wrote for the defence: he believed that Sara was suffering from an abnormality of mind – by the age of twenty-two she had made three suicide attempts. Although her personality disorder was now more stable than it had been when she was younger, it was still serious enough for her responsibility to be diminished. He was not, however, asked to give evidence on the post-traumatic stress disorder he had also diagnosed Sara as suffering from.

The last witness to be called was Dr Barbara Brockman, who had been asked by the court to prepare a report on Sara, and whom the prosecution had decided to call to endorse their view. She was younger than the two doctors chosen by the defence, who between them had a total of some thirty-six years' experience as consultant psychiatrists; Dr Brockman had been practising for just one year. She gave her evidence firmly and confidently and, like the barrister who was questioning her, stood her ground almost ferociously. She agreed that Sara was indeed suffering from an abnormality of mind but that it was of the kind that tended to improve over the years. In fact she believed that there was evidence to suggest it had improved in recent years. Since 1981 there had been no evidence of self-harm on Sara's part or anti-social behaviour to others. That, she said, was evidence that in the last seven or eight years Sara had been experiencing a period of stability. Dr Brockman concluded that although Sara was still suffering from a personality disorder it was not so substantial as to have impaired her responsibility at the moment that she killed Malcolm.

David Barker immediately sought to undermine her evidence. The easiest ground upon which to do so was her relative lack of experience. He brought out the fact that although she did some work at the Walsgrave Hospital she had been unable to obtain the notes relating to Sara's stay there. Dr Brockman said she had been told that the notes had been destroyed, but this was not the case – they had, in fact, been retrieved that very weekend by the obviously more experienced Dr Bullard. Nor, in contrast to Dr Bullard and Professor Brandon, had Dr Brockman been in court while Sara was giving evidence or indeed at any point prior to that day.

David Barker then led Dr Brockman on to Sara's attempted suicide on Boxing Day 1979. As she had not been in court when Sara was asked to display the scar on her wrist, he asked her: 'In your interview you did in fact notice the scars on the wrists, did you?'

DR BROCKMAN: And on her neck.
BARKER: Did you deal in your report with the cut wrists?
BROCKMAN: No, I do not believe I referred to it in the report.
BARKER: Did you not think it important?

Dr Brockman then asked for permission to check the notes she had made during her interview with Sara but she searched through them in vain – she had not in fact made any note of having seen the scar, which rather suggested that she had not noticed it despite her having said that she had. She admitted that she had become confused and must have muddled her own observations with what she had been told during the last few days. That, David Barker hoped, was enough to defuse her negative assessment of Sara.

There were just three further speeches for the jury to sit through. The prosecution and the defence would make their closing submissions followed by the judge's summing-up. Then it would be time for them to begin their deliberations and decide on Sara's fate.

The closing speeches took most of the morning of Wednesday, 21 February. Brian Escott-Cox rose first to make his final address. Things had gone even better than he had expected, although he always considered diminished responsibility cases were tricky for the defence to win. Juries, he found, were often reluctant to believe psychiatrists employed by the defence. If they were asked to decide whether someone was 'mad or bad' they might well, especially in a case like this where the defendant had been shown to be capable of lying, decide she was the latter. Brian Escott-Cox ran through what the jury had been told over the last week. There had been Martin's evidence that Sara had fed Malcolm six Mogadon tablets and threatened him with a knife; Helen Thomas's account of a threat to kill made just three days before Malcolm's death; and Sara's evidence which had been shown to be unreliable in places. If, as she claimed, she was in fear of Malcolm that night, why, Brian Escott-Cox rhetorically inquired of the jury, did she not just call upstairs for Martin to come to help?

The motive was still unsubstantiated, however. Allegations had been made that Sara was obsessed with Malcolm's money but the prosecution had not produced a single shred of evidence to show that he did in fact have any assets. Indeed, during the course of the trial it had been shown that Sara herself had applied for a £10,000 re-mortgage on her own property in Coventry to bolster up his business.

But despite the apparent weakness in Sara's motive the defence were no longer confident of their case. They had felt the tide turn against them when Sara admitted to lying about her exam results and then positively pull them backwards when it became apparent that she had actually withheld information from her own lawyers and psychiatrists. There was, however, still a firm conviction that the defence of diminished responsibility should work. Sara's economy with the truth on certain issues should, they believed, only serve to bolster their argument that her mind was not working as it should have been. They were worried, though, that while they felt justice to be on their side, Sara might have alienated the jury to the extent that they believed her to be capable of anything. As one of Sara's own lawyers was to remark afterwards, a guilty verdict would, in view of how the trial had gone, be wrong but not surprising.

In his closing speech, David Barker, QC, emphasized that the defence were not asking for Sara to be acquitted but for her to be convicted of manslaughter rather than murder. He also

emphasized Sara's psychiatric history, pointing out that all the
psychiatrists agreed she had a serious personality disorder, the
only difference of opinion being whether she had been suffering
from it at the time of the killing. That Sara had been called to
the witness box twice was, he told the jury, very rare and an
indication that all was not right. The fact that she'd hid 'huge
chunks' of evidence from her own lawyers was an indication of
Sara's inability to make rational decisions, as was her decision
to marry Malcolm in the first place. He sought to dismiss the
financial motive that had been pressed by the prosecution by
pointing out that Sara owned her own house in Coventry and,
according to the title deeds, half of 73 Church Walk. Further,
he pointed out, Malcolm's business account had been emptied
so that it contained only one hundred pounds. Not a lot, he
observed, for Sara to be obsessed with. He concluded that her
behaviour was irrational but that it shouldn't be seen as cold
and calculating as implied by the prosecution. Once he had sat
down it was left only for the judge to sum up the case and for
the jury to retire to consider their verdict.

Every judge lives in fear of misdirecting the jury. If they do,
and the defence spot it, they may well find their handiwork being
examined by the Court of Appeal. If they have made a mistake,
the case may be overturned. Judge Igor Judge's speech was intelligent and lucid in legal terms and clearly revealed the abilities
which have placed him on the fast track of the judicial ladder.
The purpose of his speech, as is always the case, was to sum up
the case for the jury and to make sure that they understood their
role. Whilst he could direct them on questions of law, questions
of fact were for the jury alone to decide. The same is true of
the American system, although in the United States judges are
prevented from passing any comment at all on the factual evidence, whereas in England they are not. So long as the judge
makes it plain to the jury that any comments on his part are
merely comments and can be accepted or ignored as they see fit,
he can allow the jury to get an indication of his view of various
parts of the case. So that whilst it is, of course, the jury, in the
privacy of the room to which they retire to deliberate, who

decide on the facts of the case and the verdict, they naturally carry with them an impression of what the judge's view is in certain respects.

It was their job, Mr Justice Judge told the jury, to apply their common sense. He then turned to the phrase which had prompted David Barker to request a re-trial. The jury must, he told them, ignore phrases like 'licence to kill' because it was an emotional phrase and 'it does not help very much'. That, give or take a few words, was the entire extent of his direction on a phrase which the defence believed was prejudicial enough to prevent the jury from viewing the case objectively.

The jury were then directed on the burden of proof: they were told that it was for the prosecution to prove Mrs Thornton's guilt; she did not have to establish that she was not guilty. Mr Justice Judge told them that to convict her of either murder or manslaughter they had to be satisfied so that they felt sure she was guilty, in other words, they had to be satisfied beyond reasonable doubt (although those are words the judge chose not to use). In recent years it has been accepted that directing the jury that they must feel 'satisfied so that they feel sure' is the same thing as telling them that they must be 'satisfied beyond reasonable doubt'. However, it is open to question whether the two phrases are really interchangeable and whether 'feeling sure' is really as strenuous a test as being 'satisfied beyond reasonable doubt'. It was only if they believed Sara to be guilty of murder that the jury needed to consider her defence of diminished responsibility; and if they did get to that stage, then it was for the defence to prove that her responsibility was indeed diminished. Interestingly enough, that would not have been the case had the defence been provocation. Whereas the burden is on the defence to prove diminished responsibility, if the issue is provocation then it is for the prosecution to prove that the defendant was not provoked, not for the defence to prove that she was.

Then the judge moved on to consider Sara's claim that she had not meant to injure Malcolm at all and that it was an accident. He told the jury: 'Of course, like all questions of fact, these are questions for you to decide, but if you bear in mind how deep the knife penetrated, the downward movement with the knife in the clenched hand which Mrs Thornton demonstrated . . . you will, I suspect, have not the slightest difficulty in being sure that this was not an accident.' His remarks were a perfect example of the 'doublespeak' which so often characterizes the English legal system. It was, of course, as Mr Justice Judge so correctly re-emphasized, for the jury to decide questions of fact, but his phraseology must have left them in no doubt about what conclusion he expected them to come to. Such comments reveal part of the deep-rooted judicial ambivalence which lies at the centre of English jury trials. Whilst the system prides itself on being founded on the principle that a subject should be judged by his or her peers, it is also terribly frightened of what those legally unqualified peers might get up to; they might, heaven forbid, not understand what they were doing. So while the system rests on the very fact that the jurors are lay-people, it also trembles at the potential consequences of this and makes every attempt to steer them through the correct legal hoops.

After explaining that it was Sara's intention at the moment of killing Malcolm that the jury needed to decide upon, Mr Justice Judge moved on to the issue of provocation. When deciding not to argue the defence of provocation, Sara's lawyers had pointed out that even if they did not run it the judge would be obliged to mention it. They believed on the facts of this case that not only would the defence have been unlikely to succeed if they had argued it but that also, to an extent, it might have undermined their arguments on diminished responsibility. It might well have looked as if they were saying that Sara did not know why she killed her husband and that the jury should decide whether it was because she was provoked or whether it was because she suffered from diminished responsibility. Such a two-pronged defence, they felt, might undermine and dilute their own arguments in favour of diminished responsibility. Leaving it to the judge to direct the jury on provocation might, they believed, get round that problem. But before even explaining what provocation meant in legal terms Mr Justice Judge seemed to effectively undermine it, saying, 'I come now to the question of loss of control and provocation. It is my duty to mention this to you, members of the jury, but you will notice that Mr Barker did not address you on the basis of provocation and it will, I think, be obvious to you why in a moment when you have heard what I have to say about it.' Again, although it was, of course, an issue for the jury themselves to decide, they could have had little doubt about what the judge's views on the matter were.

Mr Justice Judge went on to explain: 'You are not being asked to consider, did he lead her a miserable life?' but whether Malcolm's actions or words had actually prompted Sara to lose her self-control and, if they had, whether a reasonable woman with the same characteristics as Sara would also have lost her self-control. He told the jury: 'It may be very difficult to come to the conclusion that Sara's action was a reasonable reaction. There are many, many unhappy, indeed miserable, husbands and wives. It is a fact of life. It has to be faced, members of the jury. But on the whole it is hardly reasonable, you may think, to stab them fatally when there are other alternatives available, like walking out or going upstairs.' That was a comment which, after the trial, many were to condemn as displaying little or no understanding of the dynamics of violent and emotionally turbulent relationships.

Mr Justice Judge then proceeded to give his guidance on the issue of diminished responsibility. They needed to be sure, he told the jury, that the abnormality of mind from which all three psychiatrists agreed that Sara was suffering, was more than a mere trivial impairment, it must be substantial. He told them that they must consider the defence carefully, even though Sara herself 'would not have it'. It was seemingly apparent that he, like Sara's barristers, viewed this as the most appropriate defence.

Having made his directions as to the law, Mr Justice Judge then turned to the facts, the evidence itself. The jury must, he told them, judge the witnesses, one of whom of course was Sara. Somewhat sensitively he told them: 'Make every allowance . . . for the difficulty of her position.' It was not easy, he said, to be a witness to a car accident, so giving evidence as the accused in a case like this must be hard. 'But', he told them, 'you will have to ask yourselves: Do you believe her evidence?' They should not, he warned, conclude that Sara was guilty of murder because she had lied about her O and A Levels. But then, effectively undermining that caution, he went on: 'You have to bear in mind that on her own admission she told you lies on her oath . . . you obviously will bear it in mind as a matter of common sense in deciding when there are two witnesses, one of whom is her and one of whom is someone else, whether you choose to believe her account rather than the other witness's. It does not mean you automatically reject her evidence. It could never mean that. But you must bear it in mind and make your conclusion about her evidence.' What Sara had naïvely believed would be viewed as a genuine attempt to come clean and show that she was taking her duty to be honest seriously was being interpreted as something which cast doubt on the veracity of everything she said.

Summarizing the biographical evidence, Mr Justice Judge said: 'Her parents were stiff upper lip sort of people . . . not the sort of people to show emotion or, apparently, affection . . . but in physical surroundings, at any rate, you may think that she had a typical, pretty comfortable middle-class upbringing.' He referred, in passing, to Sara's departure from Millfield and the lack of clarity surrounding the reasons she gave for it. It would have been strange for the jury, or indeed anyone listening, not to have viewed that as compounding her initial inability to be truthful about her exam results, but what nobody (including Sara) knew was the truth surrounding her departure from the school. That alone must have had a serious impact on her ability at that point to sound convincing.

He moved on through her teens and twenties, summarizing what the court had heard about her life and commenting, rather bizarrely and some might argue prejudicially, on the three abortions that Sara had had. Having described her suicide attempts he said that 'the targets of violence at this stage were on every occasion herself, her own body . . . save, in a sense, the three terminations of pregnancy'. Abortions were, it seemed, in the

judge's mind, acts of violence. He then went on: 'The terminations of pregnancy can obviously be seen as manifestations of
inappropriate sexual behaviour. You do not need me to underline why you might want to consider that possibility, members
of the jury, and there is a question about how and why she made
herself pregnant and to have no less than three abortions. One
possible view of that is that it was very selfish of her.'

Again, Sara's sexual conduct was being placed in the dock.
As one commentator was to remark afterwards, 'She wasn't
being tried as a defendant but as a woman, and as a woman she
was found to be wanting.' It is hard to see what relevance at all
Sara's abortions had. Members of the judiciary may choose to
see them as 'selfish' or evidence of a woman's fall, but the reality
is that one in three women under the age of twenty-five is likely
to face having an abortion. And a further one in ten women is
likely to have more than one. To suggest that one possible view
of Sara's terminations of pregnancies was that they were 'very
selfish' was again undermining her reputation as a woman as
well as giving an insight into the enlightenment or otherwise of
judicial thinking.

Unfortunately, the jury were invited to collude with that prejudice. Mr Justice Judge's cosy 'You do not need me to underline
why you might want to consider that possibility' was on the one
hand flattering the jury by telling them that they did not need
him to explain the implication for them, and on the other inviting
them to consider themselves to be on a par with, sharing the
same views as, a senior figure like himself. Sara was again being
characterized as a woman who had failed to live up to the standards of the more moral majority.

Because the defence had not called any witnesses to corroborate Sara's description of the violence she had suffered, the summing-up naturally made it clear that the evidence of it had come
from 'her account'. Since it had already been suggested that her
account of things was not necessarily reliable, it is hard to know
how seriously the jury would have taken it. Any doubts they
may have had could well have been compounded when Mr Justice Judge pointed out: 'The prosecution invite you to consider

(and it is a question you may want to ask yourselves): "Well, if all these things about Malcolm are true, why did she marry him?"'

The defence, he went on, are asking the jury to accept Sara's evidence that these 'allegations and assertions against him' are true and that she married Malcolm because she hoped things would get better and they would be happy together. His summary of the defence's view-point did not carry with it an equivalent endorsement to the 'it is a question you may want to ask yourselves'. The balance on this point seems to have been tipped towards the prosecution's all too reasonable-sounding question, 'Why did she marry him?', the unfortunate implication being that either her account of his violence and drunkenness was untrue (as she would not have married him if it were) or that if her 'assertions and allegations' were true, she must have willingly taken on the burden of them and so, by extension, must only have herself to blame.

Less than a minute later Sara's version of events was again undermined. The judge said to the jury: 'Do you remember the allegation that he hit her because she had been, as she called it, bopping with the boss? He used a clenched fist to the back of her neck.' That was a fair summary of Sara's account but the sentence that was to follow must again have undermined it: 'For all the drink at this stage, he was still doing well at work and he won good promotion.' The implicit question raised by juxtaposing those two statements could only be, how does her account of alcoholism and violence square with his success at work? The judge, like most of the jury, must have known little of the tendency of alcoholics to disguise their problem, and, because the defence had not called any independent witnesses to attest to the problems Malcolm was experiencing, the jury had nothing to balance that with.

In a number of other places in the summing-up could one detect an almost subliminal process of undermining Sara's version of events? Both the prosecution and the defence case are always put together, but with the emphasis and weight attached slightly more heavily to one side did the jury see an implication either that Sara was lying about the violence or that she was a bad mother for staying around to put up with it? In relation to the period after Malcolm had lost his job at TNT Mr Justice Judge said: 'If, say the prosecution (and you might want to consider it), she might have been killed . . . by being thrown out of a window or over the balcony or maimed as a result, she would not have stayed, running the risk of her daughter being left alone.'

As for Helen Thomas's evidence about the alleged threat, Mr Justice Judge urged caution: 'We have all heard mums and, I suppose, dads say to little Johnny: "If you do that again, I'll kill you" . . . sometimes these things are said and they are meaningless . . . it is for you to say whether the fact that Mrs Thomas did not report it undermines your confidence in the truth of her evidence.' But he then went on to say: 'It is [not "It may be"] significant for your consideration that on the night when Mr Thornton died there was a telephone conversation between Mrs Thomas and Mrs Thornton and, according to Mrs Thomas, something was said that harped back to what she says was said in the De Vere Hotel.' That was, of course, a reference to Helen's assertion that Sara had said she was going to do what she had said she was going to do; which Helen Thomas had taken as a reference to her threat to kill, but which Sara herself had said must have been an allusion to the fact that she was going to leave Malcolm.

When it came to Sara's plan to feed Malcolm six Mogadon tablets, Mr Justice Judge indicated that he thought the incident might well be relevant to the issue of whether or not Sara was suffering from diminished responsibility. Indeed, reading between the lines, it may well have been his view that she was. 'You will have to ask yourselves whether this incident is an incident of someone with a personality disorder under stress or someone, whatever the personality may be, acting fairly calmly.' He went on to point out that Sara had told the court that during the course of that incident she had considered taking her own life.

It was a long summing-up. Once it had been transcribed from

the court-room stenographer's shorthand to a typed transcript it stretched to more than fifty pages. Its delivery spanned the afternoon of Wednesday, 21 February and part of the following morning.

At ten o'clock on the Thursday morning the jury arrived to hear the final portion of the judge's speech. By now there were just eleven of them. The twelfth had become ill earlier that week and it had been decided that the trial should continue without him. Mr Justice Judge entered the final phase of his summing-up. Eloquently and powerfully he summarized Sara's account of the last few hours of Malcolm's life: how Malcolm had called her a whore and accused her of selling her body; how she had cried as she told the court about it; how she said she had gone into the kitchen and prayed, taken some deep breaths and, being unable to find the truncheon, had picked up the knife; how she had not wanted to be hurt any more; how she had plunged the knife into Malcolm's stomach and how she had behaved in a bizarre and blasé manner afterwards.

The final thing he told the jury they must do was to consider the evidence relating to diminished responsibility and to examine the arguments on both sides carefully. He then asked the jury to retire and to try to reach a verdict upon which all eleven of them were agreed. He told them to take the knife with them.

It was twenty-one minutes to eleven when the jury retired. A long and nerve-racking wait ensued. Sara spent it locked alone in a cell. Six hours and eleven minutes later the jury still had not returned. Mr Justice Judge told David Barker and Brian Escott-Cox that he proposed to tell them that they need no longer try to reach a unanimous verdict and that they should now aim for a majority verdict of ten to one. He said it was also his intention to ask the jury foreman whether there was any realistic prospect of just ten of them agreeing. So, at ten to five the jury were led back into the court and Sara was led back from the cells; unlike those who had remained in court, she did not know the jury had not reached a verdict.

Mr Justice Judge told the jury he would like them to retire again and to consider whether there was any prospect of their reaching either a unanimous or a majority verdict that night. If there was not, he said, he proposed to send them to a hotel for the night. But if, he told them, they reached the conclusion that in reality there was absolutely no chance of their reaching even a majority verdict, however long they had to discuss it, he would have to consider discharging them altogether.

The jury retired again. They returned to court half an hour later. The Clerk of the Court told the jury foreman to rise and asked him whether they had reached a verdict upon which at least ten of them had agreed. The foreman said no. Mr Justice Judge then asked him whether there was any reasonable prospect of them reaching a verdict that evening. The foreman replied that he was not sure that they would be able to reach a verdict at all.

It looked as if the jury were totally split. If they were, the judge would have to discharge them and Sara would almost certainly have to go through the ordeal of another trial. Mr Justice Judge asked the foreman if they would like some more time. The foreman said they would and the jury retired for the third time that day. Another hour later, at 6.30, the jury returned once more; they still had not reached a verdict. Mr Justice Judge turned to the two QCs in front of him and asked them whether they had anything to say; if not, he said, 'I think I shall grasp the nettle.' By that Brian Escott-Cox and David Barker took it to mean that he was about to discharge the jury. Brian Escott-Cox asked him not to, and so did David Barker (if he had not, who knows what would have happened?). The jury retired for a fourth time and returned ten minutes later to say they could not guarantee reaching a decision that night and so wished to continue their deliberations in the morning.

At quarter to seven the four women and seven men were taken to a hotel, having been instructed not to discuss the case any more that evening. They were also not to contact their homes; if they needed to get messages to their families or required clothes to be picked up on their behalf, the jury bailiff would arrange for this to be done. It sounded harsh, but as Mr Justice Judge explained, it was vital that no one should get the impression that members of the jury could have discussed the case with anyone else.

They arrived at the Crown Court next morning and went straight into the jury-room to continue their deliberations. At twenty to twelve they returned; they had reached a verdict upon which ten of them were agreed. The Clerk of the Court told the foreman to stand and asked him, 'On the charge of murder, do you find the defendant, Sara Elizabeth Thornton, guilty or not guilty?'

The foreman replied, 'Guilty.'

As Sara was led down to the holding-cells the officer escorting her kept saying, 'Cry, love, you must cry.' Of course she did, and the thought that hammered and hammered in her brain was, 'I won't see Luise until she's twenty-six years old.'

9 · Reasonable Doubt

There was an audible gasp of relief from Malcolm's family. His sister, his niece, his first wife and his son had got the verdict they needed for their pain to start to recede. Nothing would ever make up for the loss of the man they loved but at least now they could feel that justice had been done.

It had taken the jury more than twenty-four hours to reach their verdict. It had been an awful, anxious period for them and for those who had awaited their decision. One woman juror wept openly as the foreman spoke. Because of the mandatory life sentence for murder, the judge had only one option: to send Sara to jail for life.

As Sara was led out of the dock Brian Escott-Cox turned to the Crown Prosecution lawyer who had employed him and said, 'That is the sort of case one gets no pleasure at all from getting a murder verdict in.' If he had successfully prosecuted a dangerous murderer he would have felt satisfied that he had done a good job, but few of those present at the trial could really say that Sara fell into that category.

Billi left the court to drive the eighteen miles to Coventry to tell Luise the result. As she walked out of Court 9 for the last time she had to pass Malcolm's relatives: their relief and jubilation were the total contrast to her sense of misery and despair. She had not expected that verdict, nor, really, had Sara's legal advisers. The older sister whom Billi had watched struggle to maintain some sort of even keel through the pain and rejection that had characterized most of her life was now to experience the most abject rejection society had to offer. By the time Billi got home Luise already knew something was up. She had turned on the radio and heard the word 'life'. She didn't know what it meant, Billi had to explain.

Arrangements were set in place for Luise to move to California so that she could live with Billi. While the paperwork was being sorted out Luise went to Devon to stay with her grandparents. Two months later, scarred irrevocably by her experiences, she would fly to the United States to try to begin a new life with Billi, her husband and their three sons.

There was one member of Sara's family who, according to Sara's probation officer, Aevril Kennedy, appeared to some to be not too shocked at the verdict: that was her father. He spoke to Aevril Kennedy soon after the verdict and so surprised was she at his reaction that she says she instantly made a note of it in her file. She recorded that Richard Cooper had expressed his relief at the conviction and the fact that 'justice had been done'. Any suggestion that he took pleasure in her conviction is emphatically denied by Sara's father, who has undoubtedly been deeply affected by the fate of his daughter.

But while he might, according to Aevril Kennedy at least, have considered that justice had been done, there were many others who did not. From that moment on they repeatedly entered the hypothetical world of 'What might have been' to ask, 'What if?'. Soon the hypotheses would start to flow from those who thought the wrong verdict had been reached. Two were common among them: the first was the belief that the jury simply hadn't liked, understood or believed Sara. That was to bring little relief – personal animosity could not really be said to be a legitimate reason for someone to be serving a life sentence. The second hypothesis was that Sara's defence should have been conducted differently.

What if Sara had felt able to tell the truth throughout the whole of her evidence? What if David Barker had not opposed the jury being discharged; would a fresh jury have decided differently (Sara certainly would not have made all the same mistakes twice)? What if the defence had decided to call evidence to dispel any suggestion that Sara could have gained financially from Malcolm's death? She had her own house, and although her name was on the title-deeds of his, it was re-mortgaged anyway. What if the knife-sharpener had been forensically tested? It might have been possible to show that Sara had not used it before stabbing Malcolm. What, too, if the prejudicial remarks and inferences that cropped up continually throughout the trial had not been made?

Or, perhaps even more significantly, what would have happened if the defence of provocation had been argued and whether it had or not, what if independent witnesses had been called by the defence to back up Sara's version of events?

A number of those witnesses had actually come to court but because the evidence they had given was not relevant to the defence's line of argument they were not called. Sara's GP was there, willing to testify to the violence he had seen meted out by Malcolm; Veronica Costelloe was there, prepared to tell the court how she had seen Malcolm hitting Sara on the back of her head and calling her a whore; Patrick Hanlon was available to explain the extent of Malcolm's illness and again to describe how he had seen Malcolm hit Sara and threaten Luise. He may also have thrown doubt on some parts of Martin's evidence: he too had seen Sara threaten Malcolm with the knife on the Sunday before she killed him, but whilst Martin had told the court that he remembers Sara actually grabbing the knife and having to disarm her, Patrick's recollection was quite different. He remembers Sara only having the knife in her hand because she was preparing a chicken and that her outburst was a fit of anger, not a genuine threat.

There were other witnesses too that the defence might have been wary about calling in case they were hostile towards Sara but who nevertheless might have helped her case. There was Diane Davies, who had been with Sara and Helen Thomas at the TNT conference. She too had heard Sara say words to the effect that she was going to kill Malcolm. But, unlike Helen Thomas, she did not tell the police she viewed them as a genuine threat. Rather, she said in a statement that Sara had just spoken out in a fit of temper, in the heat of the moment. That again could have directly undermined the prosecution case.

And what if Anne Thornton, Malcolm's second wife, had been called as a witness? The defence had not contacted her; no doubt they assumed not unreasonably that she could not help their client's case. However, if they had, they would have discovered that she had evidence that could have made a material difference to Sara's case, had provocation been the defence. Under oath, she could have described the violence she herself had endured at Malcolm's hands. She could have told the jury how Malcolm would look almost dormant one moment and then leap into violent action the next; how when he was having a really heavy drinking session he could beat her twice a day; how because of his training as a police officer he knew how to hit and where to hurt; how he would accuse her of infidelity and fly into jealous rages identical to the ones described by Sara. She did not believe that Malcolm's violence made either herself or Sara a battered woman, and she believed that the fact that Sara killed meant she deserved a prison sentence, but her evidence would none the less have provided very powerful corroboration of Sara's testimony. In particular her description of how suddenly Malcolm could switch from a passive drunken state to violence would have added weight to Sara's assertion that although he was lying down and only threatening her orally at the time that she stabbed him, she was in fear of some form of physical violence.

And there were two other impartial witnesses who could have been summonsed if provocation had been the defence – Steve Byard and Stan Clarke, who had seen Sara fly through the air from the weight of one of Malcolm's punches, and then had to stand by while the police took no action against him.

It was undoubtedly the case that Sara had not felt able to be entirely honest about her psychiatric past and events of which she was deeply ashamed, but that did not make everything she said a lie. In his summing-up the judge pointed out that there was only Sara's account of Malcolm's violence to rely on; he had already reminded the jury that when considering Sara's evidence they should remember that she had by her own admission lied on oath. But there were plenty of witnesses who could have backed up at least parts of Sara's story. Indeed, there were at least five independent witnesses to Sara being assaulted by Malcolm, none of whom were called.

There were other witnesses, too, who might have undermined any doubts about Sara's testimony that existed in the jury's minds. There was Malcolm's boss who had had to warn him formally at least twice that he would lose his job because of his drinking before he eventually sacked him. There was Keith Lee, the spiritualist to whom both Sara and Malcolm had turned for help. He again could have described the extent of Malcolm's problem and of Sara's despair, and would have provided further evidence of the lengths to which Sara had gone to get help for the man she loved. And there was Alex Patrick, the taxi driver who had been with Sara the afternoon before she killed. He too had seen the desperation and despair she had been fighting against.

There were experts who could have helped to answer one of the most obvious questions Sara's conduct posed: Why didn't she leave? There were specialists who could have given evidence on the effects of living in a violent and alcoholic relationship, but they too were not called.

Sara's lawyers would argue that since Sara's defence was not provocation, much of what those witnesses had to say was not relevant and may not therefore have been allowed by the Judge. Technically that is no doubt correct. But others might say that if someone's life is in the balance, not a single shred of evidence that could possibly assist her should have been left out. Sara's solicitor, Lesley Abell, does not go that far – he believes the barristers he instructed made a professional and proper judgment – but even he does wonder what would have happened if the defence of provocation had been argued. He believes that in law they would have had great difficulty in making the defence stand up, but he points out that arguing provocation might at least have enabled the jury to hear more about the traum that the woman they were to judge had lived through. That in t rn might well have given them the opportunity at least of returning a sympathy verdict. Indeed, the initial brief that he sent to them made it clear that at first glance provocation seemed to be the explanation for the killing. He wrote: 'This appears to be simply a case where the Defendant had been married to the deceased for a year before his death, he had been an alcoholic, unsuccessful in business and repeatedly violent towards her, and on the evening of his death after what appears to have been a normal evening for her, she returned home and was subjected to taunts and provocation from the Deceased which caused her to in her own words hold a knife above him and move it towards him . . .' After consideration of the evidence, however, the barristers rejected this defence; if they had not, things might have gone differently.

So what if those witnesses had been called? What if they had given the jury a clearer understanding of why Sara acted as she did? Could the jury then have been sure beyond all reasonable doubt that Sara was guilty of premeditated murder?

Unfortunately, it is not possible to found an appeal on the basis that one's lawyers did not call witnesses they could have done. To be granted an appeal, Sara would have to show that overall her conviction was unsafe and unsatisfactory, and to have a realistic chance of doing that she would need to point to a misdirection of the jury by the judge; a mistake to do with the law or a material irregularity. Things looked bleak: because her lawyers could have called those witnesses but did not, their evidence could never be heard. The fact that that might mean her serving a life sentence because of a legal technicality at trial rather than because she was guilty was not a concern the criminal appeal system appeared to be able to take into account. Furthermore, the appeal system specifically guards against having to consider appeals based on the claim that a lawyer has made an error of judgement. Unless it can be shown that a barrister conducted a defence with 'flagrant incompetence, leading to a lurking doubt as to the rightness or safety of the conviction', the court will refuse to hear an appeal.

From the outside, England's legal system can often resemble a game, with the judges as umpires. They are there to ensure fair play, to ensure that no one cheats or misbehaves, but so long as everything is done fairly and according to the rules, the score at the end of the day must stand, regardless of whether or not it is the right one – and seemingly regardless of the fact that it is not a question of sport but one of liberty and life.

Graham Buchanan nevertheless set about drafting Sara's grounds of appeal. Because of the legal authorities prevailing at the time, he did so with a heavy heart and little confidence that they would succeed. He still did not believe provocation was a winnable defence, and that being the case he could not see how any of the extra witnesses that could have been called would have helped. He was not happy with the verdict or the vigorous way in which Sara had been prosecuted, but he thought there was little he could do legally.

The judge's summing-up seemed to be so unassailable that he felt he could found the appeal only on the basis that the jury were prejudiced by some of the irrelevant and unfair references that had been made by the prosecution. The first and strongest one was Brian Escott-Cox's use of the phrase 'licence to kill'. The prejudice created by that phrase had, he said, been bolstered by three other improper references: Helen Thomas's allusion to Sara offering her a joint; the prosecution's suggestion that she had disappeared with a man at the TNT conference; and the question to Sara about her underwear. Taken together, he said, they were likely only to lead to prejudice in the jury's mind. He signed and dated the appeal on 16 March.

10 · Triumph over Tragedy

As the trial progressed Sara had felt increasingly as if there was nothing she could do to influence what was unfolding before her. She remembers sitting alone in the cells beneath the court and deciding that she just had to let go emotionally and allow events to take their course: 'I just had a feeling that it would all be OK. A sense of destiny took hold of me, and when I left the court for the first night in the cells, I looked out of the bus window . . . holding back the tears I thought I must remember all this because it is going to be so important, as if I knew intuitively that the trial and the verdict were not an end but a beginning.'

Many of those who were later to take up Sara's case would say that her intuition was accurate and that her imprisonment was to be the start of a powerful challenge to the English legal system. At that time, though, for Sara, it signalled the beginning of an intensely personal experience. She had to begin the difficult process of adapting to the fact that whereas the week before she had been a mother living with her daughter in Coventry she was now a convicted murderer. At times that was to be a desperate and gruelling process, but with the pain and despair that accompanied it Sara also found inner resources and strengths that she had not known she possessed. Her first year in prison would prove to be a time of growing self-awareness and self-knowledge. With that she also began to develop a strong religious faith and a spiritual awareness that have given her great comfort and peace during her time in jail. But whilst she slowly learned to cope with the outward deprivation of her liberty, one abiding pain remained: her separation from Luise.

Sara began her term of imprisonment at Risley in Warrington, nicknamed 'grisly Risley' by whose who have had to endure its appalling conditions, brutal regime and uncaring staff. On arrival Sara went through the same dehumanizing and humiliating process to which every new inmate is subjected: she was strip-searched, her personal belongings were taken away and bagged, she was given bedding and cutlery and finally assigned a number written on a white card. The colour of the card denoted her religious denomination – Church of England; had she been Catholic the card would have been red; a fine distinction for the system to be respecting. To make her new identity complete, from now on she was no longer to be known as Sara Thornton; instead she was GA 3422.

After three months Sara was transferred to Durham's H Wing. There she began to keep a diary. It not only describes her own adjustment to prison life and her separation from Luise, it also gives a more general insight into life in a women's prison.

After the sordid and brutal conditions of 'grisly Risley', Durham was relatively pleasant by comparison. H Wing had started life as a men's special security and punishment wing, but after poor conditions led to a series of hunger strikes and a major riot, it was closed down in 1971. Three years later it was reopened as a maximum security wing for women; the inmates had to live with almost constant drilling as the prison service started to try to refurbish it while they were living there. That a wing found undesirable for male prisoners was then reopened to house women must give some indication of the Prison Service's attitude towards women inmates. As women prisoners cause far less trouble than their male counterparts – they don't riot and they rarely hunger-strike – their needs are often overlooked. Then as now, the regime, equipment and facilities at Durham were geared to accommodate the larger population of male prisoners. The men are fed first, so that by the time the women are fed the food is invariably cold; when staff are overstretched (which is much of the time) it is the women who are usually the first to lose out, having their work and periods of association cancelled.

Because H Wing is a high-security unit it is completely enclosed and the women never leave it. For some the atmosphere is unbearably claustrophobic, indeed it has been compared to living in a concrete tomb. The outside world does intrude to some extent – the women are subjected to daily shouts of abuse from the male inmates housed in the other parts of the prison. Given that a high proportion of women prisoners (some studies have put it as high as 40 per cent) are victims of sexual or violent abuse prior to their imprisonment, such a situation can and does have a deeply disturbing effect. What would happen to the women if the male prisoners rioted and the staff were unable to get them out does not bear thinking about and is undoubtedly a lurking fear for many of the women living in H Wing.

The security surrounding H Wing as a 'Category A' wing is overwhelming; there are men patrolling with dogs, TV cameras, barbed wire and bright lights. Category A status is reserved for the most dangerous of inmates: prisoners whose escape would be highly dangerous to the state, the police and the general public. It is usually applied to terrorists, or serial or child-killers. Only four of the women on the wing when Sara was there fell into that category, but because the prison did not have the resources to adopt two different regimes, all the female inmates were subjected to the Category A restrictions. The heavy security did have some compensations, however, as once the women were inside, they were able to move around the block relatively freely, in stark contrast to Risley where Sara had been locked in her cell for eighteen hours a day. As the newest inmate on her wing, though, she would have to wait for a cell complete with toilet and wash-basin. The degrading Victorian process of slopping out was still in operation, and if Sara wanted to go to the toilet overnight, she would have to use the clear plastic pot provided, something she vowed to try to avoid doing. The first time she was forced to use it to defecate in she spent the night plagued by bad dreams of being found face-down, drowning in her own urine.

During the first few weeks the slow process of getting to know the other inmates and figuring out the prison routine began. All the prisoners had to work, but Sara also wanted to be able to learn. She signed up for the gym and sought out the library and waited for the opportunity to join one of the classes. After a couple of days this presented itself.

> This morning in the workroom I was asked to join an English group that meets every Monday. We've been set some home-work on newspaper-reporting but the best bit was the dis-cussion that followed. This was prompted by an article written by Martin Luther King on non-violence. . . . Considering we were three murderers and an IRA terrorist the situation was fraught with hidden dangers. I came out giggling, most prob-ably from nerves.

Getting on with the other inmates and making friends is prob-ably the most sustaining but sometimes the most difficult part of prison life. Sara immediately warmed to a number of the other women on the block. Strangely, perhaps for the first time in her life she was with people who were not offended by her but found her funny and exciting to be with. She began to make friends quite quickly and integrated into prison life; her intelligence and lack of inhibition together with a streak of bossiness meant she soon emerged as something of a natural leader. In the process she also began to recover some of the self-esteem she had lost in her two years with Malcolm: 'I know why I'm feeling happy again, my wit and humour are being appreciated. I had them laughing in that discussion group.'

Within H Wing Sara found herself with:

> Linda who strangled her daughter while drunk, Tracy who strangled her husband with her boyfriend, Ella and Martina who were convicted of the Brighton bombings, Sonia who was an East German spy, Jackie who drowned her baby in the bath, Christine who allowed her toddler to starve to death, Audrey, an arsonist with the mental age of twelve who'd been given a life sentence because the Judge 'didn't know what else to do with her' and Judy who was a convicted IRA terrorist but maintained she'd only ever been a member of Sinn Fein and had been set up, so far she'd served 17 years.

It appears from her diary that Sara became close to many of the women, trying to help and support those less able than herself, and in turn drawing support from others like Judy. They decided to do a psychology degree together: 'I've had Judy here all morning . . . we really click, she too is well read and we spend hours discussing books, history and psychology. . . . Nobody but nobody is safe from our amateur psychoanalysis.'

But most profoundly, now that the worst had happened and she was in jail, life was no longer fraught with fear: 'Why am I not at the end of my tether? . . . Is it because the quality of my life here is better than I hoped? Is it also because for the first time in three years I have no fear? No fear of Malcolm getting drunk and hitting me, no fear of prison. I'm at my lowest point in my life, this is a crossroads, now I can only go up.'

The obvious restrictions of prison life mean that inmates quickly develop a routine. Sara's consisted of gym, the workshop, study and church. As a natural athlete, she was immediately drawn to the gym and became known as the 'Jane Fonda' of the prison. Playing volley-ball, weight-lifting, doing aerobics and attempting to master her old speciality, trampolining made her fitter than she'd been for years and helped to keep depression at bay:

> We had gym this morning, a workout . . . and then . . . trampoline. The instructor said, 'I hear you are an expert' and when I pointed out that I hadn't been on one since I was 17, he said, 'What, 5 yrs ago!' I was so scared! But I did it, a sort of back somersault, I think I'm over my fear, I was sick in the toilet, and my whole body shook. I'll take it slowly though and steer clear of double back flips!

Church also became a vital part of her new life. Her growing spirituality helped to protect her from feelings of bitterness and began to help her to come to terms with her imprisonment: 'Let's see how long God wants me to do. . . . I sometimes doubt if I have the stamina, but then I remind myself that if that's what he wants he'll supply me with what I need.'

As politicians to the right of the political spectrum are always keen to point out, a life sentence rarely means life. Few prisoners given the maximum sentence the system can impose actually spend the remainder of their life in jail. When a life sentence is passed a tariff – the minimum number of years to be served – is set. Sometimes the judge will make a recommendation as to what it should be, at other times it is left to the Home Office to decide. It often takes some time for the tariff to be set; some prisoners have to wait a whole year until the decision is made. So although Sara was told that hers would probably be between ten and fifteen years she didn't know for sure. She eventually discovered that it was to be nine.

Nine years of confinement were one thing for Sara to bear for herself, and there was a part of her that was only too willing to accept punishment, but nine years of separation from her daughter were something else. She was fortunate in that Billi, as agreed, had taken over caring for Luise. But she was less fortunate in that this meant that Luise was going to live in America, making it unlikely that mother and daughter would see each other more than once every couple of years. Sara had found the initial two months when Luise had stayed with her parents in Devon especially difficult. She felt in part that Luise being there might heal her own unresolved and turbulent feelings for her father. But after a couple of months Billi's arrangements were completed and Luise travelled to California to join her. Sara records with joy in her diary the letter she received on Luise's arrival there:

Luise is safely in California. I knew it, of course, but it's great to hear it from Billi. She has settled down remarkably well, wants to learn how to change diapers and starts school in a couple of weeks. Billi is having to act as interpreter, they don't understand her English accent. I'm so relieved.

Despite that relief, though, the pain of separation remained, and as Sara tried to cope with it she began to learn more about the system of which she had become a part. She discovered that the women she found herself with in H Wing were far from typical women prisoners. Very few female inmates have committed violent crimes. The vast majority – some 80 per cent – are in prison for offences of theft, handling stolen goods, fraud or forgery. Politicians of all persuasions have frequently pleaded with judges to use prison only as a punishment of last resort: it costs in the region of £560 a week to keep a woman in jail, and Britain's prisons are already perilously overcrowded. But despite the increased range of non-custodial sentences that have been made available to judges, the proportion of women receiving prison sentences has doubled over the past twenty years. Over the last decade a third of those sent to jail were imprisoned for non-payment of fines.

With that rise comes a largely ignored tragedy, of which Sara herself was only too aware. More than half the women in Britain's prisons are mothers. Although judges are meant to take the existence of any children into account when passing sentence, thousands of children are separated from their mothers by imprisonment every year. Few of those mothers pose any serious threat to society, but every time they are sentenced to prison their children are forced to serve a parallel term of separation outside. Indeed, the imprisonment of a woman can often spell the breakdown of a whole family. Few female prisoners have a male partner outside who is willing and able to hold the home together. Some women, like Sara, do have a family member on whom they can rely, but governors of women's prisons freely acknowledge that their inmates are under greater emotional and psychological pressure than their male counterparts because of their concerns about their children.

Whatever the emotional impact on the individual inmate, however, there are wider, more worrying implications for society as a whole. Not only is the taxpayer footing an ever-burgeoning bill by the imprisonment of women who are accepted by both the prison establishment and the Government to be of very little danger in reality, there is also the threat of perpetuating a truly dangerous cycle. With each family breakdown that results from a woman's imprisonment, society risks the creation of a new stratum of socially and emotionally deprived children who could, of course, become the criminals of the next generation. Conservative Home Secretary after conservative Home Secretary has sought to reduce the proportion of women being sent to prison for non-violent crimes, but the judges have yet to hear their pleas.

As long ago as 1970, a Home Office policy document hypothesized, rather optimistically as it turned out:

> It may well be that as the end of the century draws nearer, penological progress will result in even fewer or no women at all being given prison sentences. Other forms of penalty will be devised which will reduce the number of women unnecessarily taken from their homes which so often ends in permanent disaster and breakdown in family life.

As the millennium draws to a close, that goal seems even further out of reach. The number of women in Britain's prisons has doubled since that document was circulated and continues to rise at a faster rate than for men. Similarly, women are continuing to be sentenced to prison for less serious crimes than men and with fewer previous convictions. Indeed, while only roughly 10 per cent of men will be sent to prison for a first offence, a third of female prisoners are sent to jail for their first crime. The bias that Sara felt she had experienced in the court system was seemingly by no means unique.

Criminologists have, of course, tried to discover why, despite the political pressure to limit the number of custodial sentences given to women, judges are increasingly disposed to send women to jail. One view is that whilst boys are expected to be bad and to break rules and indeed laws sometimes, girls are not. Thus a woman who commits a crime is in essence breaking two rules – one the rule of law and the other a rule constructed by society as to how she is expected to behave. The punishment she is given may well therefore be harsher, to reflect that double transgression. On the other hand, male prejudice can sometimes operate to a woman's advantage. It is undoubtedly the case that through the ages some judges, if the woman does not appear to have transgressed too harshly, may have taken a somewhat chivalrous view when sentencing. That limited and sporadic opportunity for leniency may now be on the wane, however.

Chivalry, if not dead, may well be dying. The increasing proportion of women being sentenced to prison may, some criminologists believe, reflect some sort of a backlash against feminism.
If women want equality, then judges may well now be giving
them equality and more, ultimately punishing them not only
for their crime but also for their unwillingness to conform and
for their desire to be treated as equals with men. Sara felt
that in her case this could not have been more clear. She felt
she was put on trial not only for the murder of her husband
but also for what was considered to be inappropriate female
behaviour.

Some would argue that to jail for life a woman with no history
of crime, violent or otherwise; a woman who has never been
violent in the past and seems highly unlikely to be violent in the
future; a woman whose child will suffer immeasurable hardship
by the loss of her mother, seems not only wasteful of society's
resources but inappropriate and callous. Sara herself felt she
deserved to go to jail, or at least to be punished in some way to
try to pay for the life she had taken. What concerned her, though,
was that she did not believe she was guilty of murder – of cold-
blooded, deliberate killing – only of taking a life unintentionally
in a situation that had spiralled out of control.

Sara's growing faith helped her to cope with the profound
feelings of remorse and loss that haunted her:

> Why didn't I have this faith before, then Malcolm would still
> be alive? I sat and talked to Malcolm last night, I do miss
> him. Sometimes I get a really dear feeling of him, It's hard to
> remember him when he was nice to me, the last few days of
> his life are a recurring nightmare, I hope he's forgiven me.

When Sara arrived at Durham writing and receiving letters was
governed by a complex set of rules. There were restrictions on
the numbers of letters Sara could send and receive and her mail
was subject to censorship by the prison authorities. She was not
only being kept out of society, it also seemed she was to have
to struggle to keep any contact at all with it. As a newly arrived

prisoner, she was allowed to send one letter a week on which postage would be paid by the authorities; she would have to find the money to pay the postage on any extra letters herself. Normally letters could not be longer than four sides and had to be written on instantly recognizable prison paper, with her personal prison number at the top.

Access to the telephone was also limited. The women had to arrange outgoing phone calls with the staff. The prison would pay for calls in lieu of a visit, otherwise prisoners had to pay for their own calls. Incoming calls also had to be booked in advance.

For the first couple of weeks Sara received no mail at all. Eventually a letter arrived from Billi and Luise:

> Luise wrote that she went to the creek to catch newts one of which she brought home to Billi, no other sentence could have conjured up such a happy picture for me to hold in my mind. . . . Billi wrote that she misses me but pretends that I've just gone to spend the night at a friend's house. In a way I'm glad that she misses me, but it also hurts. It makes me cry. . . . I feel better when I think Luise is still treating everything like a bit of a holiday. Is she still expecting me to come out any minute? I hope she accepts things okay. She's such a loyal little girl.

Letters, though, inevitably containing only fragments of what was happening, could often cause as much distress as they allayed:

> Had a letter from Billi yesterday, Luise is having bad dreams . . . she wants to send me a dream pillow. Can't have it, stuffed. However, I might let her send me one and keep it in property . . . tried very hard to leave my body last night, will I ever do it, I want to see Luise. . . . I'd give anything just to hug her and tell her how much I love her . . . the thought of all these years ahead not seeing her. . . . How could they deprive me of her . . . sometimes I hate Malcolm for this, all because he had to have his drink. Oh why didn't I just leave him. . . . Oh Luise, Luise.

Two months after Sara's arrival in Durham another inmate, Linda, committed suicide by hanging herself with twelve strands of wool. Suicide and attempted suicide are common occurrences in both men's and women's prisons. The effect on the other inmates, especially if the attempted suicide is successful, is profound. Prisoners face a constant struggle to hold depression and despair at bay, and very often it is a losing battle. Unfortunately women prisoners, like women on the outside, are particularly vulnerable to depression. The use of prescription tranquillizers and psychotropic drugs is much higher in women's prisons than in men's. A study of Holloway women's prison found that in one year alone nearly 33,000 psychotropic pills were given to its 335 inmates – that is, nearly a hundred per woman – whereas in Grendon, a men's prison with a population of 176, there were only 3599 prescriptions – an average of twenty per inmate, or a fifth of what women in Holloway were being prescribed. That imbalance is undoubtedly partly a reflection of the fact that while men often express their feelings of anger and frustration through violence, women tend to turn those emotions in on themselves, becoming depressed and dangerous to themselves rather than to others. Whereas violent protest is a frequent occurrence in men's prisons, in women's it is surprisingly rare, but that absence of outward unrest is balanced by a far higher rate of self-mutilation amongst women inmates. Female prisoners are far more likely than men to cut and hurt themselves. There also appears to be a higher proportion of mentally ill women in jail than men, although observers often question whether the extraordinarily high prescription rate of tranquillizers in women's jails is not also a reflection of their use as a form of control.

The institutional aspects of imprisonment are also often harder for women to cope with. Whereas men may be accustomed to living and operating in a structured group environment, women who may have spent most of their life in the home often find it brutal and alien.

Whatever the reasons that led Linda to take her life, the effect of her death on the other inmates, as Sara recorded in her diary, was deeply unsettling:

Linda has hung herself, she's dead. She looked so pretty yesterday Judy threatened to jump on her bones. She was still doing her washing last night, we sat talking till 7.45 p.m. I can't believe it. According to the officer Mrs Uttley, she was fine last night, talking out her window, she wrote some letters. Nobody had a clue, yet we all feel we failed her.

As the months went by Sara's irrepressible vitality and natural intelligence began to reassert themselves. She and another prisoner called Tracy were asked to do the administration on H Wing Enterprise Range (HER), the wing's workshop. For the first time in her life people were choosing Sara to lead and organize, and as her diary entry for that day shows, she was thrilled and somewhat taken aback: 'Dare I say they like me. I can't say it's not scary, I bubble and then run and hide in my room for a while.'

Sara and Tracy immediately started to sort out what they would need: 'We wrote out a list of things i.e. filing cabinets, etc. I also put down luncheon vouchers, health insurance and company car, but Mrs Copestake didn't really get the joke.' The women were making stuffed toys. Sara and Tracy began to whip the 'business' into shape:

I've found some awful discrepancies, for example, Mrs Helen's been letting girls make their own soft toys, etc, without filling in an order form. I pointed out that she'll have to account for the stock eventually. She saw my point immediately. . . . Also the girls are allowed to make three free things from their education grant, but that means that the Education Department must be invoiced. Honestly they haven't got a clue! I've designed and instituted a new invoicing system, including a way of invoicing between different groups, i.e. should the knitting department make clothes for toys they will invoice them. Money won't change hands, but at least the wool will be accounted for.

Thus Sara was the architect of Durham's very own internal market. She loved running the HER; it gave her something to focus on and despite her characteristic bossiness she found that the other women appreciated and admired her for the work she was doing. HER was more a charity than a business – the most the women themselves could earn for their labours was £3 per week – but Sara and the other women ran it with energy and commitment, so much so that Sara notes: 'Orders for HER toy department now total over £500. I'm very, very proud of them. Mrs Barker says I've been invaluable, she can't imagine how they would have managed without me. That makes me feel really good! It's an awful thought but I'd hate to leave now. I get so committed to things.'

Once in a while they had outside speakers come in to give them lectures to help make HER more productive. Sara writes about a talk on marketing:

> At one stage he asked if we were going to expand, I tried to tactfully point out that we have a slight shortage of labour, and if we needed more someone would have to talk to the judges. Can you imagine the courts sentencing women to life for shoplifting because HER has 20,000 Ninja Mutant Turtles to make? Where's this man's head?

Despite the release which activities like HER and gym provided, conditions in Durham were still pretty poor. The food in particular was almost inedible. Like many of the women, Sara seemed to live on chips, chocolate and the occasional piece of fruit that cropped up at mealtimes. Sara decided to start campaigning:

> Sunday a quiet day, played volley-ball this morning in the exercise yard. Whilst waiting to go we all complained about the food, so much so that when I said, 'Don't complain, do something,' Martina replied yes. I wrote out a list of foods we don't like for the chef, and a list of suggestions like more fruit, no more mushy peas, etc. . . . Lots of people in the workshop read the list and added their own suggestions. . . . Tonight we had a fabulous tea, salad and fresh fruit salad. Everyone was very happy.

Even though she was filling her time with work and study, Sara's diary reveals she was often overwhelmed by grief and sadness as she came to terms with the tragedy of Malcolm's death and the loss of everyone dear to her:

Sunday morning I opened a parcel from Ronnie [Sara's nickname for Veronica Costelloe]. She sent me some photos of Malcolm, floored me. I held back and thought later. Went straight to church – first hymn was 'Amazing Grace', I was a goner. Sobbed through that and two prayers, then walked out. . . . I came upstairs and sobbed my heart out. Oh, I do miss him, I loved him so. Sometimes I can't believe he is dead. . . . I don't really feel as if I stabbed him but I know I did, and I am ultimately accountable . . . perhaps Luise's future was my main concern, and now she's safe, I can allow myself to grieve for Malcolm and me, because it is for both of us I grieve, what we had and lost. We had so much love, such a deep understanding of each other, I can't believe it's gone, just gone.

As Sara's 'honeymoon' period started to fade, the grind of prison life began to take its toll. Unlike some of the other women who found comfort and warmth in forming sexual relationships with each other, Sara didn't feel she wanted to. As she wrote of one friendship:

It's so difficult, I like her very much, I admire her, I could, given time, love her. But sex? No. . . . Don't think I'll ever fall in love with another woman, in fact I miss the deep bond with Ronnie and with Billi. I felt I could tell them everything. I know it takes time to build up trust like that but I've never been a particularly trusting person. . . . S put her arm around me whilst we were waiting to leave the workroom, I broke out in a cold sweat! I cannot accept physical love like that. It makes me feel very, very uncomfortable.

The loneliness of a lifer is deeply felt as they never know how long it will be until they see their loved ones again. The constant waiting for letters that have already been opened and read by a stranger, having to plan phone calls weeks in advance and then when the long-awaited call comes having to cope with the noise and lack of privacy, make it hard for anyone to open up and talk of love or difficulties or simply to cry when continually surrounded by other people. And after a phone call or a letter is finished, the harsh reality of the lifer's situation descends: they are in prison and their loved ones are on the outside, and who knows when they will speak to or hear from them again?

Although there may be some benefits for women in crisis in being in an institution where they do not have to make any decisions, just fit into a larger discipline, these benefits are short-lived. Living in an environment where one has little or no control over one's surroundings is extremely stressful. For example, the heating at Durham is centrally controlled and is switched on and off at a certain time each year. So even if it is very warm outside, the prison's heating system may still be turned on: 'It's so hot in the prison. . . . It's 85 degrees outside and the heating's still on, I've had three showers today!'

Although Sara found the prison staff at Durham far more humane than the staff at Risley, she, like the other women, was at the mercy of their whims and moods:

> Those bloody screws have destroyed my harmony. . . . I was sitting watching TV when I heard my name called, I went to investigate and found it was Mrs G, she said she'd been calling my name for half an hour. When I told her I hadn't heard her she said, 'Book the doctor, I think you're deaf.' I told her I am deaf and that it's in my medical records, she did have the grace to say sorry, but one of the clerks started shouting at me about my attitude. Who does she think she is, 21 years old and one year in the prison service? She should go to Risley, they appreciate beasts like her there.

A chronic shortage of resources combined with an often disgruntled prison staff means that prisoners can spend up to twenty-three hours locked in their cells. The prison regime is focused around staffing requirements not prisoners' needs, thus for example evening meals are served at 4 p.m. so that the prison staff can have their own evening meal at a more normal time. This often means that prisoners are left without any food until 8 a.m. the next day. While at Risley Sara spent eighteen hours a day alone in a filthy cell with no heating. At Durham conditions were better, but the women never knew for how long they would be let out during the day and when they would be locked up. Sometimes it would be 8 p.m., sometimes 4 p.m. Access to the outside was also limited, they were given an average of forty minutes a day in the fresh air.

However arbitrary and petty the rules may be, a prisoner senses early on that it is not a good idea to rebel. The system rewards those who submit and punishes those who rebel. During her first month at Durham Sara was sent to clean the newly built punishment cells: 'They are frightening. One cell is just fibre-glass walls with a chair . . . the other, the bunk is a concrete block, one window, no heating. I know I'll never be in there again.' She had seen women sent to the punishment block in Risley, where they would spend weeks at a time, alone and totally at the mercy of prison staff.

The fear of being injured or falling ill in prison creates a great deal of anxiety for prisoners, especially those serving long sentences. As Sara noted early on, 'It's essential to take care of your health. They are very loath to take anyone to hospital because of the security involved. So you have to be really ill.'

The Prison Medical Service has been the subject of much recent criticism, at the heart of which lies the fact that it is part of the Prison Service not the National Health Service. This obviously becomes problematic in establishing an open and trusting doctor–patient relationship. As the Prison Medical Association says, 'The doctor's primary relationship must be to the patient and it is to the detriment of the doctor–patient relationship that the doctor is also seen to be involved with management.' As one Senior Medical Officer at a Bristol prison admitted, staff shortages can affect what the Medical Service is able to offer patients. He admitted that sometimes when doctors asked for a prisoner-patient to be brought to them for examination, 'We are just told, "sorry, no staff, sir. Try again tomorrow" . . . It's a funny way of delivering medical care.'

One of the women on H Wing told Sara that she had broken her knee-cap, but it was left for three days before it was x-rayed and put in plaster. As a result the woman walks with a limp.

As a prisoner Sara was at the bottom of a pyramid of power, virtually defenceless and inhabiting a closed world. She soon discovered that there was very little to protect her and to ensure that the system did not abuse the power it had over inmates. If she wanted to complain about an officer's actions she had to make an official complaint. The prison authorities could decide that by making that complaint she was 'offending against good order and discipline', put her on report and ultimately punish her if they so chose. Even if her complaint was accepted as genuine the prison officers themselves could retaliate, by holding back letters, constantly searching her cell and generally making her life miserable. So prisoners learn early on that it is not in their best interests to complain. In prison Sara was left feeling that the system believed inmates have forfeited their basic human rights as well as their liberty. Even in the outside world the temptation for power to corrupt is strong; in such an enclosed environment as prison there is plenty of scope for those who wield power to abuse it, and that can often take petty and spiteful forms. At one point Sara pulled a muscle in her back and was unable to walk, and made the mistake of going to a nurse.

> I went to see the nurse today, she was very abrupt with me. Said no painkillers and after inspecting my back she started to pummel it. Hurt like hell, but I didn't let out a squeak. . . . In fact she was so unfeeling that she has depressed me. . . . I can't get over her unkindness. Why was she like that to me? She doesn't know me, I've never spoken to her before. . . . Martina said she's an evil bitch and is known for her sadism. . . . It was the same at Risley almost as if we get the dregs here.

Through her work and the friendships she was forming with the other women, however, Sara was beginning to shed some of the deep self-hatred she had carried around with her for most of her life.

I'll know I'm better when I can accept people liking and admiring me. It embarrasses me. I almost prefer if they criticize and dislike me. Is that a trait learned from my childhood? Will I be able to say, 'I am a good, worthwhile person'? I jokingly say to Judy, 'Today I am going to be assertive' and she laughs, but she understands that with humour I can see myself. . . . I can't say no, because I don't want to hurt. . . . I've even slept with men just to give them comfort. I'm ashamed of that, I know they misconstrued my motives.

She began to feel that prison had become 'a sanctuary, a place to put my life on hold and come to terms with the emotions that led to Malcolm's death'. Her childhood, her relationship with her father, her desperate search for love and acceptance, all began to reveal themselves to her. Prison, she wrote, 'is helping me to be more tolerant . . . without the distractions of the outside world one becomes more attuned to one's spiritual needs', and she added, 'At Risley I learnt all about cheque-card fraud.'

Armed with her sense of humour, a growing awareness of her own self-worth and a firm belief that her imprisonment must be for a reason, Sara embarked on what was to be a hard but significant struggle.

On 1 August 1990, Sara read an article about domestic violence in the *Independent* newspaper. The Home Office, the article said, had issued guidance to every police force in Britain to try to improve the way incidents of domestic violence were handled. The Government minister launching the circular criticized the previous attitudes of the police to the problem: 'With domestic violence we are where we were ten years ago with rape ... brutality in the home is just as much a crime as any other sort of violence. The victims of this hidden crime must be helped and offenders must be punished.'

This was, quite simply, to change the course of Sara's life. The following day she wrote to the paper in reply. Because of the significance that letter was to have for her and for thousands of other women it is reproduced here in full.

Sir,

In response to your leading article 'Violence in the Family' (1 August) I am a 35-year-old woman in my first year of a life sentence. I was found guilty of the murder of my husband by a jury at Birmingham Crown Court in February. I had no previous record.

My husband drank heavily and repeatedly attacked me. Although the police were summoned on many occasions he would only be verbally warned.

After a particularly vicious assault, which resulted in my being treated at hospital, I insisted that charges be pressed. My husband was arrested, charged and then released; he came home again.

A quiet two-week period then erupted in a weekend of

violence. As a result I stabbed my husband once; he later died.

I've never denied inflicting the fatal wound. I had no intention of killing my husband. On the contrary, I summoned an ambulance straight away.

For the eight months preceding the trial I lived on bail with my 11-year-old daughter.

I am one of three women here, and many more in other prisons, who feel that if the police had taken our complaint seriously, our husbands would be alive and we'd be free to live with our families today. Instead we've lost our children, our husbands, our homes and our freedom.

Yours sincerely,

Sara E. Thornton

HM Prison Durham

2 August

Sara posted her letter more in hope than expectation; it took forty-eight hours just to leave the prison because it had to be vetted by the prison authorities. Her diary records: 'I always said that Malcolm wouldn't die for nothing. Is it strong enough, will they publish? Everyone here is behind me, praying that this will start the ball rolling to change the law.' The prayers of those women in Durham's H Wing must have reached the ears of the *Independent*'s editor. Six days later it was published. Sara's expectations had been so low that she didn't even bother to check the letters page. She only realized it had appeared when the following day she received a letter from a woman pledging to start a pressure group. In her diary that night she wondered, 'Is this the start of something? . . . I can't believe it! It's wonderful. We are all on such a high . . . I'm so excited that I'll never sleep. I might be in prison, but you can't shut me up! . . . I feel very close to Malcolm tonight, darling Malcolm, I swore your death would not be in vain!'

The next day a bunch of flowers was brought to the prison by two women from Durham's Women's Aid and the mail brought two more letters. Letters were to continue to arrive almost every day from women all over the country, some of whom had themselves been battered and abused and some of whom were just writing out of sympathy and concern. Sara's letter to the *Independent* was indeed to be the start of something.

Someone else had also read that letter, someone who was to have a significant impact on Sara's appeal and on her life. This was George Delf, a veteran and passionate campaigner. He was born in 1933 and, like Sara, spent the early part of his childhood abroad. His father was an army officer and until George was eleven the family lived in India. Returning to the austerity of an English public school education and a year's National Service, he developed a political awareness and an anti-establishment attitude. He has kicked out against the establishment order and his own background ever since, writing of his father in a book published in 1985, 'He exchanged his soul, or most of it, for a mess of khaki potage.'

He went to Cambridge University to study languages but his main passion was politics. After years spent campaigning for the peace movement both at home and abroad he ended up settling in Durham. He read Sara's letter in the *Independent* and was moved by her plight and impressed by her eloquence. He wrote to her offering to visit; she sent him a long and honest letter in reply.

I've been in prison five months ... I've spoken to many women who like myself lived with violent men, and who, when denied assistance or support, cracked and committed murder, manslaughter, whatever. I never realized how widespread it is, how many children suffer the loss of both parents, how ignored we are.

It strikes me we are breeding another generation of wife-beaters, children who will grow up to believe that violence is a normal way of life. In order to stop this (don't I sound arrogant!) I feel that society's view of women must change. At present it is fairly acceptable for a man to beat his wife! As long as they do it behind closed doors (and that is where it happens, without witnesses) it is fine ...

I never believed that I would be found guilty of murder
... I do have grounds for an appeal. Would you believe the
prosecution asked me if I wore knickers? ...

I am in prison in Durham because it is the top security prison
in Britain. Thirty of Britain's most dangerous women! ...

I guess you could say I am not your average British house-
wife. My eccentricities did me little good during my trial. I
have a healthy disrespect for authority (that looks worse than
it is) and I am at a loss as how to proceed from here. I have
no outside help, apart from the friends I've left behind. ...
All I have to go on is my faith in God, and the overwhelming
feeling that I just have to do something. ... Do you
understand?

Defence in a domestic murder is a very delicately balanced
issue. If one puts the violence forward too strongly then the
jury feel that you had a good reason to murder. My counsel
decided it was safer to plead guilty to manslaughter while
balance of the mind was disturbed (diminished responsibility).
Consequently two eminent psychiatrists took the stand and
made me sound as mad as a hatter! When the prosecution
counsel, in cross-examination, said that 'anything less than
life would give her a licence to kill' I thought, 'Broadmoor,
here I come.' When we asked for a re-trial it was denied. My
husband's violence was very understated. I was made out to
be a tart and a greedy, cold, calculating murderer. So now
they just want to say, sorry and all that but you are in the
system. I guess eventually, in about ten years' time they'll let
me out the other end, thoroughly cowed, demoralized and no
use to anyone!

I'd like it very much if you came to visit ... please bring a
packet of cigarettes. I can roll my own but I'm not very good
at it. ... I'm receiving a lot of encouragement from the girls
in here, though I can see many are bewildered by my actions
and determination. It simply doesn't occur to them to question
anything. They accept so meekly the condemnation of the
establishment they profess to despise and distrust. It's
frightening.

By the time the visit became due Sara did not know what to expect. She had already received a number of letters from George Delf. They were eloquent, powerful and sympathetic, and she was very excited. Her friends got her ready, one doing her hair, another lending her shoes, and dressed in peach she waited in the Visitors' Centre for George to enter.

To get there, George was taken through eight different sets of bolted doors. He was immediately struck by Sara's petiteness. Her hair was curled and courtesy of her friends, she looked unusually glamorous. She had watched anxiously as the visitors entered, and spotted a scruffy man with long greying hair. Her first thought was, 'My God, he's a tramp.' Then the warder asked him, 'Are you George Delf?' A voice inside Sara's mind screamed, 'No, no, please let that be one of someone else's disreputable relatives.' But once he opened his mouth she relaxed. Out came a melodious cultured voice and she knew it was George. They sat together and talked. She spoke of her love for Malcolm and showed him a photograph of them together. He gave her a copy of one of his books and a postcard with Sigmund Freud's house on it. She was struck by his intelligence and compassion. He immediately wanted to know why her defence had not been Malcolm's violence, and he wrote out a list of questions that he asked her to try to answer. She handed him a copy of her grounds of appeal. The two of them clicked.

When Sara got back to her cell and read through the list of questions, she found he had written at the end that, like her, he thought everything needed to be changed. It would be hard work and unpaid. They would have to 'reach into our own parched souls and find what moisture is there. Shall we do it?' Her immediate response was yes, yes, yes.

To George, the life-time crusader, Sara offered many things. He felt the injustice of her case strongly. Taking it on would drain and exhaust him but he had never been one to shy away from battle. And in any case it offered him the chance to become involved in a meaningful campaign again; to use the skills he had already developed to challenge the law and to harness the press; and perhaps somewhere, on an emotional level, he sensed

Sara's vulnerability and what he might well have interpreted as a need to be rescued.

For Sara, who was indeed vulnerable at that time and in need of help, George appeared as her saviour. Not only was he intelligent and committed he was also – once she got past the shock of the grey locks and worn clothes – an attractive man. Piercing, deep blue eyes and a healthy, brown face that seemed to have weathered many a storm gave her an instinctive trust that she was later to say she regretted. At that point, though, there was little to stop either of them, and they formed a relationship.

George had the experience and the confidence that Sara lacked. With his backing she decided to sack her old lawyers. She convinced Durham's governor to allow George the status of 'legal adviser' – that ensured extra meetings and when added to the bi-monthly visits she was already allowed it enabled them to see each other every week. Some other prisoners were supportive but some were jealous, a problem Sara was going to experience increasingly as her campaign gathered momentum. One complained to the governor that George was behaving in a decidedly unlegal way at the end of each visit. The governor was obliged to approach George and discreetly ask him to kiss Sara only when he was visiting as a friend – not when he was visiting as a lawyer.

Sara's letters to George show how she gradually opened up and began to confront the reality of her imprisonment and her crime.

I can't stop thinking about Luise and her birthday. I remember how tremendously excited she used to be in the days leading up to it, the endless questions, and little hints from me as to what I had bought her. . . . All this is remembered with ineffable sadness, it clouds everything, I feel bogged down, unable to formulate even the simplest plans. I've just my spirit. I shall probably sob my heart out on Sunday when I speak with her . . .

I guess many of us, including myself, tend to blame others. It's only since I've been in prison that I have understood how wrong I was. So many people felt that Malcolm deserved to die, but nobody, George, deserves to die, at least not like that. . . . Some of the girls feel very angry and bitter, very negative feelings. They cannot see the positive aspects of prison. I love being locked up alone for twelve hours. . . . Never before have I had such a chance to really get to know myself and perhaps understand. But the main point I want to make is that we mustn't make life appear cheap. . . . Life is very precious. No matter how badly Malcolm behaved he was entitled to his life and I took that away, however accidentally it was. . . . I don't think I am an easy person, I think nothing of being the first on the dance floor, going to a pub on my own, wearing shorts, going topless. . . . I think a lot of it had to do with being brought up to treat men as equals – not as prospective lovers/husbands, etc. . . . I sometimes think that prison has saved my life. I wonder if I could have coped with the guilt and trauma of Malcolm's death if they had only given me probation?

Have you ever had a flash of understanding that was so deep it took your breath away? Lying here thinking about prisons . . . I started thinking that my real prison is the past, the way I think of myself, why Daddy doesn't love me, why he always calls me a liar, etc. Well, it hit me – whenever Mummy had been hitting us she always explained our tears, punishment (whip, locked room, cupboard, no supper, etc.) as the result of our lying, cheating, etc. I guess Daddy believed her, or wanted to. Poor Daddy, poor us. I feel like crying . . .

The only time Daddy was nice to me was when he was drunk – or had been drinking heavily. Maybe, just maybe, that's why I tolerated Malcolm so long.

As the honesty and intimacy between Sara and George developed, so did talk of love. Sara, though, was wary.

Let me give you a warning – some men only love what is unattainable, i.e. a woman serving a life sentence. . . . Don't feel sorry for me, pity I don't need. I'm not brave, I'm just trying very hard to understand why I am here, what went wrong, and can I ever put it right.

Together they went through the grounds of appeal that had already been lodged on Sara's behalf. To both of them they appeared to be misconceived. They did not reflect her experience and did not go to what they both saw as the heart of the matter – violent cumulative provocation, in other words acts and words of provocation that had been repeated over time. They decided to change the defence and find lawyers who would be prepared to argue Sara's case in the way they both believed it should be fought. That was not as easy as it sounds. Sara wrote numerous letters to the Registrar of Criminal Appeals explaining that she needed new lawyers. That part of her correspondence was studiously ignored until she wrote saying that she had decided she would conduct her own defence if she was not to be allowed new lawyers. That precipitated what must have been an unprecedented phone call to Durham's H Wing from the Registrar of Criminal Appeals himself. Master McKenzie said that he could not of course offer Sara any advice but perhaps it would be as well if she did have a new lawyer, and would she like to be able to instruct a QC as well? Her first battle was won.

The next would be to find those new lawyers. George and Sara originally decided to ask one of England's most high-profile female/feminist barristers, Helena Kennedy, to represent Sara. When she was not able to, they decided to try to find someone else, and at a seminar at the London School of Economics George Delf met a solicitor called Rohit Sanghvi. The seminar had been arranged by the Southall Black Sisters, a collective of Asian and Afro-Caribbean women who run an advice, campaigning and resource centre in Southall. As well as campaigning tirelessly on behalf of women who are victims of domestic violence and murder, they have campaigned for women who killed their violent and abusive partners. The conference focused on a case that had many apparent similarities to Sara's. Kiranjit Ahluwalia, after being subjected to the most terrible domestic violence for some ten years, had poured petrol over her husband's feet. She too was serving a life sentence for his murder. Rohit Sanghvi was Kiranjit's solicitor and he said he would be happy to be Sara's too. George also met Kiranjit's barrister, Andy Nicol, a former LSE law lecturer, at the conference. He suggested that a colleague of his, Edward Fitzgerald, should take on Sara's case.

George contacted Ed Fitzgerald and was impressed. In his thirties and exceptionally bright, he had chosen to devote his legal talents to cases which many other barristers are reluctant to touch. Championing the cause of those who have least rights, and often working without pay, his practice consists largely of actions on behalf of prisoners serving life sentences or patients confined to mental institutions. Already he can claim credit for forcing the British Government to reform its laws on prisoners serving life sentences by successfully challenging the Government in the European Court. He immediately sympathized with Sara's case and the arguments that she and George wanted to present.

To complete the legal team, Sara wrote to Tony Gifford. A radical QC and member of the House of Lords, he was renowned for handling the most highly political cases. Sara's case had obvious political dimensions and he too was happy to take it on.

As soon as Sara and George started to look at the defence of provocation with their lawyers, they could see that their battle was not going to be an easy one. For the defence to be available to Sara she would have to prove that she had stabbed Malcolm while suffering from a 'sudden and temporary loss of self-control'; in other words that she had acted in the heat of the moment.

Sara believed that was undoubtedly what had happened but legally she faced a problem. She had gone into the kitchen for a brief period before stabbing Malcolm. That, from the law's point of view, could constitute a 'cooling-off period' during which Sara had time to regain her self-control. And, if she had done so, she could not have been said to have been acting in the heat of the moment.

The law in this area tries to tread a difficult tight-rope. It has to distinguish between genuine cases of provocation and killings which are motivated by revenge. If Sara had had time to think before stabbing Malcolm then she might have killed because she had decided to 'get Malcolm back' or 'put an end to his threats once and for all' rather than just having acted on the spur of the moment because she had 'snapped'. Sara had said in her interview to the police and under cross-examination at trial that she had gone into the kitchen to calm down. Indeed, that was one of the factors which influenced her original lawyers not to argue provocation; the time she had spent in the kitchen, looking first for the truncheon and then picking up a knife, looked, to them, like a classic 'cooling-off period'; the period which according to legal precedent meant the effect of the provocation had worn off. The fact that Sara believed she'd anything but 'cooled-off' by the time she went back into the living-room did not seem to matter.

Sara was by no means the first woman to be convinced that she had killed because she was provoked and yet who seemed unable to avail herself of that defence. It had been argued for quite some time by certain lawyers, most notably those who worked with battered women, that the law in this respect was harder for women to use than for men.

Since the vast majority of murders are committed by men, the defences to the crime developed by the law were naturally based around the typical male offender. Viewed against that backdrop, the notion of a 'sudden and temporary' loss of self-control can be seen to be particularly apt to describe the sudden rage of a man, of the husband who loses his temper and kills his adulterous or nagging wife on the spot. But women who are provoked by their partners rarely react on the spur of the moment. Often they are unable to as they are physically smaller and weaker than their provoker. Thus they may react by finding a weapon or waiting until their partner is drunk or asleep, and although they may be suffering from the same loss of self-control at that point as at the point when a man kills immediately, the time-lapse is taken by the law to be a strong indication of premeditation.

Similarly, many women simply do not lose their self-control in the same way as men, perhaps because they are physically less strong, perhaps because their conditioning teaches them to suppress rather than express angry and violent emotions; many women react to provocation over time. This can particularly be seen to be the case with women who have been victims of domestic violence. Cowed and brutalized, they may well lose their self-control over a long period of time. That 'slow-burning' emotion experienced by a woman driven slowly but surely to the end of her tether does not fit easily into the current definition of provocation. The loss of self-control can be clearly evident but it does not come suddenly in a fit of rage but cumulatively over a period of time. Similarly, what the law views as a 'cooling-off' period may in fact be a 'boiling-over' period in which the woman has time to brood and mull over what has happened, and it may be during that period, which could last for some time after the provocative words or acts, that she finally snaps – not there and then on the spur of the moment.

So, if Sara had lashed out and killed Malcolm while she was being beaten by him; or if she had been gripped by a sudden jealous rage at the thought of some real or imagined adultery on his part, she could have used the defence of provocation, but because she had not reacted suddenly, it appeared that she was going to face considerable difficulties.

That seemed to be unfair. She could of course turn again to diminished responsibility as a defence, but she fervently believed she had not killed Malcolm because she was mad. She had killed him because his behaviour had made her snap, and she wanted that to be her defence. She became determined not to force herself to conform to what she saw as a stereotype of a neurotic or crazy woman to get justice. And her resolve to use the defence of provocation was strengthened still further when she realized that the restriction that any loss of self-control be 'sudden' is not to be found in any legal statute.

Much of England's criminal law is the product of an uneasy liaison between common law – the law as it has been developed gradually by judges in the courts – and the laws that have been laid down by Parliament in statutes. English judges are not meant to make law: that is for Parliament to do. Their function is only to interpret it and apply it. That process can inevitably involve some filling-in of the gaps and some modifications but only if it can be viewed as putting into action the intention of Parliament. Judges are not free to set off on their own excursions into judicial interpretation – they have to follow the wisdom of those who have gone before. Thus, they are bound by precedent – the judgments of higher courts laid down in earlier cases. Those precedents, which set out the correct interpretations and procedures, must be followed by all judges in the lower courts. Only when a case reaches the Court of Appeal is it possible to argue that a previous interpretation is wrong or out of date, but even then, if that previous interpretation is the result of a ruling of the House of Lords, it must still be followed. Only when a case reaches the House of Lords – the highest court in the land – can arguments about changing the law really be entertained, and then only if it can be shown that those changes would in fact only be interpreting the intention of Parliament in a more accurate way. It is for politicians to make the law and for judges to apply it. And judges, notoriously resistant to change in any case, are keen to avoid doing anything that could remotely be interpreted as usurping the role of Britain's elected Parliament.

The statute governing the defence of provocation is the 1967 Homicide Act. Section three sets out the definition – and remarkable for their absence are the words 'sudden and temporary'. Section three states:

> Where on a charge of murder there is evidence on which the jury can find that the person charged was provoked (whether by things done or by things said or by both together) to lose his self-control, the question whether the provocation was enough to make a reasonable man do as he did shall be left to be determined by the jury.

It goes on to say that the jury should take into account everything said and done and the effect they think it would have on a reasonable person. Taking that definition, it would seem there was little to stop a woman like Sara using the defence, there being no requirement that she react immediately and suddenly and an explicit instruction that the jury should consider everything that was said and done, which presumably would include the whole history of Malcolm's violence and alcoholism. However, because English law is not just made up of statutes, to understand its application it is necessary to look to its bedfellow – the common law – to see how the statute has been interpreted and applied.

The most significant case – which was decided in 1949, way before the 1967 Homicide Act – was the case of *R* v. *Duffy*. In that case a woman, whom it was accepted had been brutally treated by her husband, had attacked and killed him while he was in bed. He had beaten her earlier that evening and prevented her from leaving the house with their child, but her plea of provocation failed. She was convicted of murder and hanged the following year. The judge in that case was Mr Justice Devlin, who was later to become one of England's most respected law lords. In directing the jury he gave them what from that case on came to be the classic definition of provocation. Mr Justice Devlin told the jury that the provocation must be such as 'to cause in any reasonable person and actually causes in the accused, a sudden and temporary loss of self-control, rendering the accused so subject to passion as to make him for the moment not master of his mind'.

Thus the words 'sudden and temporary' came to be integral to the definition of provocation, until, that is, Parliament decided to come up with its own definition in Section three of the Homicide Act. The Act not only did not include any requirement that the loss of self-control be 'sudden and temporary' but it specifically downgraded the relevance of any lapse of time to being just one of a number of factors which the jury should refer to when deciding whether or not the accused was provoked. Thus a lapse of time or any apparent 'cooling-off' period would be relevant but not fatal to someone claiming the defence of provocation. On the face of it it would seem that the Act abolished the 'sudden and temporary requirement', indeed its commentary specifically states that Section three was 'intended to abolish all previous rules of law as to what can or cannot amount to provocation'. That was expressly pointed out by the House of Lords when they considered the wording of the Act in a case in 1967, albeit in relation to another issue.

However, the judiciary, having developed what it felt to be a useful direction to give to juries, was unwilling to let it go. In at least two cases since the Act was passed the Court of Appeal has ruled that Mr Justice Devlin's 'classic' direction on provocation is still the right one to apply. So the 'sudden and temporary' requirement has effectively been grafted on to the statute, and is still applied by judges throughout the country today, years after an Act of Parliament by implication abolished it.

It seemed to all those looking at Sara's case that at least one of the arguments they should raise on appeal must be that Parliament had not intended that restriction to remain. The argument had the force of logic, but neither Ed Fitzgerald nor Rohit Sanghvi was confident it would succeed. Court of Appeal judges being notoriously reluctant to disagree with each other, they were not predicting success just on the basis of that argument.

They were also acutely aware of the fact that removing the judge-made requirement could well be perceived by the judiciary as broadening a defence to murder. Whatever the merit and force of their arguments, they felt they would confront a profound unwillingness to make any ruling that could be interpreted as making it easier for murderers to 'get off', a resistance which they felt their arguments on the grounds of equality were unlikely to override. Although they would argue forcefully that it was unfair to allow the defence to operate in a way which made it easier for men to use than women, they could see judges falling prey to the same prejudice that had been raised at Sara's original trial – namely, that a 'licence to kill' or, more specifically, a 'licence for women to kill their husbands' might be being introduced through their back door. The fact that husbands already had that licence (if one believed it to be one) was unlikely to be enough to convince them.

With Sara in Durham, it fell to George Delf to do a lot of the necessary liaising with lawyers. He had strong ideas on how Sara's defence should be conducted. Rohit Sanghvi, Sara's new solicitor, who was ferociously diligent and committed to his work, went through Sara's papers very carefully. His work on Kiranjit Ahluwalia's case and with battered women over the previous ten years had left him totally convinced that the law relating to provocation needed to be changed. However, he immediately felt that Sara had another ground of appeal and he wanted to pursue it. He thought that the whole way in which the psychiatric evidence had been handled at her trial was wrong. He told George and Sara that he wanted to contact the prosecution's psychiatrist, Dr Brockman, to see if she might possibly concede that her opinion at trial was wrong. But Sara refused to allow him to make even the most tentative approach. Sara had a passionate mistrust of psychiatrists, and George had a rabid and seemingly pathological hatred of them. He was to describe the work of the psychiatrists at Sara's trial as a 'witches' brew of half-truths and pseudo-science', accusing one of them of having 'a vindictive capacity for opening rather than healing wounds'. Sara refused to have any further psychiatric evidence sought or discussed on her case.

That was a view both Rohit Sanghvi and Ed Fitzgerald fought desperately to change. They both agreed that provocation should be their main argument but as veterans of many a vain battle to persuade the English legal system to reform itself they were not overly optimistic. They wanted to have a safety-net so that if their arguments on provocation were rejected they had something to fall back on that would enable them to gain Sara's release. They were both highly committed legal reformers but to both of them their first priority was to get Sara out of jail. There seemed to be little point in her languishing in prison for the sake of a political point if there were grounds upon which they could get her out. They both wanted to persuade Sara to make her political argument powerfully and effectively whilst still obtaining her release. They felt it was one thing for her to decide to offer herself as a martyr to her cause, and they respected her for it, but they felt she should not have taken that course of action. Indeed, Ed Fitzgerald drafted no fewer than three sets of advice in an attempt to persuade her to allow him to make not only the arguments on provocation but also the others that might get her out or at least reduce her life sentence. If he was allowed to pursue diminished responsibility as a fall-back, he believed it would not be necessary to argue it as it had been at trial, namely, that Sara was suffering from a serious long-standing abnormality of mind. Instead, he believed, it would be possible to show that she was suffering from a temporary manic depressive illness induced by the stress of looking after a dangerous and violent alcoholic who had repeatedly abused her. But by that stage Sara's attitude had hardened. Whatever her lawyers' advice and misgivings, Sara was adamant that she would rather remain in jail than compromise on a point of principle.

She was moved from Durham to Bullwood Hall Prison in Essex to be nearer her legal advisers and so better able to prepare her defence. She was determined to fight her case on principle alone and also to be able to address the court. Pleading diminished responsibility again and calling psychiatric evidence to enable herself to walk free would be selling out. With a characteristic disregard for any legal etiquette, she again wrote direct to the Registrar of Criminal Appeals, who the year before had helped her to change lawyers, explaining how she felt.

HMP Bullwood Hall
Hockley
Essex

23 May 1991

Dear Master McKenzie,

In a sea of doubt and confusion, I once again turn to you for advice.

I stand convicted of murder, sentenced to life imprisonment. Any person who knows me, reads my case, and the surrounding circumstances, is all too aware that I had no intention of killing my husband. I have a lot of public support and sympathy from men, as well as women and children, who can see, all too clearly, the overwhelming

male bias within the judiciary which worked so effectively
against me.

I wish to appeal my conviction and sentence and clear my
name. I want nothing more than to be recognized as a
woman who tried her hardest, with no outside help, to save
an emotionally crippled man from himself. I am not bad, I
am not mad, I was subjected to intolerable pressure,
enhanced by a society that for reasons of its own, did not
want to care. When my husband threatened to kill me I
cracked.

My appeal seems to me to be a morass of legal definitions,
implications and unjust contradictions. I am not happy. I
do not wish to be freed under the banner of diminished
responsibility. I do not want to be freed because the judge or
the prosecuting QC made an error. I want and demand
justice.

It is becoming increasingly clear to me that I cannot hope
to find justice in the Court of Appeal. The appeal judges
are regarded as 'gods'. I was under the impression that our
courts were to reflect public opinion. The public who feel
strongly enough to voice an opinion, feel I have been unjustly
convicted and imprisoned.

Freedom, for me, means being true to myself. Honouring
myself, and recognizing that I alone am solely responsible
for my life and my actions, knowing truth in my heart gives
me strength. I do not want the 'freedom' of the Court of
Appeal if it entails arguing legal and at times archaic
definitions and technicalities, when true justice stares the
judges in the face; I am a modern woman and I ask for
modern justice.

Is there any reason . . . why I cannot speak for myself at
the Court of Appeal? I would do so firmly and above all,
with dignity. If I lose I will have lost honourably. I don't
want to be squabbled over like a piece of meat, by grown men
who have no sense of justice, no sense of moral duty, no
feeling for truth. I'd rather stay in prison and work towards
a better understanding of women.

Please don't curse me, stop a minute and listen with your heart. Sometimes a person just gets to the stage where they have to try and do what is right – often against overwhelming odds. I'm not really interested in rules, regulations and precedents. I am fighting for myself and I wish to be heard. Simple, really. If you can't answer my questions perhaps you would be kind enough to pass my letter on to Lord Lane, or the Lord Chancellor – to anyone you think can help.

> Yours sincerely
> Sara E. Thornton

Within a week a typewritten reply arrived from Master McKenzie. Formally but courteously he told Sara that permission to address the Court was sometimes given, but that it was given at the discretion of the Court. She would have to wait to hear what the Court said when the time for her appeal came, but she instinctively felt positive and wrote in her diary:

Since deciding to speak at the Court of Appeal, I have felt a strong conviction that I will be freed. At first, I thought that I would have to present my own case, but, as a result of my letter to the Registrar, I now know that I can speak in addition to Lord Gifford. In my gut, I feel that is what I must do! I know if I ask for my liberty, it will be granted. So strong is this belief that I have started to mentally plan to leave here. I've tried to explain my deep feelings but no-one except for Kiranjit [Ahluwalia] really understands. She's convinced I'll be freed, everyone else just thinks it's wishful thinking. But it isn't! It's as strong as strong as the feeling I had when I knew before my trial that I'd end up in prison . . . this feeling is simply that it's time to leave prison all together.

12 · The Appeal

Sara's appeal was set for 19 July 1991. At 5 a.m. she left the prison in Essex, carrying with her all her belongings in case she was released. Her destination was the Royal Courts of Justice on the Strand in London. To most people this is just the sandstone arched set for tumultuous and emotional television scenes when celebrated prisoners walk free, or perhaps the calmer backdrop for an earnest interpretation by a seasoned legal observer of their Lordships' latest pronouncement. To barristers, many of whom work in chambers just a few minutes' walk away, this is a place where careers are made or broken; where appeals are won or lost; where the strength of legal argument succeeds or fails. Here their faces look unusually earnest and careworn, barely recognizable as the same ones which on another day at Isleworth or Nottingham Crown Court can be seen laughing and joking with those whom they oppose in court. There, only a jury will assess their performance; here, they will face some of the best legal minds in the land, and the outcome of their battles will be noted down and most probably printed as a record in the Law Reports for all to read. They can be seen scurrying into the courts at almost any time of the day, sometimes already bewigged, clutching large blue notebooks and carrying black robes. The more senior are followed by their clerks, towing huge trolleys full of legal tomes, their masters' intellectual capacity to interpret and analyse their contents apparently in inverse proportion to their ability to carry them themselves.

Once up the steps and forward through the arch they find themselves back in time, their gowns and wigs no longer out of place. The Great Hall, designed and built a century ago, stretches ahead for over two hundred feet. The polished marble floors, the sweeping arches, the hush and semi-darkness, the sudden coolness after the throng of the street outside lend an air of reverence to the atmosphere. Indeed, there is more of the cathedral to this building than of the real and human world. As if to emphasize that, one end of the hall is lined with stain-glass windows decorated with the arms of past Lord Chancellors. While those who know their way whisk confidently past, heels tapping self-importantly on the marble floor, others stand in awe, fear and confusion. This is not a place for the lay-person, for the ordinary human being, although it is them the system is meant to serve. This is where their fate may be decided but where only those so ordained can speak and supplicate. The height and epic proportion of the architecture is seemingly designed to reinforce a sense of humility, if not blind faith, through which confidence in the antiquated system can be maintained.

Sara was not led through the sweeping central hall and up the spiral stone steps to the designated court-room. As a convicted prisoner she was naturally taken straight to the cells in the base-ment to await her turn for justice. Ten cases were listed to take place in Court 7 that day. Sara's was the eighth. She was not brought upstairs to take her place in the stand until 3 p.m. By then it was too far into the day for the case to be begun and finished. Their Lordships do not like to sit late without good reason. So justice was postponed until the following Monday. Sara's trip and anxious wait had been for nothing, and she returned to jail with her bag of optimistically packed belongings. Those who had travelled many hundreds of miles and taken time off work to be there with her received no acknowledgement and no apology. The barristers and solicitors themselves would still at least be paid, although ultimately it would be the tax-payer who would foot the bill.

On the Monday Sara returned to Court 7. This time the entire day had been set aside for the court to hear just her appeal. The public gallery was full of people both sympathetic and hostile to her case. Among those who had returned for the hearing were members of Malcolm's family; George Delf; Billi's natural parents, George and Joyce Caddy, who were to become a resili-ent and steady support to Sara; a cousin of Sara's and her husband; and Sara's father and stepmother who had made the journey up from Devon, this time declaring their presence openly by sitting in court. The remaining seats were filled by supporters and well-wishers.

Outside the court a demonstration had been mounted on Sara's behalf. It was to be the first of many designed to highlight her cause and the cause of women like her. It had been organized by two women's groups: Justice for Women and Southall Black Sisters.

Justice for Women had heard about Sara's case shortly before the appeal. One of its members had written to Sara after hearing her story on a Channel Four documentary, 'The Provoked Wife'. As a pressure group committed to fighting violence against women and sexism in the police and the judiciary, they were very interested in Sara's story. The campaign was not new to this type of case; in 1981 a branch of Justice for Women based in Leeds had become involved in the Maw sisters' trial. In that case two women who had killed their violent father as he attacked their mother were given lengthy prison sentences. The two daughters had themselves been abused by the father, and with the help of a campaign mounted by Justice for Women they successfully had their sentences reduced. The group was also concerned with the way the defence of provocation was seemingly being used by violent men who had killed their wives.

Justice for Women immediately offered Sara their support, which she readily accepted. They set about producing leaflets and generating publicity about her forthcoming appeal. Over one hundred women turned up at court that day; none of them knew Sara personally but all believed fervently in the justice of her case. A huge crowd of supporters stood on the pavement in the Strand, chanting and singing their protests: 'Free, free Sara Thornton, Free, free Sara Thornton ... change the law on provocation' to the tune of 'What shall we do with the drunken sailor'.

As passers-by stopped to watch the colourful spectacle, barristers scuttled embarrassedly past, heads down, not knowing quite how to deal with the startling display of emotion being enacted outside their High Court. The energy, commitment and lack of inhibition of those protesting could not have provided a more marked contrast to the dry and soulless atmosphere inside Court 7 itself. High ceilings and ornate mock gothic architecture enhanced the impression that all were gathered for some form of ritual. Raised high behind a bench across the centre of the room sat the three men who were to decide Sara's fate: Lord Justice Beldam in the centre flanked on either side by two High Court judges, Mr Justice Saville and Mr Justice Buckley. Priest-like, they listened as Lord Gifford, QC, Sara's leading counsel, began his submission.

Tony Gifford is renowned throughout the legal profession for both his intellect and his politics. He had set up the only truly radical set of barrister's chambers in the country. All barristers are self-employed and most work from offices (known as chambers) where they can pool their overheads and share the services of a clerk. They are paid what they manage to earn, there is no sick pay, no maternity leave and no guaranteed income. It is hard for anyone without an independent income or some sort of outside financial support to survive their first few years in the profession, something which in no small part explains the preponderance of barristers from comfortable upper-middle-class backgrounds. The chambers established by Tony Gifford were run as a co-operative, with everyone being paid a salary regardless of what they earned. This experiment in genuine equality did not last, however, and by 1991 Tony Gifford had started to do a lot of work in Jamaica, dividing his time between there and here.

He was in the West Indies for most of the period leading up to Sara's appeal, returning for a hurried twenty-four-hour pit-stop at the end of June before flying out to South Africa as a guest of the ANC. Instructions to Ed Fitzgerald on how to prepare the case had already been faxed from Jamaica. Tony Gifford was keen to see the political dimension emphasized. He had no illusions about how difficult it was going to be to win on provocation, but he thought it was certainly an arguable case. And, besides, this angle fitted in with his client's wishes. Unlike Ed

Fitzgerald and Rohit Sanghvi, he did not find the idea of pursuing diminished responsibility by a different route promising, and he dismissed as very weak the grounds that had been submitted originally – namely, that the jury at trial had been prejudiced. Sara had certainly found someone who was as keen as her to argue the most political dimension of her case.

Before embarking on his crusade, Tony Gifford had a request of the utmost importance to Sara to put to the court. He asked the judges to exercise their discretion and allow Sara to speak. The three wise men, sat high upon their bench, were not visibly impressed. After a brief period of murmured consultation they declined the request, and Tony Gifford did not press the point. Sara was bitterly disappointed. This seemed to confirm her worst fears. What was happening in the court did not seem to be to do with her or with her personal experience; rather, she was being allowed to eavesdrop on the slow whirrings of some arcane and anachronistic machine which seemed content to decide her fate without even acknowledging her existence. As if to emphasize the point, she could barely be seen from the raised wood-panelled dock in which she had been placed. For those in the public gallery, who had come to observe justice being done, the only evidence that the appellant was in court was a few reddish-brown curls peeping over the top of the dock.

Thus the appeal began with Sara unheard and virtually unseen. For four hours Tony Gifford argued the case for change. His tenor was dry and to some observers seemed somewhat flat, but their Lordships seemed content to listen, interjecting occasionally to engage in bouts of intellectual cross-fire with the country's leading radical legal mind.

Tony Gifford was persistent but respectful and the power of his intellect, if not the points he was making, was in its turn greeted with respect. His argument began with a catalogue of the provocative acts that had taken place in the course of the day and night preceding the killing. He described how Malcolm had thrown away his wedding ring; told Sara to get out of the house and take Luise with her; called her a whore; threatened to kill her if she'd been sleeping with other men; threatened to kill her while she was asleep. Just from examining the record of what Sara had said – remarks like 'I felt I did not know how much more I could take from him': 'I was feeling terrible, terribly hurt'; 'I wasn't thinking clearly, not thinking anything . . . upset . . . angry, there is no doubt I was angry' – there seemed to be clear evidence that she had lost her self-control. In view of those remarks, Tony Gifford submitted, the judge should have given a full direction to the jury on provocation. Instead it had been perfunctory, loaded against the appellant, and full of errors.

The first mistake he said Mr Justice Judge had made was not to direct the jury to take into account the whole history of Sara and Malcolm's relationship. Although he had begun that part of his direction to the jury by saying that they must 'take into account the whole picture, the whole story, everything that was said, possibly anything that was done, if there was anything done, on this night', it was those last three words, 'on this night', that Tony Gifford objected to. The law was clear on this point, it was the jury's duty to consider the entire factual situation, everything that was said and done. The judge had therefore erred, he said, by telling the jury only to look at everything that had happened on that night. In the case of a woman subjected to a violent and alcoholic husband, he submitted, it was even more important that the jury take everything into account. What happened on the night of the killing might by itself not seem to be enough to provoke a reasonable person, but when looked at in a context of persistent violence and abuse its impact could change.

After raising a number of other points, Tony Gifford moved on to consider the judge's approach to the issue of provocation. He had dealt with it, he argued, in a dismissive and perfunctory way and should never have invited the jury to draw an adverse inference from the defence's failure to raise the issue. If there was enough evidence to suggest that Sara had been provoked, then, Tony Gifford argued, the judge should have left the jury to decide, rather than undermining the evidence with comments like 'There are many, many unhappy, indeed miserable husbands and wives . . . but on the whole it is hardly reasonable, you may think, to stab them fatally when there are other alternatives available, like walking out or going upstairs.' The judge's own negative view of the defence must, he submitted, have been apparent from that remark, which would have had a clear impact on the jury. What few in the court other than the judges realized was that as Tony Gifford was delivering his assault on Mr Justice Judge's summing-up, Mr Justice Judge was himself sitting as a Court of Appeal judge, just a few doors down the corridor in Court 4.

Next Tony Gifford took the three Lord Justices of Appeal through the arguments against restricting the defence of provocation to only those whose loss of self-control was 'sudden and temporary'. He pointed out that there was no foundation for it in the relevant Act and that it operated in a way that could discriminate against women. It reduced the defence, he argued, to one that was 'apt to describe the sudden rage of a male but not the slow-burning emotion suffered by a woman driven to the end of her tether'. He also pointed out that many High Court judges seemed prepared to accept pleas of manslaughter by reason of provocation where there had been a history of domestic violence, and so as well as being wrong it was anomalous to have grafted on the requirement of suddenness.

During the break for lunch Sara complained that she could not see what was happening in court. She says she was told by one of the prison officers that if she made a fuss she would be removed from the court and spend the rest of her appeal downstairs in the cells. So, as no cushion appeared to be forthcoming, Sara took a blanket with her when she went up to the dock, folded it up and sat on it. With the aid of that make-shift cushion her face was now visible. She sat there silently as hour after hour the trauma of her marriage became the subject of an intellectual debate by people whose experience seemed as far removed from hers as it was possible to imagine.

By this point Tony Gifford had turned his arguments away from judicial misinterpretation of statutes to allegations of inadequacies on the part of Sara's barrister. Criticizing another

member of the legal profession is something that is rarely done
in public, let alone in court. Whilst the public might choose
to make lawyers the frequent butt of their grievances, lawyers
themselves tend to stick together and refrain from criticizing
each other unless it is totally unavoidable, the argument being
that it is difficult to distinguish between genuine miscalculation
and professional misconduct; if barristers are to be instructed
for their independence and judgment they should not be subjected to attack by anyone who is unhappy with the way their
case has gone. Cases of gross incompetence are one thing, but
a constant sniping at those who every day have to stand in front
of a court and make weighty decisions on their feet is something
the profession would prefer to avoid. It is arguable whether the
profession and the legal system have resolved satisfactorily what
happens to those cases where a judgment by a barrister which
in hindsight may appear to have been mistaken (though not
negligent) could be responsible for someone serving a lengthy
jail sentence.

Tony Gifford correctly made no allegation of incompetence or
negligence, he merely stated that Sara's counsel (whom etiquette
dictated he did not mention by name) should have argued the
defence of provocation. There would have been no conflict had
it been run in combination with diminished responsibility, he
submitted. The jury would simply have been asked to decide:
was Sara's responsibility impaired because of an abnormality of
mind? Or, did she lose her self-control because of her husband's
threats and goading?

Such a line of defence would also, he pointed out, have
changed the weight of the evidence. There would have been less
emphasis on Sara's mental state and more on Malcolm's violent
and abusive behaviour. That would have enabled evidence to be
submitted to back up Sara's account of Malcolm's violence. The
court had already been given copies of statements by Sara's GP,
Dr Farn, who had witnessed Malcolm attacking and threatening
Sara, by a Dr Weston, who had given Sara a sick note after
Malcolm knocked her out, and by Veronica Costelloe.

There was one other piece of written evidence which Tony

Gifford submitted to the court: a report from Dr Max Glatt, the specialist who had treated Malcolm when he had been admitted to the Charter Nightingale Clinic for alcoholism. The court was privileged to have available to it an opinion from a world authority on the subject, the author of some seven hundred papers on alcohol and dependency, who had also actually treated the alcoholic in question. In his thirteen-page statement prepared especially for the court, Dr Glatt listed the impact alcoholism could have on the partner of an alcoholic. In particular, he described how it could make someone 'snap':

> An alcoholic's very inconsistent and unpredictable behaviour – often rapidly changing from a loving to an utterly aggressive one – verbally often very abusive and offensive and sometimes physically violent – necessarily leads, in time, to reaction from the wife, with the development of an increasingly vicious circle of increasing mutual distrust, suspicion, resentment, bitterness and frustration. Even the most submissive and meekest wives are driven to a pitch where they answer or scream back, or even fight back when at the end of their tether, although physically they are no match for their husbands . . . whatever the original state of their emotional stability, they have gradually been worn out by long periods of emotional strain and stress, their stability has gradually been seriously eroded, living on the edge of a volcano, feeling angry and loathing themselves for not having walked out long ago and for not being able to cope. Such a wife might frequently lose her self-control which might snap suddenly, more or less seriously, by something which for her may become the last straw, and such last straw may not necessarily concern what outsiders may consider a large matter, because such 'sudden' loss of control may be the response not to the last provocative act but to a long series of provocative acts, or attitudes, to chronic provocation which the wife may have had to suffer and tolerate in humiliation because she could not see a way out.

Dr Glatt remembered Sara visiting Malcolm regularly while he was being treated in his clinic. His report concluded that her behaviour, characterized by bouts of hope and then despair, of struggle and then resignation, was very consistent with that of many of the wives of alcoholics he had seen, and he pointed out that most experts now accepted that alcoholism was a family illness.

Brian Escott-Cox had listened patiently to Tony Gifford's arguments. His submissions in reply for the Crown were to take only about a quarter of the time Lord Gifford's had. He did not, as he had originally anticipated, have to defend himself against the use of prejudicial language, that ground of appeal not having been pursued. In the more refined atmosphere of the Court of Appeal Brian Escott-Cox seemed to have lost some of his sparkle. Lord Justices are not as amenable as juries to persuasion based on charm and bluster, and so his chief weapons were largely impotent. Perhaps, too, he felt little joy in defending a conviction that he had gained little pleasure in obtaining.

After sitting through the arguments that had been presented to them, their Lordships reserved their judgment; they would deliver it the following week. Sara left with a heavy heart and no hope. George Delf left incensed, as he was to write later in an article in the *Guardian*:

> The appeal hearing itself proved that it is not only evil which can be banal. Even at the highest level, our law contrives to wring boredom out of personal suffering ... the medieval pomp of British justice is a dusty and decrepit relic; without feeling and mature emotion.

Emotion was again noticeable by its absence when the three judges returned to Court 7 the following week to make their decision public. Lord Justice Beldam, the presiding judge, whose gentle and cultured manner completely belied the severity of what he had to say, delivered the judgment. Ensconced on the high podium beside him sat Mr Justice Buckley, who throughout the hearing had stared down without expression, saying little and certainly nothing encouraging, and Mr Justice Saville. Of the three judges Mr Justice Saville (who was only hearing the case by chance, having been drafted in when it was realized the appeal would have to be postponed) seemed to be the most sympathetic. His questions to Lord Gifford during the hearing had been direct, concise and alert, seeming to draw him out in the most important areas. It was on him that Sara's supporters had been pinning their hopes. As Lord Justice Beldam delivered his judgment, Mr Justice Saville looked down at his hands, his tanned face blank.

As is the custom – and some would dispute its logic – Lord Justice Beldam gave his reasons before his decision. So it was more than thirty minutes after he had started to speak that those present heard what by that stage they already strongly suspected: Sara's conviction against appeal was dismissed.

The judgment began with an account of the facts, a neutral and commentless account, starkly in contrast to that given to the jury by Mr Justice Judge. However, two events that were relied upon as factually correct are worth mentioning because both might have been viewed quite differently if the court had heard from some of the witnesses who were available but not called upon to give evidence at trial. The first was Martin Thornton's account of the threats Sara made to his father with the knife. Lord Justice Beldam, understandably in the absence of any contradictory evidence, relied upon Martin's recollection of the incident. It was therefore accepted as fact that Sara deliberately picked up the knife to make the threat and that she had had to be disarmed by Martin. The episode had of course been witnessed by Patrick Hanlon from Alcoholics Anonymous, who would have disputed that Sara had deliberately picked up the knife or had to have it taken away from her.

Similarly, the evidence of the taxi driver, Reg Kimberley, who after dropping Sara home on the evening of the killing had concluded she was in a 'quarrelsome and arrogant' mood, might well have been modified if the court had also heard from another taxi driver, Alex Patrick, who earlier that day had seen Sara in a desperate, forlorn, tearful state.

As had been anticipated, the Court of Appeal declined to find that there had been any misdirection in Mr Justice Judge's use of the phrase 'sudden and temporary loss of control'. Similarly,

Lord Justice Beldam ruled that Mr Justice Judge's three words, 'on this night', objected to by Lord Gifford as unduly restricting how much of the history of the relationship the jury should consider, could not be held to be incorrect. He accepted that it was correct that the jury should look at the whole picture, not just what happened on the night of Malcolm's death, but concluded, in a twist of what can only be described as judicial logic, that the jury would not have concluded that the words 'on this night' restricted their deliberations to things done only on that night.

He also said that the judge had not been wrong to comment upon the fact that David Barker, QC had not raised provocation as a defence: 'The learned judge was doing no more than telling the jury that counsel may not have felt able to advance the defence of provocation because of the clear evidence which the appellant herself had given.' Thus he seemed to observers to effectively condone the pre-emption of the jury's role as arbiter of fact by both Sara's own lawyer and the judge.

Turning finally to the conduct of Sara's counsel and his failure specifically to raise the defence of provocation, Lord Justice Beldam referred to what was then the leading authority on the topic. In the case of Ensor in 1989, he said, the court had ruled that

> if defending counsel in the course of his conduct of a case made a decision or took a course which later appeared to have been mistaken or unwise, that normally would not be regarded as a proper ground for an appeal, but that if the court had any lurking doubt that the appellant might have suffered some injustice as a result of flagrantly incompetent advocacy the court would quash the conviction.

Thus he affirmed the view that unless a barrister could be shown to have been 'flagrantly incompetent', the justice of the appellant's case was really immaterial.

Lord Justice Beldam agreed with Lord Gifford's argument that it was not incompatible to argue both provocation and diminished responsibility, but said that as there was no suggestion in the evidence that Sara had reacted suddenly, and as she had consistently maintained she had not meant to stab Malcolm any-way, most barristers would have done as David Barker did. One might wonder why, if indeed there was 'no suggestion in the evidence', he had earlier agreed that because the facts raised the question of provocation it was right for the judge to have put it to the jury.

His ruling may have absolved an experienced and respected barrister of liability but even some of those involved in prosecuting Sara were unable to agree with his conclusions on the question of provocation.

The judgment made no reference to the statements from Sara's GP, Dr Max Glatt and Veronica Costelloe. It is unclear what, if any, consideration they were given.

As Lord Justice Beldam announced that 'The appeal against conviction will be dismissed', George Delf shouted out, 'Shame on you' from the back of the court. Sara herself spoke for the first and only time at her appeal, saying, 'Thank you' with as much sarcasm as she could muster.

Lord Gifford asked Lord Justice Beldam for leave to appeal to the House of Lords on whether it was appropriate for the 1967 Homicide Act to be restricted by the words 'sudden and temporary'. He was effectively asking Lord Justice Beldam for permission to try to overturn the judgment which he himself had just delivered. After a brief adjournment Lord Justice Beldam declined to give his leave: 'Lord Gifford, we have given very serious consideration to this but we do not think the circumstances of this case raise a question of law of public importance.' Many members of the public were soon to take issue with that view of what was indeed important.

As Sara was led from the dock to continue her life sentence, one of the prison officers who was escorting her broke down in tears.

Sara was whisked back to Bullwood Hall Prison, more convinced than ever that the courts were not the place for her to seek justice. Her experience in court, she was to say later, made her feel as though she was no more than 'a lost bet over a game of golf'. She felt the judges had only been interested in investigating the trial, not in asking whether justice had been done.

Sara's case had become well known to women working in the field of domestic violence, but other than her letter to the *Independent* it had received virtually no national news coverage. That night some national television news programmes decided to run pieces on it even though at that time it was far from being a high-profile celebrated case. One of these was Channel Four News. The programme editor that night was initially reluctant, saying, 'She didn't win, there's been no change in the law, so where's the news value? The Appeal Court turns down appeals every day.' To his credit, however, he agreed to run the piece anyway. If he still had doubts about how newsworthy Sara's case was, the events that were soon to follow certainly assuaged them.

13 · The Patience of a Saint

Two days after Sara's appeal was turned down a man walked free from Birmingham Crown Court. Joseph McGrail had been given a suspended sentence for killing his alcoholic common-law wife. He had taken Marion Kennedy by the throat as she lay drunk, thrown her on to the bed and kicked her. Freeing him, the judge, Mr Justice Popplewell, told Joseph McGrail that he had 'every sympathy' for him and that the woman he had killed 'would have tried the patience of a saint'. The disparity between this case and Sara's was brutal and obvious. When George Delf spoke to her on the phone that evening and told her about it, she broke down in tears. The justice that had just been denied to her was, it seemed, freely available to members of the opposite sex. She had exhausted all the legal remedies that were open to her; after spending the night meditating in her cell, she phoned George Delf and told him that she would not eat until she received the same understanding and justice that had been shown to Joseph McGrail.

Sara had sympathy for Joseph McGrail who, like her, had been trapped in a difficult relationship with an alcoholic. He had lived with Marion Kennedy and her alcoholism for ten years until he eventually snapped as she lay in an alcoholic stupor demanding more drink. His plea of guilty to manslaughter was accepted on the basis that he had not intended to kill her. The provocation the court believed he had experienced was taken into account when sentencing him. The judge did not ask him why he did not leave.

The rejection of Sara's appeal had attracted some media attention, and now that she was on hunger-strike and had apparently been so unfairly treated, every newspaper wanted to tell her story. The national press started to give space to the feminist arguments that were being raised on her behalf: to virtually every newspaper editor the contrast between the life sentence she had received and the apparent leniency with which Joseph McGrail's case had been handled smacked of blatant injustice. The *Guardian* printed a letter from Harriet Wistrich, a member of Justice for Women:

> I was horrified to read that Joseph McGrail was given a two-year suspended sentence . . Can anyone now refute the evidence that the law operates by a double standard, reflecting the male bias of the judicial system? It is high time the criminal law system was overhauled, and the refusal by the Appeal Court to give Sara Thornton leave to appeal to the House of Lords must be reconsidered.

Sara was temporarily transferred from Bullwood Hall to Holloway Prison in London so that her medical condition could be monitored during her hunger-strike. While in Holloway she continued to refuse food, and supporters held vigils outside by the prison gates and mounted regular, noisy demonstrations outside the Home Office and the Court of Appeal. Justice for Women set up a Sara Thornton Support Group and letters of support started to flood in, often from women who had themselves experienced violence. An anonymous note handed to a demonstrator outside the Court of Appeal was typical:

> I only wish I had known sooner, I would have been here with you. After eight years of physical and mental abuse I know how it feels to be worn into the ground unable to see any way out and to live in constant fear. I too have a child. My thoughts and hopes are with you and all other women who suffer at the hands of violent men.

Sara's case seemed to have struck a chord with many women who had never before dreamed of demonstrating or protesting about anything. Offers of support also flooded in from academics and lawyers who viewed her fate as clear evidence of social injustice and discrimination.

Sara's solicitor, Rohit Sanghvi, started to speak publicly on her behalf. Joseph McGrail had been given sympathy, he said, but Sara had not. The support and understanding that her sentence was attracting enabled him and her campaigners to argue in the media the case that had been rejected by the courts. 'The problem for provoked women who kill is that prosecutors will not accept pleas of guilty to manslaughter as easily as they do in the case of men, and once the case goes to trial, the jury's hands are tied. Women are subjected to a double injustice.' Juries should not, Rohit Sanghvi told the *Independent* newspaper, be forced to convict if it could not be shown that someone had lost their self-control immediately.

From prison, Sara saw as much of the coverage of her case as she was allowed to. Whilst most of those who spoke out supported her, some pointed out that Joseph McGrail had been with his partner for much longer than Sara – some ten years – whereas Sara had only been with Malcolm for just over two. In a letter to George Delf from prison she wrote:

I am sick of it all. I am sick at not quite coming up to the standards required. Because I didn't suffer ten years of abuse ... because I am not a pathetic figure of a woman who languishes quietly in prison. Because I take responsibility for my life, because I dare to fight, I am being ignored like a bad debt, in the hope that I'll eventually get the message.

She believed that in turning down her appeal the authorities were in reality saying: 'Women like you don't achieve anything, you've broken the rules, dared to step out of the boundaries we men have set for acceptable female standards of behaviour, so we'll show you the consequences of your actions.'

If Malcolm had killed me they would have used everything they are using against me now in Malcolm's defence. I'd have been portrayed as a woman who nagged him over his drinking, who didn't always wear knickers, who went off to a conference and left him. Oh, I can just see the case they would build. And Malcolm, being the good upstanding citizen, despite his illness, oh yes, he would have walked free. Perhaps would be advised to go for help and treatment.

Sara's spirit was strong but she carried very little extra weight. The authorities at Holloway were certainly monitoring her condition. Every day without food brought her more letters from people offering their support but begging her to stop her hunger-strike. Justice for Women and the Southall Black Sisters continued to hold candle-lit vigils outside the prison. Sara even received a two-page letter from the then Home Office minister, Angela Rumbold, explaining with some sympathy why the Home Secretary felt unable to intervene and assuring her that the Home Secretary would review any new evidence in her case very carefully. So many people wrote to her that the prison staff had to give her black bin-liners in which to store all the letters.

Ten days into the hunger-strike Billi brought Luise over from the States. It had been a year and a half since Sara had last seen her daughter. The authorities at Holloway, the most progressive of England's women's prisons, were sympathetic. They gave mother and daughter almost unlimited visiting time, allowing them to use one of the manager's offices. Luise believed her mother might die, she pleaded with her to stop. It was that plea, from her twelve-year-old daughter, that persuaded her to do so. On 20 August, after nineteen days without food, Sara ate a tuna-fish sandwich and drank a glass of milk, thereby ending her hunger-strike. She told the *Guardian* newspaper a few days afterwards:

> I had hundreds of letters from people asking me not to go ahead with it, but they were just pieces of paper. Seeing her saying she did not want me to die crystallized it for me. Also, I felt that as long as I was on hunger-strike I was not trusting the people who were supporting me, and letting them help.

But she had mixed feelings about stopping; part of her had wanted to carry on and felt she was ducking out by stopping, but another part of her realized that she had achieved all she could hope to. The Home Office were not going to give in to what they would term the 'emotional blackmail' of a hunger-strike, but she had at any rate succeeded in generating an extra-ordinary amount of public sympathy and pressure. The momentum to attempt to change the way the law was applied, if not the law itself, had definitely begun.

In the House of Commons, the Labour MP Jack Ashley had written to the Lord Chancellor asking that Sara be given leave to appeal to the House of Lords. Later he was to introduce a Ten-minute Rule Bill which attempted (unsuccessfully) to get the law changed. That autumn both the Labour and Liberal Democratic Party conferences passed resolutions calling for the law to be reformed. Some Conservative MPs, notably Theresa Gorman and Emma Nicholson, also expressed sympathy.

The campaign to change the law was building up steam. Sara's was not the only case to highlight the apparent inequities of the system. There were two others which came to be closely associated with hers: Kiranjit Ahluwalia and Amelia Rossiter were both also battered women who had killed. They too had been given life sentences for murder and they were serving them in the very same prison as Sara.

Kiranjit Ahluwalia was born in India into a middle-class family. After completing an arts degree and beginning a law course she came under pressure from her family to marry and duly agreed to enter into an arranged marriage with Dipak, who she had not previously met. After spending some time in Canada the couple moved to England and settled in Crawley in Sussex.

From the beginning of the marriage Kiranjit suffered violence and abuse. Her husband tried to beat her and strangle her; he threatened her with knives; pushed her downstairs; tried to run her down at a family wedding; sexually abused and raped her. The law had been of no use, she had got two court orders against him but failed to get them enforced. Finally, at the end of her tether, she had gone out and bought some petrol, waiting until the small hours of the morning to take it upstairs together with a stick and an oven-glove for self-protection. She threw the petrol into her husband's bedroom, lit the stick and threw that in too. A week later Dipak died in hospital from the burns. Like Sara,

Kiranjit had told the police that she didn't intend to kill her husband, she had just wanted to cause him pain. But, also like Sara, she was seemingly barred from using the defence of provocation – because, in the eyes of the law, her loss of self-control was not sudden. She spoke very little English and had not given evidence at her trial. Sara befriended her in prison, encouraging her to speak English and to fight for her freedom.

Amelia Rossiter remained quite distant from Sara and Kiranjit. She was older than them – in her sixties – and she had suffered violence and abuse for most of her long married life before stabbing her husband, Leslie, more than fifty times. She was being physically assaulted at the time that she killed him but out of a sense of guilt and shame she was reluctant to make public and so use in her defence the full extent of the violence and brutality she had suffered. Her defence of accident and self-defence had failed.

The Southall Black Sisters had taken up Kiranjit's case in January 1990, visiting her regularly in prison. Since Sara's failed appeal they had worked very closely with Justice for Women and once her hunger-strike had ended the two groups together had ensured that fortnightly pickets outside the Home Office kept the profile of their cause high. Like the demonstrations that had taken place outside the Court of Appeal, they were noisy, powerful and emotive. Their obvious visual impact ensured that they got frequent coverage on television news.

On 23 November 1991, a day which had been designated International Day to end Violence Against Women, three thousand women marched through the centre of London calling for the release of Sara, Kiranjit and Amelia. At the rally in Trafalgar Square a tape-recorded message from Sara was played out over the public address system to her supporters. Sara's disembodied voice floated through the crowd. Her message was that she wanted every woman and child to live without fear. As many of those who had gathered had come from refuges it was a moving occasion.

The Justice for Women campaign was being run from the living-room of a small flat shared by two feminists in north

London. One of the women, Julie Bindel, had organized the original demonstration outside the Court of Appeal. She started to visit Sara in prison and wrote to her regularly. George Delf had begun to feel uneasy about the involvement of these feminist campaigners; in particular he was unhappy about the fact that some of their demonstrations were organized for women only, thereby excluding him and, he believed, a large section of Sara's supporters. For their part the women were equally suspicious of George's motivations; they felt he projected himself as a knight on a white charger, coming to what he thought was the rescue of a poor forlorn Sara.

The situation became increasingly difficult for Sara, who was being torn in different directions by her two closest friends, and she pleaded with them to meet and work together. They did indeed meet when they were both invited to appear on Central TV's audience discussion show, 'The Time and the Place', and for a while an uneasy alliance was maintained. Both sides, though, were becoming increasingly concerned about the situation, and Sara's immediate instinct was to trust George: in one angry moment she 'sacked' Julie from her campaign. However, she gradually began to feel that George was attempting to isolate her from her other supporters. As Sara became more questioning of his motives, George became more outspoken in his accusations against her female campaigners. He seemed to Sara to be clearly threatened by Julie's lesbianism and upset by the fact that Sara was not put off by it. Sara became increasingly suspicious of George and eventually they parted, not without acrimony. It had been a relationship which captured the public's imagination, seeming to fall into the epic mould of love triumphing over insuperable odds; a love story to delight every newspaper editor. Its demise soon became public knowledge and, as is all too often the case, seemingly public property as well.

An article in the *Birmingham Post* quoted George Delf as warning that Sara had linked herself with a women's fringe group and would lose public support: 'The effort I put into this campaign was to try to get middle-ground opinion behind her which she needs if she is ever going to get the courts and the

Home Secretary to release her. By focusing her attention on this really way-out fringe group, she is going to lose tremendous support.' Sara herself had already written to the *Guardian* that 'Mr Delf's inability to look to the broader implications of my case as far as the treatment of women both in judicial and social terms, has played a major role in the break between us.'

Certainly Justice for Women felt George had taken too individualistic an approach to the issues raised by Sara's case. They believed it was crucial to draw parallels with similar cases of injustice and to provide a broader political context which would show that Sara's case was not a one-off. Neither they nor Sara were fighting just for her freedom; they wanted change on a larger scale: a reinterpretation or change in the law and a more consistent and enlightened approach on the part of judges.

At its top end the judiciary is almost exclusively male. There are no female law lords, only one female Lord Justice of Appeal, and 98.5 per cent of High Court judges are men. Legal history is littered with evidence of judicial sexual stereotyping. Whilst taking a sympathetic view of the plight of men provoked by nagging or lazy wives, judges have often refused to allow women who have been battered for years to plead provocation. The origins of such attitudes can be found in the law itself. Until 1867 it was perfectly legal for a man to beat his wife, the only guideline being that the stick he used to hit her with should be no thicker than his thumb. Although this 'rule of thumb' is no longer in existence, Sara's campaigners argued that, for women facing domestic violence, little has changed and that recent legal history seems to provide similar examples of judicial prejudice.

In 1987 Thomas Corlett was sentenced to three years in prison for the manslaughter of his wife, who had provoked him that day by moving the mustard-pot to the wrong side of the table. Judge Gerald Butler had said at the trial that Corlett was 'a hard-working man who snapped after skivvying after his wife for years'.

Similarly, there was uproar at the Central Criminal Court when Peter Lines was cleared of murder on the grounds of provocation after killing a woman with whom he had had a three-day affair. She was seven months pregnant and the jury had heard how he had half-strangled and then stabbed her seven times in the chest and throat when she refused to accept that their relationship was at an end.

In 1988 the Reverend Shirley Freeman killed his wife when she refused to tune in to his favourite radio programme, 'Desert Island Discs'. After considering the evidence in the case, the judge accepted his plea of provocation and released Freeman with a suspended sentence. More recently still, in January 1992, Rajinder Singh Bisla was convicted of manslaughter after being cleared of the murder of his 'nagging' wife. He had strangled her in front of their three children to 'shut her up' after more than two hours of verbal abuse. He'd told the police: 'I killed her. I put my hands around her neck. I didn't mean to hurt her. I just wanted to shut her up.' The judge gave him an eighteen-month suspended sentence.

As well as prejudice, the campaigners highlighted inconsistency. Not all battered women who kill are treated unsympathetically by the courts and the Prosecution Service. In some cases pleas of guilty to manslaughter are accepted without the ordeal of a full trial; in others women are cleared of murder despite difficulties in conforming to the narrow legal definition of provocation. As Helena Kennedy, QC points out in *Eve was Framed*:

> Much depends on the attitude of the judge and indeed the prosecutor. In some cases, because of the background, the prosecution and the judge accept a plea to manslaughter even where there has been some premeditation, as in the Maw sisters' case, where their violent father was lying unconscious on the mattress upstairs when agreement was reached that he must be killed (Court of Appeal, December 1980). Similarly, a plea to manslaughter on the grounds of provocation was accepted by *R* v. *Radcliffe*, May 1980, where the accused borrowed a knife from her neighbour, intending to kill her husband, and did so six days later.

However, such understanding is usually reserved for cases where women conform to stereotypes that make their responses acceptable. If the woman conforms to the image of the 'good and loving' wife she is more likely to find herself dealt with sympathetically, with the compassion she deserves. Thus Elizabeth Line, a former nun, was given a suspended sentence in 1992 after stabbing her violent husband seventeen times. The court had heard how she had come from a strict Catholic background, entering a convent at seventeen and later becoming a nurse. The headline in the *Daily Star* the following day made the stereotyping apparent: 'Mercy for Ex-nun who Killed Sex Monster'. In the article that followed she was described as a 'sobbing ex-nun' and 'tall and slender', both presumably attributes that militated against her being convincingly portrayed as a cold-blooded killer. Her husband, the article pointed out, had 'even killed her pet kitten' when in a drunken rage.

Mary McShane was similarly freed in November 1990, despite killing her violent husband, after she was described as an 'angel' by a relative of the deceased. Her mother-in-law had written to the court saying: 'We do not blame you. You are still the same sweet, lovely person you were when we first met you.'

Sara, of course, had failed to conform to those stereotypes. She was not capable of being portrayed as 'sweet', nor could she claim the purity of a former nun. But her case highlighted not only the plight of someone left at the mercy of judicial and societal prejudice but also problems with the sentencing relating to murder. Commentators began to point out that if there was no mandatory life sentence for murder, then Sara could have received a sentence that would better reflect the circumstances in which she had killed. The automatic life sentence for anyone convicted of murder was introduced in 1969 as a sop to those who opposed the abolition of capital punishment. It was meant to satisfy the demands of those who thought murder should be clearly marked out through the sentence which attached to it as the most severe and heinous of all crimes and also to allay the fears of those who believed that too lenient a sentence might encourage some murderers to strike again. But it has increasingly attracted criticism for not allowing courts to distinguish between different degrees of culpability. The mandatory life sentence for murder, it is argued, means that mercy killers and battered wives receive identical sentences to terrorists and serial killers unless they are able to bring themselves within one of the defences that reduces the crime to manslaughter. The very existence of defences such as provocation and diminished responsibility, critics have argued, show that not all killings can be treated as being equally bad, which in turn means that the argument that murder required a unique sentence because of its unique and absolute nature has been undermined. Opponents of the mandatory life sentence include some powerful figures, perhaps most notably the former Lord Chief Justice, Lord Lane. But as Kenneth Clarke made plain to journalists soon after he was made Home Secretary in 1992, reforming the law for murderers, whatever the merits, is unlikely to appear near the top of any Conservative Home Secretary's political agenda. Shrewd Conservative politicians do not wittingly court the wrath of their own party's powerful law-and-order lobby.

But even if that change had been a realistic possibility it was not enough to allay the fears of Sara's supporters who felt that it would just give too much power to judges, thereby increasing the vulnerability to their prejudices of the women who appeared before them. 'Men', Julie Bindel argued, 'would still walk free after saying, "She nagged me", but women who fought back against violence would still in most cases be classified as murderers unless there was a change in current definitions.'

In particular, it has been argued that a new defence should be developed to deal with cases in which there is a history of domestic violence. At the moment battered women are often hampered in their defence by the 'proportionality of force' rule which says that a person cannot use a deadly weapon in self-defence unless one is being used against him or her. The rule, which clearly assumes an equality of fighting skills and strengths, was designed to deal with situations where a man was fighting a man. It is clearly of little if any use to a woman or child being attacked by a man of superior strength. Similarly, it takes no account of the greater degree to which many men are skilled and socialized in the use of violence.

Criminologists sympathetic to the campaign's aims drafted a submission to the Royal Commission on Criminal Justice. They called for a new defence of 'self-preservation' to be established, which differed from the established defences of diminished responsibility and provocation in that it allowed any history of violence and abuse to be used as part of the defence. Jill Radford and Liz Kelly who drafted the submission argued that 'self-preservation' should be allowed as a partial defence to a charge of murder if the defendant honestly believed that she or he had no other course open to them and that their life was in danger. They argued:

> Our starting-point for the new defence is women's experiences. The common theme which emerges is that women who have been subjected to continuing abuse or violence reach a point where they come to believe that it is a question of 'It's my life or his.' Both the history of the violence and the many attempts women make to avoid or escape it, play a part in their reaching this desperate and despairing conclusion ... the new defence, if accepted by the jury, would then allow a judge to pass sentence according to his discretion in much the same way as currently happens in relation to other manslaughter verdicts. Clearly, we are not asking for a licence to kill.

Other feminist groups argued that there did not even need to be so dramatic a change and that judges merely needed to remove the requirement that they themselves had created: that any response to provocation should result from a 'sudden and temporary' loss of self-control.

With George Delf now absent from her campaign, Sara became increasingly involved in the largely feminist movement that had sprung up around her. Whilst she welcomed and encouraged the activities of her many male supporters, she began increasingly to see her predicament as being the result of her sex.

14 · The Backlash

The town of Atherstone has still not forgiven Sara. Despite the relatively short period of time she spent there, she has become their most famous and their least favourite daughter. The stories about her are apocryphal. Most concentrate on her reputation as a woman, as if by showing her as a fallen woman they can prove that she is an evil woman. In one pub it is said that she took off her clothes while standing on a pool table. In another it is remembered that on one occasion, when wearing a fur coat, she did not appear to have very much on underneath.

True or false, for many of the people of Atherstone, such stories bear directly and irrefutably on Sara's propensity to kill. If she can transgress sexual mores, the logic would seem to run, she is capable of anything. The same men who were prepared to take advantage of her 'easy virtue' are now content to see her 'rot in jail'. On one level such attitudes are, of course, just one small town's reaction to a woman who did not conform to their view of how women should behave and who ultimately killed. On another, though, they are symptomatic of a wider ill present in society at large. They evince a collective denial of the problems battered women and partners of alcoholics face.

Rather than face the difficult and perhaps uncomfortable process of trying to understand why what happened happened, it becomes easier to latch on to notions that offer an apparently easy though totally fictitious answer. Thus, few of those who lived around Sara, the very people who might have been best placed to help her and her family, acknowledge that there was really any problem at all. Some deny altogether that Malcolm was an alcoholic – 'He just liked a drink' – others accept he had a problem but chose to blame it on Sara. A number of his close friends say his drinking only got out of hand when he met Sara, before that he had been fine. If that is true, it is hard to see why he twice attended an Alcoholics Anonymous programme while working in Saudi Arabia some five years earlier, and why his work records reveal that he received a formal written warning about his drink problem the year before he met Sara. It may be more comfortable to think that if a man is drinking it is because a woman drove him to, but in Malcolm's situation that certainly was not the case.

By the same token, even fewer people were prepared to recognize that Malcolm was violent towards Sara. She herself uses the expression 'street angel and home devil' to describe Malcolm. Their friends, either fooled by the angel into being unable to recognize the devil, or simply not wanting to accept that someone they knew and respected was capable of violence, are adamant it did not happen. Again, the few that are prepared to accept it may have happened blame Sara: if Malcolm hit her, she asked for it. One neighbour denies totally that there was anything wrong with the way Malcolm treated Sara, stating with disgust that if his wife had gone out dressed the way Sara had, she too would have deserved everything she got. That same neighbour's wife turned the lights off and pretended not to be at home when Sara ran to them seeking help and needing to call the police.

One friend who knew Malcolm was hitting Sara denied that this fact made her a battered woman: 'I've known many battered women and Sara simply isn't one of them.' The problem from her point of view seemed to be that Sara did not fit the stereotype of a quiet and timid woman, cowed into subservience and submission. She wasn't nearly meek and mild enough and she hadn't suffered for nearly long enough. The woman taxi driver who so often came to take Sara and Luise away from Malcolm's violence and drunkenness doesn't believe that there is such a thing as a battered wife. 'If a man beats his wife then she knows he's going to do it before they get married. She makes him do it. My last husband used to beat me but I asked for it. Any woman can get their man to hit them if they really want to.'

Similarly, Malcolm did not conform to the stereotype of the

brutish husband. He was cultured, intelligent and respectable, and it was almost impossible for his friends to accept that he behaved like that; if he did, it was inconceivable that it could have been his fault.

The denial of Malcolm's violence doesn't stop at those who were close to it, it also extends to those who experienced it. Anne, Malcolm's second wife, frequently suffered at his hands. Her description of his violence ties in almost exactly with Sara's. But she doesn't believe that either she or Sara was a battered woman. Malcolm never, she says, 'gave me a beating for nothing. If he was violent I provoked it.' Tall, glamorous and strong, Anne is as far removed from the stereotype of the 'battered woman' as Sara. She rationalizes the violence Malcolm meted out to her by blaming herself. More often than not their rows would centre on his drinking, but, she says, if she said nothing he would not become aggressive. She believes that if she had just left him to it and been prepared to watch him drink himself into the ground, she could have escaped his brutality. The problem was not him, she said, but her – she couldn't just leave him to it. 'Everyone else thinks someone sitting drunk in a corner is funny. It's not your responsibility and you can go home. But when you're the person who has to go home with him it is a problem.' She also had to deal with Malcolm's sexual jealousy, his taunts and his suspicions. If she had just stayed in the kitchen accepting her role as a conventional wife rather than going to work in a hospital, things could, she believes, have been a lot easier. Like Sara she would often fight back, throwing things at Malcolm and then running for cover, and that too, she believes, makes her equally to blame. She says the only reason she didn't need to have hospital treatment for the injuries she'd 'brought on herself' was that she was a nurse.

Just as Sara's friends and neighbours were able to attribute Malcolm's abuse to her behaviour, so Anne was able to convince herself that she had 'asked for it' in some way every time he hit her. In the same way that individual women can blame themselves for men's violence towards them, so can society. Hence the question is continually asked of battered women: 'Why didn't she leave?' Or, as Mr Justice Judge put it in Sara's case, why didn't she just walk out or go upstairs?

Such questions, of course, put the onus and ultimately the blame on the woman. If the man is being violent, she should leave her home. If a man is insulting and upsetting her, she should just walk away. If she does not or is not able to, what can she expect? While the violent partner's behaviour is explainable, the victim's is not. Thus, when Sara called the police out, they suggested that she leave. When they ultimately decided to prosecute Malcolm, they told her it would be wisest if she went somewhere else, somewhere safer, for a while. Her doctor gave her a certificate to enable her to stay off work. The police and the medical service however unintentionally effectively colluded in enabling Malcolm to drive her from their home with violence. If it is the man who is breaking the law, assaulting and terrifying someone, surely he should be the one to be removed, the woman should not have to suffer the double jeopardy of first being beaten and then being forced to flee? One can imagine few other criminal–victim relationships that would be handled in this way.

Attempts are being made to tackle the problem of domestic violence in a more appropriate way. In August 1990 Sara read in the *Independent* that the Home Office had promised a revolution in the way police deal with domestic violence. The then minister responsible, John Patten, launching a new policy circular, said he wanted all police officers to realize that 'brutality in the home is just as much a crime as any other sort of violence. The victims of this hidden crime must be helped and offenders must be punished.' Too often assaults in the home were not even treated as a crime but left to the couple to sort out themselves, in other words the batterer was enabled to continue unimpeded. John Patten acknowledged: 'With domestic violence we are where we were ten years ago with rape.'

Two years after that update in policy was announced, a working party which included senior police officers, social workers and representatives from Victim Support, found that:

The nature of police culture can make it difficult for the investigating officer to deal well with domestic violence. The police tend to be a male-dominated, action-orientated organization who like decisions to be clear-cut and problems to have a solution. Constables tend to see dealing with domestic violence as a low-grade activity unlikely to attract either prestige or excitement.

The result of that, they concluded, was that much domestic violence was still not treated as seriously as it would have been had it taken place outside the home, and that on some occasions it was not recorded as a crime at all. What action the police take is still ultimately left to the individual (usually male) officer. Many officers base their decision not to take action on the fact that women are often reluctant to give evidence against their partner – either because they don't want him to go to court or because they fear further violence if he does. Thus the perpetrator soon discovers he can 'get away with it'. In Canada, however, if the police are called and there is evidence of abuse, the offending partner is automatically arrested and prosecuted, thereby removing the burden from the woman in deciding whether or not her lover should be criminalized. Since the policy was introduced violence has dropped by a dramatic 25 per cent. In Britain, the Government's only recent initiative has been the policy pronouncement mentioned above, and despite its fine words the Home Office has not even yet begun to collect separate statistics on the crime.

Like rape, domestic violence continues to be a largely hidden problem, taking place behind closed doors and with, as in Sara's case, few people knowing or being prepared to accept that it happens. The Home Office acknowledges that women are more likely to be attacked by their partner than by anyone else. Figures show that in London alone, in 1990, more than 100,000 women were forced to seek hospital treatment for injuries that resulted from domestic violence.

For women trying to flee violence there is very often literally nowhere for them to go. Some local authorities refuse to provide accommodation for a woman who has been beaten unless she first proves this by taking out an injunction against her partner. While she does so, of course, the violence continues. Similarly, the number of places in refuges remains unacceptably low. In 1975 a Government Select Committee on Violence in Marriage recommended that there should be at least one family place per 10,000 in the population. By 1990 there were still little over a thousand places in the whole country – less than a third of those recommended seventeen years before.

By the time a woman does find a place in a refuge she will have endured, on average, thirty-five assaults. It is not just the lack of physical resources that affects a woman's ability to leave a violent relationship. Economic, social and emotional factors also all play a significant role. Leaving a male partner, no matter how brutal he may be, can spell financial ruin for a mother. For many women, deliberately choosing single parenthood and poverty, putting their own physical safety over the financial and material well-being of their children, is not an easy choice. The woman may escape violence, but to what? To poverty, to being alone to look after children, to living in temporary over-crowded accommodation, perhaps to having to move out of the area, thus disrupting their children's education and possibly having to give up their job. To face the uncertainty that leaving would bring takes immense courage. And often by the time the woman realizes she should go, her self-esteem has sunk to such a low ebb and her confidence has been so shattered by the way she has been treated that she finds it impossible to go.

Similarly, women usually love or have loved the man they are with. Their partner may express constant remorse and make repeated pledges to reform, making it even harder for the woman to give up her hope that he will change. The more she has invested in the relationship, the harder it will be for her to walk away; the more she has endured for the sake of trying to make it work, the more difficult it will be for her to give up hope and recognize that it has not. That can be compounded in the case of an alcoholic batterer: the woman may often blame the alcohol rather than him; or she may even blame herself. As Dr Max Glatt wrote in relation to Sara's own case:

> The question 'to leave or not to leave' is more or less continually on the wife's mind and she may, in fact, often threaten to walk out, but then relent because she may still love him or at least care for him enough not to want him to destroy himself. By then she has often lost her self-respect, especially as the alcoholic projects all of his own failings on to her, the ever-available scapegoat. She may even feel in some way responsible for his state and that she must therefore stand by him for as long as he needs her.

Putting the emphasis on the woman to leave rather than on the man to end his violence has been called 'victim-blaming'. It is also a question that courts only seem to ask of the battered woman and never of the 'hen-pecked' or jealous husband who would, of course, be in a far easier position to actually walk out. It is also a question which, according to the Working Party on Domestic Violence which reported in 1992, people should be able to answer by simply examining their own experience:

> With a little reflection, anyone who has endured even mild abuse in a situation of relative powerlessness should be able to understand the problem. Most people have had the experience of trying to deal with a difficult boss at work or a difficult and demoralizing teacher at school or college and should be able to understand, with a little imagination, how unhelpful it is to think that the situation could be cured by simply leaving the scene. The positions we find ourselves in are not easy to escape from. Too many reasons, too much history, have led us into those situations for simple escape ever to be an easy or practical proposition.

The tendency seems to be to criticize women who stay, whereas in reality women are often only doing what at other times society expects of them. As the American academic Angela Browne points out in her book *When Battered Women Kill*:

Perseverance in the face of hardship; attempts to understand, soothe, and smooth over; assigning a higher priority to the care of others than to one's own well-being are qualities that have been taught and valued for decades as a vital part of a woman's role. Unselfishness and self-sacrifice – asking little and giving much – are held as virtues, especially in relation to one's family. Thus, it should not be surprising that the first coping strategies women utilize when violence occurs in their relationships most typically are attempts at peacemaking and resolution.

Sustained violence does also inevitably take its toll on the victim's emotional and mental health. It may well be in a woman's best interests to leave but, if the effect of brutality has left her unable to act in her own self-interest, not leaving does not make her more culpable than the man who brutalized her.

The 'Why doesn't she leave' question seems to walk hand in hand with the fear that, if a woman like Sara Thornton were found guilty only of manslaughter, it would be an invitation for any battered woman to take up arms against her brutalizer. That fear, it seems, is all too real amongst judges; hence their frequent references to the possibility of giving battered women a 'licence to kill'. That presupposes, of course, that battered women want to kill the men they live with, whereas in reality most will say that what they want is a lot more straightforward: they simply want the violence to stop. It also ignores the fact that a woman who is in a violent relationship is in reality much more likely to be killed by her partner than she is to kill him. In the five years up to 1990 478 women were killed by their partners; the number of men killed by women was a quarter of that.

For many, Sara's case has become a symbol for the ways in which society fails battered women and then deals with those who are ultimately driven to kill. But in some ways she is far from epitomizing what she has come to represent. She does not fit the stereotype of the cowed and submissive woman; she did not endure decades of violence. Just as her failure to conform to the archetypal woman may well have affected her conviction in court, so her failure to conform to society's image of a typical battered woman leaves her vulnerable to hostility now – both from those who knew her in Atherstone and from certain sections of the press. Not all the coverage of her case has been sympathetic. Journalists, ever hopeful for a new angle on a by now (in their terms at least) old story have begun to question whether or not Sara is a suitable symbol for such a cause. Trickle by trickle articles are starting to appear, all written by people who profess themselves to be sympathetic to the plight of battered women who kill, but all of whom raise questions about the merits of Sara's case. In August 1992 an article in the *Spectator* revived the arguments used by the prosecution at trial, repeating, with apparently no attempt to substantiate them, claims that Sara had killed for money. It also pointed to her split with George Delf and her lack of support from her father as evidence that there must be something awry with her cause. Authors of such articles always profess themselves to be sympathetic to the cause but sceptical of Sara. She did not, as far as they were concerned, endure Malcolm's violence for long enough; she did not play the meek and helpless wife role undefiantly enough. If she is to be an icon, then it seems that purity is what is required. The issues surrounding Sara's case have inevitably been simplified to some extent and in some respects the campaign that has grown up around her has itself distorted her story to fit the epitome.

Sara herself has often been offended by the way Malcolm has been portrayed. To make her story easier to tell, countless journalists and the campaigners they feed from have portrayed Malcolm as no more than a brute. That is a misconception Sara has struggled to correct. 'I get upset when I see him described as a "violent brute" because when he was not drinking he was a lovely man. He was very funny, had a great sense of humour, and was extremely intelligent. When he was sober he never hit me once.' By the same token she is also frequently angered by the way she herself has come to be presented: 'I want to be seen for what I am, a real, imperfect woman who was battered and who killed, not some virginal figure waiting for a judge to charge in on his white stallion and rescue me.'

Whatever the simplifications that have taken place, the fundamental issues remain the same, and in many ways Sara's failure to conform to the role of icon sets the legal system the sort of challenge upon which it should itself be judged. For if a system of criminal justice is to be truly fair, it has to be able to deal with the atypical as equitably as with the typical. When it comes to that atypical case there is now some evidence to suggest that attitudes are shifting.

Two cases in particular stand out; both were decided after the publicity and outrage surrounding Sara's failed appeal. In both, the women concerned had killed while their partner was drugged or asleep, and in both expert evidence was presented to show the traumatic effect domestic violence can have.

June Scotland had put ground-up sleeping and travel sickness pills into her violent and sexually abusive husband's food; when that had failed to kill him she had beaten him to death with a rolling-pin. With her daughter's help she then buried his body in the garden, and the crime was only discovered when the next-door neighbour accidentally excavated his corpse during building work. Three psychiatrists told the court that Mrs Scotland's mental state had been impaired by years of sustained abuse. Relying on that, the court was prepared to accept her guilty plea to manslaughter rather than making her stand trial for murder. She was given two years' probation in 1992.

Pamela Sainsbury had also been given probation. She had strangled her partner with a nylon cord as he slept, sawed up his body and dumped the remains in a field. Earlier that evening he had subjected her to two hours of punching and kicking. Although her plea of guilty to manslaughter was accepted on the basis of diminished responsibility, the emphasis of the case had turned more on her husband's behaviour than on her mental state. Indeed, Mr Justice Auld appeared to accept that her mental state had been caused by her partner's behaviour – which was one step closer to provocation: 'You killed him in a sudden and impulsive act, driven as much by fear and hopelessness as anger.'

That was closer to the sort of interpretation campaigners were looking for. Although in both cases the women were found guilty of manslaughter on the basis of diminished responsibility rather than provocation, the emphasis of the defence had rested firmly on the man's violence. Psychiatric evidence had been used not to show a long-standing abnormality of mind on the part of the woman but the extent to which the husband's abuse was responsible for affecting the woman's mental state, putting his behaviour rather than her mental health centre-stage.

The defence used by June Scotland and Pamela Sainsbury comes very close to the specialist evidence that is now admissible in American courts to prove the existence of 'battered women's syndrome', which according to criminologist Susan Edwards, writing in the *New Law Journal* (October 1992) is 'something akin to a state of fear, trauma and shock, characterized by anxiety and depression, a perception that death is likely, a total inability to escape and a feeling of helplessness'.

In terms of English law it represents a crucial blurring of the distinction between provocation and diminished responsibility; the abnormality of mind is found to be present because of sustained provocation. For the woman who kills because of battering but fails to fall within the law's restrictive definition of provocation it represents a step forward. However, it still forces a woman to plead mental abnormality in a way that a man pleading straightforward provocation would not have to. The psychiatrist who gave evidence for both women, Dr Nigel Eastman, has lent his backing to the calls for the defence of provocation to be made more equally available to both sexes. Although he was successful in those two cases his fear is that women may be in danger of falling between the two defences to murder: they may not have developed a mental disorder serious enough to plead diminished responsibility, and at the same time may not have acted with the suddenness required to plead provocation.

Two more significant inroads were to follow. In April 1992 the Court of Appeal released Amelia Rossiter, accepting that she had been provoked. And on 25 September Kiranjit Ahluwalia, after more than three years in prison, was freed by the Old

Bailey. Two months before, the Court of Appeal had ordered a re-trial. It did so on the basis of diminished responsibility, with the Lord Chief Justice, Peter Taylor, rejecting Kiranjit's lawyers' arguments on the issue of provocation. But few felt the referral would have happened without the high-profile campaign that had highlighted the deficiencies in the law of provocation. As Kiranjit left the court, her supporters released dozens of coloured balloons, symbols of all the women still in prison. Kiranjit herself turned to the press who were waiting packed together outside and made an impassioned plea for those she had left behind. Chief amongst them, of course, was Sara. Two of the three women on whom the campaign to change the law on provocation had focused were now free. Only Sara, the woman who had perhaps done most to highlight the issue, remained in jail.

15 · The Wait Continues

When you turn into the long drive that leads to Bullwood Hall it is easy to think you have made a mistake. The approach seems too grand; it is lined by trees which are in turn banked by rolling green fields, creating the impression that you are about to visit a stately home. Half-way up the drive on the left is a small flock of goats, grazing carelessly; a little further on a cluster of nicely built houses around a circle of grass; but once past them there is no mistaking your destination. Jarring harshly with its gentle green environment, the huge white fences and bare brick architecture of one of Britain's twelve women's prisons greets you. From inside its confines the green fields are reduced to a tantalizing blur by the mesh of the wire that encloses the prison.

If you go there in the early afternoon you might well find a small group of friends and relatives, huddled outside the enormous prison gates and dwarfed by the size of them. Some will be with children; some will be alone; but almost all of them will be carrying bunches of flowers as gifts for those they are to visit inside. When the time comes for the visitors to be admitted, the gate will be opened and the motley stream will proceed inside, first depositing the flowers by the gatehouse so that they can be searched before being passed on to the inmates. Before Sara came to Bullwood Hall prisoners were not allowed to receive flowers. Sara could not believe the pettiness of the rule that forbade such a simple comfort. She demanded to see the governor, and instead had a meeting with a more junior administrator who refused to change the rule. Sara persisted, however, making an official complaint, and eventually the authorities caved in. It was one of many battles Sara was to fight and win in prison. Whereas many of her fellow-lifers were cowed into submission by the system, she refused to let her energies be dissipated. To an outsider many of the issues she has fought about may seem insignificant, but to those whose lives are spent within the concrete prison walls they have made a significant difference.

Bullwood Hall seems to visitors and inhabitants alike to be a miserable prison. Slopping-out has only just been abolished there. Stuck out near the Essex coast it is not easily accessible, and many inmates have to go for long periods without receiving any visits. On Sara's wing there were a number of other women who had killed their partners, indeed five of the twelve lifers Sara was placed with had killed in similar circumstances. Two of them, Kiranjit Ahluwalia and Amelia Rossiter, have already been released. There were also a number of other women who had been given life sentences when others had killed their partners. One woman's boyfriend had killed her unfaithful husband in a fight after he had seen him hit her. The boyfriend had been given a life sentence with a ten-year tariff, the woman, who had a young baby, a life sentence with a sixteen-year tariff, even though she had not physically participated in the attack.

All the prison's inmates are accommodated in single cells, but long-running problems with the Prison Officers' Association over staffing levels mean women are locked in their cells for longer than elsewhere. Prisoners are given their main evening meal at 4 p.m., leaving them with sixteen hours to wait until their next meal. The Chief Inspector of Prisons has described such a regime as 'ridiculous and apparently wholly geared to suit staff shift systems' rather than inmates' requirements. For at least half the week there are not enough staff to allow prisoners out of their cells to mix with each other in the evenings. That means women are often locked away alone from 4 p.m. until 8 a.m. It is a relentlessly lonely and wretched experience. At night the corridors of the wing reverberate with the sound of women crying. No inmate is strong enough to cope with such incarceration without breaking down from time to time.

It was against that backdrop that Sara decided every small concession she could wring from the system would be worth fighting for. As far as she was concerned, depriving inmates of their liberty was one thing but subjecting them to a regime that was for many too much to bear was another. Having won the right to have flowers, Sara's next battle was over music. While she was in Durham she had been allowed to have a small compact disc-player in her cell. Bullwood Hall took a far less enlightened view and refused to allow her to have it. Again she challenged that decision and eventually was allowed to set the CD player up in the lifers' recreation room. From then on, at certain times and on certain days the prisoners could listen to it, and sometimes even the incongruous spectacle of prisoners and officers dancing together took place. Sara also took on the issue of make-up. For many inmates it was a simple but important way of cheering themselves up, but their only access to cosmetics was via friendly prison officers. They would have to ask an officer to buy a particular lipstick or eyeshadow and hope that he or she returned with the right one. Sara persuaded the authorities to allow the women to buy their own make-up direct from Avon.

When Sara started to work in the factory workshop making plugs she found the light was appalling. The work was close and would have been eye-straining even if there had been enough light. On one particular day there was no artificial light at all as there was a power-cut. The inmates were still expected to work. Sara complained about the conditions and said she would not work unless more light was provided. The officer who ran the workshop was strict and authoritarian; he was renowned for sending women to the punishment block for even minor misdemeanours and no one else had dared to challenge him about their working conditions. He was furious with Sara, but when the prison governor was called up to adjudicate she sided with Sara. It was another battle won.

Every inmate has a key to her cell, which she is expected to lock, but Sara refuses to lock her door, saying she trusts her fellow inmates. Inside her cell it is hard to see anything beneath the sea of papers. It is equipped with the standard prison furniture: one small bed, one table and one wardrobe, and every available inch is covered with neat stacks of correspondence and legal documentation. On the small noticeboard above the table are pinned two photos: one of Luise and one of Mahatma Gandhi; around them are pinned numerous newspaper cuttings and notes reminding Sara of letters she has to write. The cell does not just function as the headquarters of Sara's own campaign, it is also the place to which other prisoners often come in search of advice and support. Having tirelessly researched the law relating to her own case, Sara now devotes much of her time to helping other prisoners prepare theirs, encouraging them to fight, and where necessary finding them a lawyer. She was a major force in Kiranjit Ahluwalia's case, helping her to build up the confidence to challenge her conviction, and now that Kiranjit is free she is doing the same for others.

Sara's battle to achieve her own freedom continues. The sense of peace and calm which she initially experienced on entering prison has now all but evaporated. Although she continues to battle against the system, the misery and brutality of prison life seem unbearable at times. When she is not campaigning, much of her time in prison is spent in quiet meditation, trying to find the strength to endure what seems unendurable. Having lost her appeal, her legal options are severely limited. On 25 September 1991, she submitted an application for a pardon to the then Home Secretary, Kenneth Baker. She has still not received a reply. Its submission was accompanied by a petition signed by over 5000 women. Her advisers are not at all hopeful that a pardon will be granted; the last time a Home Secretary exercised his prerogative to grant one for a convicted murderer was in 1956.

The application was drafted by Ed Fitzgerald, the barrister who had been Sara's junior counsel at her appeal, and ran to some twenty-three pages of foolscap. In it he argued that granting of a pardon would reflect 'the public sense of injustice which her case had engendered'. He highlighted the flaws in Sara's trial: the fact that her representatives had not argued the defence of provocation; the fact that the trial judge had effectively withdrawn the defence through his negative comments; and the fact that the Homicide Act itself carries no requirement that any loss of self-control be 'sudden and temporary'. He also argued that the injustice of Sara's case was compounded by the fact that in many other cases judges had been prepared to accept pleas of provocation and diminished responsibility in similar circumstances. It was, of course, that apparent lack of consistency which contributed to the public perception that Sara had been found guilty of murder rather than manslaughter not because of guilt but at worst because of prejudice and at best because of very bad luck.

If, as seemed likely, her application for a pardon fell on deaf ears, her only other alternative was to try to get another appeal. Since she had already lost one appeal she would only be granted another if the Home Secretary could be persuaded to refer her case back to the Court of Appeal.

In the period that followed the application for a pardon Sara and her supporters provided the Home Office with further evidence which they hoped might influence the Home Secretary's deliberations. Statements from witnesses who were available at trial but had not been used were handed in. One of them was from Patrick Hanlon, describing the threats that had been made against Luise and Sara by Malcolm on the Sunday before his death; another was from Diane Davies, describing Sara's alleged threat to kill at the TNT conference in Coventry as an expression of anger. Further evidence had already been submitted from Dr Max Glatt: as the Court of Appeal's judgment had made no reference to the report that had been laid before it during Sara's appeal, there was nothing to suggest it had actually received full consideration. In it Dr Glatt reiterated his view that the impact of Malcolm's alcoholism on Sara had been totally ignored.

No answer came from the Home Office but the attitude it was taking was clear: there was nothing that could in legal terms be classified as 'new' in what Sara and her representatives were saying. Once an initial appeal has been turned down, a distinction which many may see as arbitrary is brought into play – a distinction between what was theoretically available at trial, which is viewed as 'old' evidence, and anything that has subsequently emerged and can be viewed as fresh, untried evidence.

Sadly, it is that somewhat arbitrary distinction – between the old and the new – which can sometimes seal a defendant's fate; not whether they are truly guilty. Sara's arguments about provocation had been dealt with by the Court of Appeal as, in theory at least, had Max Glatt's evidence. Although the witnesses whose statements had been submitted had not been called to give evidence, their existence was known to Sara's lawyers. Indeed, Sara's lawyers had received copies of the statements witnesses had made to the police. That being the case, they did not fall into the category of fresh evidence.

Surprisingly, though, nothing in the legislation sets out the basis upon which the Home Secretary can refer cases back to the courts, according to which there must be new evidence. The criterion has been introduced by civil servants, to keep what they see as the 'floodgates' closed. Their justification for introducing the restriction is that if there was no such limitation they would simply be swamped by a deluge of alleged injustices. As it is, the resources that are devoted to examining potential miscarriages of justice are woefully small. One small Government department, known simply as C3, is charged with the responsibility for assessing and reviewing all the cases that are of concern. It has fewer than sixteen staff, none of whom are trained lawyers, and they have to deal with up to 800 cases each year. Some prisoners wait years to get a reply from the department and very few of those that are dealt with are ever granted a new appeal. The department's administrators believe not only that it is necessary to keep the floodgates closed but also that defendants should not be given two 'bites at the same cherry': if evidence that was available at trial but was not used can be presented at a later appeal, defendants are effectively being given two opportunities to make their case. That in turn, it is argued, could undermine the role of the jury at the original trial, as it would effectively be asking a different court to look at the same case and arrive at a different conclusion. The logic seems to be that it is worth risking a few wrongful imprisonments rather than allowing the system, if necessary, to duplicate its efforts to discover the truth. In this area, as in a number of others, the system that is meant to exist to administer justice seems to become too entangled in its own rules of administration to recognize the requirements of justice.

The possibility of Sara persuading the Home Office to re-open her case did not look strong and all the signals coming from the Home Office indicated that her submissions were going to be rejected. However, at the end of 1991 her fortunes improved. A solicitor who has perhaps done more than any other lawyer to expose the failings of the criminal justice system took over Sara's case. Gareth Pierce has been behind many of the successful revelations of miscarriages of justice that have in the last few years shaken the legal establishment to its core and led to the setting up of a Royal Commission. The Guildford Four, the Birmingham Six, Judith Ward, the Tottenham Three and the Cardiff Three are just some of the cases that bear her hallmark. Where other lawyers have failed or given up she has succeeded. Whilst many radical lawyers have used their success in such notorious appeals as a boost for their profile or their career, Gareth Pierce has chosen to remain out of the public glare, her energies instead channelled into helping those who find themselves the powerless victims of a system that is meant to administer justice. Her tenacity and the quality of her work has earned her the respect of those whose failings she has exposed; both the Home Office and the Courts are aware that the very fact she has taken on a particular case indicates a serious likelihood that there is substantial cause for concern.

Looking through Sara's papers Gareth Pierce became convinced that justice had not been done. Her concern was not just that the issue of provocation had not been raised but also that at no point had any court considered the full facts of Sara's case. Reading through the summary of the prosecution's case at the trial, she saw that it made no reference to the physical abuse that Sara had endured at Malcolm's hands; the only reference she could find was to 'violent arguments', which did not, of course, convey either a full or accurate picture of what had happened. At this initial stage it seemed clear to Gareth Pierce that not only should there be real disquiet about the way Sara's trial had been conducted but also about whether she had received comparable treatment with others who had behaved similarly. Additionally, the fact that police officers who, whilst acting entirely professionally, also had a personal interest in the case had been so intimately involved in its investigation also seemed to be grounds for grave concern. She felt very strongly that both the outcome of the trial, namely Sara's conviction for murder, and the length of the minimum tariff that it had been decided Sara must serve did not properly reflect Sara's culpability.

However, while she became utterly convinced that Sara's case should be re-opened, she was also aware that as things stood this was unlikely to happen. None of the evidence that had so far been submitted on Sara's behalf seemed likely to satisfy the criterion of being 'new'. To prevent Sara's whole case being thrown out because of this she wrote to the Home Office and asked them to suspend making a decision until she had had time to investigate the case further.

Some nine months later, after full consultation with Sara and with her backing, the fruits of those investigations were submitted to the Home Office together with a lengthy and substantial critique of the way the trial and appeal had been conducted. Gareth Pierce's enquiries had uncovered a number of serious issues and, most importantly, what she believed to be some crucial 'new' evidence. Much of it related to the issue of provocation. Because of the line of defence chosen, none of the psychiatrists who gave evidence during Sara's trial had been asked one simple question: whether, given the stress that Sara was under and the violence she had endured, she had been provoked.

In his initial report Professor Sydney Brandon had actually told Sara's lawyers that in his view she had been provoked, but he was not asked to repeat that view in court. Neither of the other two psychiatrists, Dr Bullard and Dr Brockman, was asked to offer an opinion on the issue of provocation at any stage. Both have now said that in their view Sara had almost certainly been provoked. Dr Bullard is of the view, and would have said in Court had she been asked, that in the light of Sara's vulnerable mental state and the cumulative violence she had endured it seemed likely she had been provoked into stabbing him. Similarly, when asked recently, Dr Brockman said that whilst she still remains unsure that Sara's responsibility was diminished she too believes that Sara could have been provoked. Thus while the three psychiatrists had disagreed on the extent to which Sara's responsibility for the killing was diminished they are, apparently, unanimous on the issue of provocation. The fact that the prosecution's psychiatrist agrees with the defence's experts on this issue is clearly of immense significance. It now seems possible, therefore, that had provocation been argued by Sara's lawyers, and had the psychiatrists' views been sought, the jury could have been faced with a unanimous body of expert medical opinion backing up Sara's defence.

Not only would this have had significance at Sara's trial; it could also have altered the whole course of her appeal. At Sara's appeal, Lord Justice Beldam specifically referred to the absence of any psychiatric evidence on this point:

> We cannot help feeling that if after the very detailed study which they [the two defence psychiatrists] had made of the case they had held the opinion that her mental disorder made it more likely that in the face of verbal insult she would have given way to impulsive tendencies or aggression, they would have said so, and would have stressed this characteristic as significant in her loss of self-control.

What, of course, the Court of Appeal did not know was that one of the psychiatrists, Professor Sydney Brandon, had indeed stressed that very factor in his pre-trial report but had not been questioned about it during the trial, and that the other two psychiatrists, neither of whom had been asked to express their view on the question during the trial, would also have supported the defence of provocation.

The importance of that unheard psychiatric evidence is bolstered by the Court of Appeal's judgment in Kiranjit Ahluwalia's case. Whereas expert evidence was not called in Sara's case on the issue of provocation, the court made it clear that in certain circumstances that evidence could be relevant and could be called. When considering the question of provocation juries are meant to ask themselves two questions.

First, they are meant to consider whether the defendant was indeed provoked, and then they are meant to ask whether a reasonable person with the relevant characteristics of the defendant would have been provoked. Historically the sort of relevant characteristics juries have taken into consideration when looking at the second part of the test have been physical ones. So, for example, if the defendant was a hunch-back and is being taunted about the deformity, the jury would be told that they should consider whether a reasonable person, with a hunch-back, would have been provoked. It now seems that the sort of characteristics that can be taken into consideration include mental traits. In Kiranjit Ahluwalia's case the Court of Appeal apparently accepted that conditions like post-traumatic stress disorder or 'battered woman syndrome' could constitute characteristics akin to physical traits like hunch-backs. Thus the jury would need to ask themselves in a case like Sara's not, 'Would a reasonable woman have been provoked in the same situation?' but 'Would a reasonable woman who was suffering from "battered woman syndrome" have been provoked in the same situation?' To help the jury understand the nature of such conditions the Court of Appeal accepted that expert witnesses could be called. If such an argument had been pursued on Sara's behalf, it now emerges, the psychiatrists concerned would have backed her case up.

In addition, the very fact that the existence of 'battered woman syndrome' has now been accepted by the courts may in itself be grounds for justifying the presentation of evidence on the issue; evidence that could be interpreted as 'fresh evidence', given the developments in the law that have taken place since Sara's trial.

Gareth Pierce also commissioned further psychiatric reports from experts whose evidence had been crucial in two earlier cases: that of Judith Ward, who had spent sixteen years wrongly imprisoned for IRA bombings, and of Engin Raghip, one of the so-called Tottenham Three wrongly convicted of murdering PC Keith Blakelock at the Broadwater Farm riots in 1985. The reports were based on further examinations of Sara; transcripts from the trial; tapes of Sara's interviews with the police (which had not been played in court) and all the other evidence relating to the case that had not come to light until after the trial, such as Dr Max Glatt's report. The reports contained a number of significant conclusions. The first was that, at the time of the killing, taking into account both the evidence that had existed before the trial and the evidence that had come to light during and after the trial, Sara was suffering from a severe personality disorder that substantially impaired her mental responsibility. In other words, with the benefit of a fuller profile, they backed up the views of the defence's two psychiatrists at the trial that Sara's responsibility was diminished. The reports also point out that the stresses Sara was under and her mental condition were not relevant only to the issue of diminished responsibility, they were also highly relevant to the issue of provocation. For a sensible understanding of why someone like Sara had killed, it was, they argued, essential that the two strands – diminished responsibility and provocation – were considered together. That was a view to which Gareth Pierce herself subscribed and that the prosecution's psychiatrist, Dr Brockman, also endorsed. She too felt that it was a complex case and not one that could be described as either straightforward diminished responsibility or provocation. The pity was that the jury had not had the benefit of having evidence backing up both strands presented to them at the trial.

The further psychiatric investigations also threw up another issue that Gareth Pierce believed threw into question the whole basis upon which the trial had proceeded. On the basis of all the evidence and further fresh interviews with Sara, the reports concluded that Sara's personality disorder, including her disassociative behaviour after killing Malcolm, suggested that the evidence she gave, particularly in interviews with the police and also in the witness box at her trial, could not and should not have been relied upon without the benefit of expert interpretative advice. While in both highly stressful situations Sara had been able to present an outward impression of a person who was coping rationally and competently, that in fact was not the case. Just as in the case of Judith Ward, who was eventually shown to have had a personality disorder at the time of her arrest and trial which prevented her from being able to give a reliable account of herself, Sara's capacity to do so was also affected. The only way to know for sure whether her account could at the time be relied upon would have been to seek expert psychiatric advice, and that was not done. Had it been, the reports concluded, Sara might well have been considered unfit to be questioned by the police or even to take the witness box during her trial, and the outcome of her trial might have been very different. In both Judith Ward's and Engin Raghip's cases the Court of Appeal had emphasized the importance of expert evidence to assist lawyers, judges and juries on the issue of whether a person who appeared to be coping was in fact able to give a reliable account of themselves or might instead be in a disassociative or hysterical state.

In addition to the evidence submitted by Gareth Pierce, there are also at least three new witnesses whose evidence in relation to the provocation Sara suffered could well be crucial. Two of them, Steve Byard and Stan Clarke, who saw Sara fly through the air as a result of one of Malcolm's punches, were unknown to the defence at the time of Sara's trial. The third, Anne Thornton, who herself experienced prolonged violence at Malcolm's hands, had been interviewed by the police but not by the defence.

There are other issues relating to the issue of diminished responsibility that similarly have still not been raised in any court. Any neutral observer watching the psychiatric evidence that was given in Sara's original trial must wonder how the prosecution's psychiatrist's position could not have altered as a result of Sara's court-room revelation of her full psychiatric history, including the fact that she had attempted suicide a number of other times by the time she was twenty-two. Such an observer might also question how that psychiatrist's view may have been affected by the fact that the psychiatrist in question had neither been in court to hear Sara's evidence nor re-examined her in the light of what had emerged.

Similarly, no jury and no court have considered the full effect which the domestic violence Sara experienced had on her mental state. At her trial no psychiatric evidence was sought or presented to show whether her responsibility might have been diminished as a result of the mental impact of the violent relationship she was in. If it had been, it might well have shown that the trauma of the violence had affected Sara's mind. Indeed, in many respects, the whole distinction between the defence of diminished responsibility and the defence of provocation in cases where battered women have killed is open to question. If the woman has been clearly affected by the violence she has experienced, then that violence is likely to have affected both her mental state at the time of the killing and the likelihood that she would be provoked.

The potency of such arguments is already now being accepted to a greater extent by the courts. On 29 October 1992, a fifty-two-year-old grandmother, Janet Gardner, was released by the Court of Appeal after it heard medical evidence which showed that she had been in a state of helplessness and depression as a result of the physical and verbal abuse she had suffered from her husband. The judges accepted that she'd been suffering from 'battered woman syndrome'. For the first time a British court accepted the full medical impact sustained violence could have on a woman.

If all the issues surrounding domestic violence had been raised, backed up, argued and most importantly accepted at Sara's trial, there must be very serious doubt as to whether Sara would still be in jail today.

From prison Sara continues to fight for justice. She has no legal aid and until she has an appeal pending no right to receive visits or even phone calls from her lawyer. Every day brings fresh letters of encouragement from those around the country who support her case. The rest of the evidence relating to her case has now been submitted; it only remains for the civil servants, the Home Secretary and, if an appeal is allowed, the courts, to reach a decision.

While the slow cogs of justice turn to deliberate these issues, Sara grows older in prison while 5000 miles away a daughter grows up without her mother.